Conversations with Ian McEwan

Literary Conversations Series
Peggy Whitman Prenshaw
General Editor

Conversations
with Ian McEwan

Edited by Ryan Roberts

University Press of Mississippi   Jackson

www.upress.state.ms.us

The University Press of Mississippi is a member of the Association of American University Presses.

Copyright © 2010 by University Press of Mississippi
All rights reserved
Manufactured in the United States of America

First printing 2010
∞

Library of Congress Cataloging-in-Publication Data

McEwan, Ian.
    Conversations with Ian McEwan / edited by Ryan Roberts.
        p. cm. — (Literary conversations series)
    Includes index.
    ISBN 978-1-60473-419-5 (cloth : alk. paper) — ISBN 978-1-60473-420-1 (pbk. : alk. paper) 1. McEwan, Ian—Interviews. 2. Authors, English—20th century—Interviews. I. Roberts, Ryan, 1973– II. Title.
    PR6063.C4Z46 2010
    823'.914—dc22
    [B]   2009026952

British Library Cataloging-in-Publication Data available

Works by Ian McEwan

Novels
The Cement Garden. London: Jonathan Cape, 1978.
The Comfort of Strangers. London: Jonathan Cape, 1981.
The Child in Time. London: Jonathan Cape, 1987.
The Innocent. London: Jonathan Cape, 1990.
Black Dogs. London: Jonathan Cape, 1992.
Enduring Love. London: Jonathan Cape, 1997.
Amsterdam. London: Jonathan Cape, 1998.
Atonement. London: Jonathan Cape, 2001.
Saturday. London: Jonathan Cape, 2005.
On Chesil Beach. London: Jonathan Cape, 2007.

Short Story Collections
First Love, Last Rites. London: Jonathan Cape, 1975.
In Between the Sheets. London: Jonathan Cape, 1978.
The Short Stories. London: Jonathan Cape, 1995.

Children's Fiction
Rose Blanche. London: Jonathan Cape, 1985.
The Daydreamer. London: Jonathan Cape, 1994.

Plays
The Imitation Game: Three Plays for Television. London: Jonathan Cape, 1981.

Film Scripts
The Ploughman's Lunch. London: Methuen, 1985.
Soursweet. London: Faber & Faber, 1988 [Based on the novel by Timothy Mo].

Librettos
Or Shall We Die?: Words for an Oratorio Set to Music by Michael Berkeley. London: Jonathan Cape, 1983.
For You: The Libretto. London: Vintage Books, 2008.

Contents

Introduction

In May 2008, Ian McEwan and Steven Pinker talked on stage as part of PEN American Center's World Voices Festival. Their discussion centered on communication, evolutionary psychology, and how, in Pinker's words, "if you look at the transcript of a conversation, it's remarkable how little communication of data there is. So much is innuendo and euphemism, and we count on our listener to fill in the blanks." Context matters in conversation, as does nuanced phrasing and tone, and the process of transferring verbal exchanges to the page undoubtedly results in some minor loss of meaning or intent. McEwan is sensitive to this fact, and his engagement in the conversations gathered in this collection reveals his focused attention to the specificity of language and exactness of meaning. The conversations are extremely informative, but, more importantly, they document an ongoing dialog between the author, his works, and his readers. Through this series of compelling and open discussions, McEwan offers a unique view into his writing process and provides insights into his multifaceted nature as a celebrated public figure, scholar, parent, and writer.

Ian McEwan shocked his way onto the literary scene in the early 1970s with two collections of short stories (*First Love, Last Rites* and *In Between the Sheets*) that detailed humanity's inherent darkness and complexity. Critics and reviewers were quick to comment on his macabre themes of death and incest and the isolation of many of his characters. Two short novels quickly followed (*The Cement Garden* and *The Comfort of Strangers*), and their subject matter further solidified McEwan's reputation in the press as a writer of quality with a penchant for controversial or disturbing plots. In 1989, when Rosa González Casademont asked McEwan whether his early reputation affected his later work in a negative way, McEwan acquiesced, saying, "Yes, I have found it difficult, due to the insistence of certain newspapers to sensationalise what I do, and to portray me as some kind of literary psychopath. Once this set of expectations is set up round my work, people read it in this way." His works continued to sell and he was already a growing force when, in 1983, *Granta* magazine and the Book Marketing Council named him one of the "Best Twenty Young British Novelists," along with contemporaries Martin Amis, Salman Rushdie, Pat Barker, William Boyd, Kazuo Ishiguro, and Julian Barnes.

In the early 1980s, McEwan felt a need to break from the claustrophobic world of his early works and took a lengthy break from writing novels. During this time he wrote *Or Shall We Die?*, an oratorio about the threat of nuclear war, and *The Ploughman's Lunch*, a film directed by Richard Eyre. Such experiences helped alter McEwan's approach to writing novels by bringing his subject matter into a more public arena. As he explains in his interview with *Études britanniques contemporaines*, "*The Comfort of Strangers* edged into a slightly larger world, and by the time I'd written an oratorio about the threat of nuclear war and came to start *The Child in Time*, I thought I could find ways of bridging the earlier, small canvases of intense psychological states with a broader public reality."

With the publication of *The Child in Time* (1987), McEwan entered a fertile period of writing that witnessed the publication of several commercial and critical successes, including *The Innocent* (1990), *Black Dogs* (1992), *Enduring Love* (1997), and the Booker Prize–winning *Amsterdam* (1998). His reputation and fame grew throughout the 1990s, and he continues to flourish in this decade with a string of bestsellers, including *Atonement*, *Saturday*, and the critically acclaimed *On Chesil Beach*. McEwan often finds himself the subject of public scrutiny, a result of his tremendous commercial success and his consistent ability to write about matters relevant to contemporary society. He has dealt with a wide range of human experiences, including the effects of losing a child, religious fervor, psychological obsession, the intricacies of relationships, euthanasia, and happiness in a modern world bent on conflict and destruction. Once considered a writer of macabre subject matter, McEwan now finds himself more often described as England's greatest living author.

When evaluating selections for a volume in the Literary Conversations series, one quickly becomes aware of the different levels of conversations offered by a writer of McEwan's stature. This collection avoids the standard book tour profiles and interviews writers submit themselves to as they travel between cities to promote a new publication. McEwan's popularity ensures that countless publications of this kind exist—so many, in fact, that he admits in the final interview of this collection, "I spend a lot of my time avoiding interviews, and still I end up doing an awful lot. I probably refuse five times as many or ten times as many as I do." Despite this claim, McEwan frequently consents to lengthy and more intimate exchanges, and such pieces form the foundation of this collection. They include interviews with English, French, and Spanish scholars, conversations with artist Antony Gormley and psychologist Steven Pinker, and discussions with fellow authors Ian Hamilton, Christopher Ricks, David Remnick, Zadie Smith, and Martin Amis.

The interviews collected in this volume provide McEwan numerous occasions for self-reflection and clarification of the essential themes of his writing and, taken as a whole, provide the greatest opportunity for readers to understand the complexities of his works. McEwan approaches each of his novels with deep consideration and insight and is especially forthcoming about the creative impulse that sparks his narratives. "I looked for extreme situations, deranged narrators, obscenity, and shock—and to set these elements within a careful or disciplined prose," he tells Adam Begley in reference to his earliest stories. Of his first novel *The Cement Garden*, he explains to John Haffenden, "It has a definite genesis in one paragraph of my notes, at the doodling stage, where I suddenly had a whole novel unfold about a family living 'like burrowing animals . . . after mother dies the house seems to fall asleep.'" He describes to Begley how *Enduring Love* began, "with random scenes and sketches, whistling in the dark" and how an early draft of *Atonement* contained biographical information about the author Briony Tallis, a character he tells Jonathan Noakes was, "the most complete person I'd ever conjured." McEwan also provides detailed information about his other works, including his screenplay *The Ploughman's Lunch*, his children's stories, the oratorio *Or Shall We Die?*, and the libretto *For You*.

The act of creating features heavily throughout these interviews as McEwan discusses the intimate nature of his writing process. In his conversation with David Lynn, McEwan muses, "I write to find where I'm going." He elaborates by saying, "I do see writing, the actual physical matter of writing, as an act of imagination. And the best days, the best mornings are the ones in which forcing down a sentence might generate a surprise." Similarly, he tells Begley that writing is "a process you can't have, and don't want, under your full conscious control." About the tools of writing, McEwan explains to Noakes a crucial shift in how his thoughts are transferred to the written page: "Word processing, I think, delivered me into a wonderful virtual space. The chapter that is in the computer, but not yet printed, has the same—or the equivalent—virtual quality as an idea in your head that you've not committed to paper yet." McEwan likewise admits to Begley, "Word processing is more intimate, more like thinking itself. In retrospect, the typewriter seems a gross mechanical obstruction." Such examination of the physical act of writing and creating texts leads Zadie Smith to conclude that McEwan "is rather an artisan, always hard at work; refining, improving, engaged by and interested in every step in the process, like a scientist setting up a lab experiment."

While McEwan views writing as a "private, obsessive business" and prefers such privacy in his personal life, he also fully understands the role writers sometimes play in a larger society. The final interview in this collection pays special attention to this issue. When asked about submitting to interviews, McEwan replies with exquisite honesty, "It feels more like a duty, part of one's professional terms of engagement." McEwan is also aware of the dangers associated with such engagement, admitting, "[T]here's never anything final if you say something in public. You are likely to get misquoted, then attacked on the basis of something you never said." On occasion, McEwan struggles with the difficulty involved in finding a suitable balance, suggesting that writers "have to be careful about being drawn in to a celebrity-opinion culture that has a view about everything. Yet, on the other hand, sometimes it's important to speak up when certain public issues cross your own concerns."

The conversations selected for inclusion in this volume reveal several common themes, including relationships between men and women, the notion of time and space, truth, sexuality, terror, the darkness of human nature, religion and science, history, and the relationship between writing and life. The interviews were originally published in a variety of locations (Great Britain, North America, Canada, France, and Spain) and span thirty years, thus representing various phases of McEwan's career. In their totality, the interviews discuss the full range of McEwan's writings and elaborate on his interest in music, film, theatre, children's stories, the management of his celebrity, politics, and science, specifically evolutionary biology and environmental issues.

As editor, I selected the most in-depth, substantive, insightful, literate, and wide-ranging interviews and attempted to provide a balanced mix of less accessible interviews with those more frequently cited in scholarly studies. I have tried to avoid, as much as possible, repetitions, though in a few instances the material covered may overlap. The interviews included here appear in their original form, with only minor editing to improve clarity or to establish uniformity of presentation. They are arranged in the order in which they were conducted, from 1978 to 2008. The interviews originally appeared in a variety of publications and formats, including books, literary journals, weekly publications, and audio recordings.

Three of the interviews were previously available only in audio format and therefore provide exclusive material to scholars. McEwan's 1987 conversation with Martin Amis for the Institute of Contemporary Authors provides unique insights into his views on nuclear annihilation, while his conversation with David Remnick highlights McEwan's thoughtfulness and humour. The final interview in the collection addresses several topics of interest not covered elsewhere, including McEwan's views on the politics of environmentalism, plans for his papers, and his views on interviews as a genre. Each of these audio recordings were transcribed and jointly edited with Ian McEwan for clarity and precision of language. I trust readers and scholars will find these interviews of particular value. Not only do they offer insight into McEwan's work, but they also give a sense of his literary personality and growth as a writer. Taken as a whole, the interviews in this volume show how Ian McEwan constantly explores, articulates, and refines his views about writing, science, relationships, politics, and humanity.

This book would not have been possible without the contribution of all the people who have interviewed Ian McEwan, and I thank each of them for facilitating the use of their conversations. I would like to thank my best friend and beloved wife Tricia for her continued support on this and many other projects. Special thanks to Vanessa Guignery and Barbara Burkhardt for their encouragement and friendship, and to Lincoln Land Community College for supplementing my travel costs to London so I could interview Ian McEwan. My thanks also to Walter Biggins at the University Press of Mississippi for his assistance in making this volume possible.

I am indebted to Ian McEwan for his gracious interest in this collection, his suggestions of past interviews with merit, his tireless work editing audio transcripts, and for granting me the final conversation that concludes this volume. I greatly appreciate his consistent generosity and friendship.

RR

Chronology

1948   Ian Russell McEwan born 21 June in Aldershot, England, to David
        and Rose McEwan. Spends early life in military outposts in the Far
        East and North Africa.
1959   Attends boarding school at Woolverstone Hall, Suffolk.
1966   Enters the University of Sussex. Read English and French and be-
        gins writing fiction.
1970   Graduates from Sussex with an honors B.A. in English literature.
        Enters University of East Anglia and studies modern fiction and
        creative writing under Malcolm Bradbury and Angus Wilson.
1971   Receives M.A. in creative writing.
1972   Publishes first short story, "Homemade" in *New American Review*.
        Travels to Afghanistan.
1974   Meets Ian Hamilton, who later publishes a few of McEwan's short
        stories in *The New Review*.
1975   Publishes first collection of stories, *First Love, Last Rites*.
1976   Receives Somerset Maugham Award for *First Love, Last Rites*.
        "Jack Flea's Birthday Celebration" airs on the BBC on 10 April.
        Travels to the United States.
1978   Publishes second collection of stories, *In Between the Sheets*, and
        first novel, *The Cement Garden*.
1979   BBC halts production on filming of television adaptation of "Solid
        Geometry."
1980   "The Imitation Game" airs on the BBC on 24 April.
1981   Publishes *The Imitation Game* and *The Comfort of Strangers*,
        which is shortlisted for the Booker Prize for Fiction.
1982   Marries Penny Allen, with whom he has two sons.
1983   Named by *Granta* and the Book Marketing Council as one of the
        20 Best Young British Novelists. London Symphony Orchestra
        performs *Or Shall We Die?* Film release of *The Ploughman's
        Lunch*, which receives the *Evening Standard* Award for best film,
        best director (Richard Eyre), and best screenplay.
1984   Fellowship of the Royal Society of Literature.
1985   Publishes *Rose Blanche*.
1987   Publishes *The Child in Time*, which wins Whitbread Book of the

the Year award. Visited Soviet Union with delegation from END (European Nuclear Disarmament).

1988 Publishes *Soursweet*, a film script based on a Timothy Mo novel.

1990 Publishes *The Innocent*. Release of the film adaptation of *The Comfort of Strangers*.

1992 Publishes *Black Dogs*, which is shortlisted for the Booker Prize for Fiction.

1993 *The Good Son* is released, as are film adaptations of *The Cement Garden* and *The Innocent*. Awarded the Prix Fémina Etranger (France) for *The Child in Time*.

1994 Publishes *The Daydreamer*.

1995 Divorces Penny Allen.

1997 Marries Annalena McAfee. Publishes *Enduring Love*, which is shortlisted for the James Tait Black Memorial Prize.

1998 Publishes *Amsterdam*, which wins the 1998 Booker Prize for Fiction.

1999 Awarded the Shakespeare Prize (Germany).

2000 Distinguished as Commanders of the Order of the British Empire (CBE).

2001 Publishes *Atonement*, which is shortlisted for several prizes, including the Booker Prize for Fiction, James Tait Black Memorial Prize, and the Whitbread Novel Award.

2002 *Atonement* makes shortlist for the Los Angeles Times Book Prize and wins the WH Smith Literary Award.

2003 Receives the National Book Critics' Circle Fiction Award (USA) for *Atonement*.

2004 Release of the film adaptation of *Enduring Love*.

2005 Publishes *Saturday*. Shortlisted for the Man Booker International Prize.

2006 Receives the James Tait Black Memorial Prize for *Saturday*.

2007 Publishes *On Chesil Beach*, which is shortlisted for the 2007 Man Booker Prize for Fiction. Release of the film adaptation of *Atonement*.

2008 Publishes *For You: The Libretto* with performances by Music Theatre Wales. Receives British Book Awards Author of the Year and Book of the Year for *On Chesil Beach*. Receives the Good Housekeeping Book Award for Best Author. Film adaptation of *Atonement* receives seven Academy Award nominations, wins for Best Original Score, and also wins the BAFTA Film Award for Best Film.

Conversations with Ian McEwan

Points of Departure

Ian Hamilton/1978

From *The New Review* 5.2 (Autumn 1978): 9–21. Reprinted by permission of the Ian Hamilton Estate.

Ian Hamilton: You have published two volumes of short stories and now your first novel, *The Cement Garden*, has appeared. I'd like to ask you about these later on, but first perhaps we could talk about your "background," as they say . . .

Ian McEwan: Well, it was an army background, I suppose. I was born in Aldershot in 1948 and my first years were spent in a married quarters prefab. My father was a Scots sergeant-major. He'd joined the army in 1932 as a regular, simply because of unemployment in Glasgow. My mother was a local girl who had lost her first husband in the war, so I have a stepbrother and stepsister. She'd known extreme poverty, especially after her first husband died. In 1947, life was extremely difficult for a widow with two children. She was about thirty when she married my father—he was twenty-nine.

Hamilton: What are they like, are they similar in personality?

McEwan: No, not at all. My father was, and still is, a very well built, handsome man with a military moustache. And, like his own mother, he's very domineering. My mother, even though she'd looked after her own large family of sisters when she was a girl, and had also had this hard stretch during her twenties, was—and is—a very gentle woman, very easily tyrannised.

Hamilton: I suppose that although you had a stepbrother and a stepsister you probably still viewed yourself as an only child?

McEwan: Yes, I did in a way. For a start, they were so much older. And in any case my stepbrother lived with his grandmother—rather an ogre of a lady, who'd offered to take on one of the children when my mother's first husband died. So he was brought up in a council house full of gleaming and intimidating objects: china dogs and a vast polished stereogram.

Hamilton: Unenviable comforts. So the family was really split up from the start.

McEwan: Yes, and all the more so when my father was posted to Singapore. I was about three or four at the time. The stepbrother stayed behind.

Hamilton: How do you remember your father from those early years? You've said he was domineering.

McEwan: Well, initially he was something of a stranger to me. He would go off all week to work and only come back at weekends. He always had a very rough manner, although in fact he is a very affectionate man. He finds it hard to be directly affectionate. As a kid, he scared the shit out of me. One of my earliest memories is of seeing this figure in the rain, pushing his bicycle past the prefab window; when I saw him, I'd run behind the settee and call to my mother to send him away. As far as I was concerned, he was an intruder into my rather intense, pleasant relationship with my mother.

Hamilton: You all moved to Singapore when you were three. Do you remember much of that?

McEwan: Not a great deal. I think it was like many army places abroad. They're like small council estates anywhere in England. The sense of being somewhere foreign is down to things like the sunshine and one or two servants. I had a nanny, which I think of as one of my greatest accomplishments. She was seventeen years old, and very beautiful. She used to sleep in my bed or, rather, at the bottom of it. She taught me Chinese, which I like to think I could recover under intense hypno-therapy.

Hamilton: You were there for how long?

McEwan: Oh, until I was about six. For a bit after that we lived in various postings in England. By the time I was eight my father had received his commission—he was now an officer.

Hamilton: Did he ever hope that you'd end up in khaki?

McEwan: He may have done, but I think he knew right from the beginning that it was not my kind of scene at all. He would probably have been delighted if I'd shown the slightest interest, but I didn't. And in any case, he was very keen that I should get an education. He had won a scholarship to Grammar School when he was fourteen but couldn't go because the family couldn't afford the school uniform.

Hamilton: So he sent you to boarding school.

McEwan: Well, yes, but that was later on, when I was about twelve. In between there was a spell in Africa. This was a very happy time for me, that pre-teen stretch of childhood. I had many very close friends, and I used to do a lot of things with my father—physical things. Life was very open air, a great deal of running free, swimming, exploring the coast and the desert. Compared to the years that followed, say thirteen to seventeen, it was bliss. I read a lot, a huge amount. My mother worked briefly in the YMCA bookshop and she used to bring me books back from the shop. I read Jennings and Enid Blyton books. I didn't read any of the books that everyone else I met later on had read—C. S. Lewis and Winnie the Pooh or *The Hobbit*—I missed out on the great middle class English read. I read indiscriminately and with great pleasure: Biggles, Gimlet, all the comics, and Billy Bunter.

Hamilton: So you had some kind of notion of what being sent back to boarding school in England would be like?

McEwan: Yes, I was quite excited. I remember looking at all those pamphlets; I suppose they must have been for public schools, but I wasn't at all sure. In the end I was sent to a state-run boarding school in Suffolk. My mother wasn't at all happy about the whole thing, but she didn't say anything.

Hamilton: It must have been strange, setting off.

McEwan: It was. I remember leaving. We flew in a DC3 from a little army air strip. I remember sitting next to two old ladies. I was sitting by the window and I was weeping and blubbering quite copiously and they started to weep and blubber too. Then I looked out of the window and I realised with horror that my mother, who was standing about fifty yards away on the sand, was also crying. I think it was then that I had a strong sense of what it was really all about, that it wasn't just some sort of Jennings adventure. I mean, I really had left home.

Hamilton: And the school, what was that like?

McEwan: Well, it was a peculiar school—it's a place called Woolverstone Hall—in the sense that, although its intake was mostly intelligent working class London kids, it was still run along the lines of a minor public school. Although I'm sure it was more liberal than most public schools of the time.

Hamilton: All boys, I suppose? And all obsessed with sex, one way or another?

McEwan: Yes, and all that came as a complete shock. However, at first I was so innocent that I didn't even notice it, or when I did notice it didn't seem to have anything to do with me. I think it was only after I'd been there for a couple of terms that I began dimly to understand what people meant by "wank." Even then, wanking didn't seem to be something that I might conceivably ever do. It's odd, but much of that time between twelve and, I suppose, sixteen or seventeen I remember as just *empty* time—we had a lot of time to ourselves and much of it I spent feeling rather at a loss.

Hamilton: Were you a studious type?

McEwan: No, I was a very mediocre pupil—at any rate, during that middle period I've just described. I was always twenty-sixth out of thirty or twenty-first. I was ignored, really. I remember there were some boys who were taken up by individual masters—who were pederasts, presumably. They never buggered the kids but they took a lot of time over them. I was always a very quiet, extremely shy, pale kid who didn't get taken up by the teachers or bullied by the bullies. There were far more obvious victims. There were thin kids, or fat kids or very cocky kids, and somehow I always seemed to get missed. But just as I avoided the bullying, I also missed any kind of direction from the teachers. Most people seemed to have a great deal of difficulty remembering my name. I was always being confused with some other kid who looked vaguely like me.

Hamilton: Did all this offend you?

McEwan: No, not at all. I just wanted to survive. I didn't want to get beaten up. There's nothing else really I can say about that stretch of my adolescence. It wasn't until, I suppose, I was about sixteen or seventeen that things began to happen. The hormones started to flow. I became intensely competitive and started to read books and became good at all the things I was doing. And then suddenly teachers started to take some notice of me, and I won prizes. I also made some very intense friendships with other boys. Because the school was completely girl-less, one started to eye little boys with passion. That took up quite a bit of my time.

Hamilton: What kind of thing were you reading at that time?

McEwan: Oh, anything noble, superior, and tragic. I fell in love with the countryside and read *The Prelude*. I read Keats, Shelley, and, because this was Suffolk, George Crabbe. Life suddenly had an edge to it. This was now about 1965 and sneaking out to the pubs I discovered just how much fun it was to do things which people didn't approve of. I started to write poems, poems modelled on Shakespeare's *Sonnets*, I suppose because of the pederastic element. I'd write poems that had names of little boys spelled out in them.

Hamilton: Risky stuff: Were they efficiently decoded?

McEwan: Well, in fact, I discovered much later on that some little boy had written a letter to my parents telling them that I was a wicked fellow. Luckily my mother intercepted it before it reached my father, but it certainly made her very unhappy in ways that she couldn't ever tell *me* about. She mentioned it a year later after I'd brought my first girl home. She was immensely relieved. I'd always wondered why girlfriends received such special treatment, were fêted almost. I mean, few other mothers at the time would make sure that a double bed was available when your girlfriend came to stay. It was simply because she thought I was destined to become a raging gay.

Hamilton: How much of all the swinging sixties stuff got into your day to day life at school? It would all have been at its height about the time of your hormonal upsurge, I suppose.

McEwan: We didn't even realise it was happening. By the time we were in the sixth form we were writing long solemn pieces in the school magazine about the legitimacy of homosexual relationships and the need for everyone not to wear uniform and how power should be spread and decisions should be taken by the students. But we had no idea *why* we thought that.

Hamilton: Did you have the traditional very special English master that most writers seem to have had?

McEwan: Oh, do they? Well, yes, I did. He was twenty-six or twenty-seven, and cynical and well read and a Leavisite. It was through him that I *got* English, or however you'd describe it. I read, needless to say, *The Great Tradition* and *The Common Pursuit* and *Reading and Discrimination*. I became very excited about English Literature as a monkhood and became determined to go to University and teach the stuff.

Hamilton: What did your Leavisite teacher make of the Beatles and all that? Disapproving, I assume.

McEwan: Yes, I became awfully torn. I remember pitching quite violently between, on the one hand, loving rock and roll and, on the other, feeling it was my *duty* to be more critical. The whole time I was at school, from the time I was eleven, there was always Buddy Holly, Elvis Presley, Eddie Cochran, and so on. By the time I was fourteen I had been to my first rock and roll concert. I paid 3s 6d to see the Rolling Stones play the Church Hall in Guildford. And yet I refused to listen to the Beatles' third album because I had suddenly decided it was all manipulative trash. A couple of months later I changed my mind. I couldn't line up my excitement about the poetry, about "serious books," my involvement with this élitist aesthetic of the inner life, and with the teachers who believed in such an élite—I simply couldn't square all this with my interest in rock and roll music. I was quite unnecessarily confused.

Hamilton: After school you went to Sussex . . .
McEwan: Well, I took a year off. At first I went home but I felt too excited to stay around. I went to London and more or less read my way through the Sussex book list. For a while I was a dustman with the Camden Council. Then I went to Greece for a time, and when I came back I did some more time as a dustman. This was about 1967, the time of *Sergeant Pepper*, which I regarded as very important. At the time, though, I was a dustman all day and I'd come back at night totally exhausted and all the things that were going on in London at that time simply passed me by. I was just too tired to go out. I didn't know anything about that whole upsurge of whatever it was. In fact, I simply felt pleased with my independence; I thought it was remarkable to be earning money each week and not sleeping in a dormitory.

Hamilton: Why was *Sergeant Pepper* so important?
McEwan: Well, it was a unity, it had shape, it was allusive, it was exhilarating music. It resolved for me the ambivalences I felt about pop music.

Hamilton: I've always understood that a lot of the allusions in *Sergeant Pepper* were to drugs, the drug scene . . .
McEwan: I didn't know anyone at that time who had any drugs so they weren't in my life at all . . . I certainly would have tried anything or everything. In a way that whole era, which was at its peak around 1967—psychedelia, the Arts Labs—it all passed me by.
Hamilton: You read English at Sussex. What was that like?

McEwan: Yes, English and French. Sussex was something of a disappointment to me. After a year off, it was like arriving at school again. I expected to be up all night having wild or serious conversations and I was naively horrified to find myself in a totally unintellectual environment: the student union was full of pinball machines and table football. Most of my contemporaries in tutorials didn't even know what century Alexander Pope wrote in, let alone know anything about his work. So, no seminal conversations. I found myself trooping off every night to small terraced houses, jam-packed with people on the stairs all trying to get into a party. Worst of all, Sussex had this very debby and snobbish element, more so probably than in Cambridge—a thriving nucleus of upper middle class girls and boys who wanted to become media kings and were involved in the London season, or what was left of it. Still, I was very happily in love with a beautiful girl, and I had some good friends there.

Hamilton: What about the teachers?
McEwan: They were rather remote. The tutorial system bred a paternal atmosphere in which you might meet your tutor socially once a term over a glass of sherry. There weren't any teachers there who made me feel very excited.

Hamilton: Were you reading modern fiction?
McEwan: Yes, a certain amount. I'd started reading modern fiction in my last year at school—Iris Murdoch, William Golding. *The Catcher in the Rye* was very important and *Catch-22*. On the whole, though, when I got to Sussex I stopped reading. I felt I had a lot of time, now, because I seemed to have read a lot more than most of the people around me, and I started handing in my school essays with the teachers' comments rubbed out, and kept getting A's for them.

Hamilton: What did you get for them at school?
McEwan: B minus.

Hamilton: So you went around feeling a bit superior and contemptuous?
McEwan: Not particularly. I just found the place unexciting. There was no sparkle. And the effect of that, fortunately, was that my commitment to the idea of Eng Lit began to wear a bit thin.

Hamilton: What about your donnish ambitions?

McEwan: Well, they just vanished, quite slowly without my quite realising it. Not that I could think of anything else to be—except a writer. But everyone I knew wanted to be a writer.

Hamilton: Were you in fact writing then?
McEwan: Yes, by my third year I'd written a stage play and a radio play and I'd adapted a Thomas Mann short story for television. None of these was commissioned, I should say, nor performed. With the television play, for instance, I thought it would be a simple matter of sending it to the BBC and they'd send me a cheque by return of post. I think its opening line was "Dawn. Lubeck. A huge crowd flows over a bridge." It would have needed a budget of two million pounds. I also started to write a novel and I thought the best way to do this would be to go into a wood and simply write it. I'd get to this dank little wood near the Library at Sussex and sit on an ant-infested log. I thought if I write a page a day of this it will only take me less than half a year and then I'll have one of those thin Penguin novels. The desire to be a writer really did precede the material. It seemed that this might be a way out. I toyed with various impossible ideas for M.A. dissertations but luckily none of them was accepted, and then just a week before the Autumn term was about to start, I read that the University of East Anglia were offering an M.A. for which one could submit a little bit of fiction instead of the written thesis. Even though it only made up a sixth, I think, of the M.A. it seemed like a chance . . . so I went there.

Hamilton: So at this stage you were to some extent committed to the idea of fiction as opposed to plays, or poetry?
McEwan: Yes, well, I did feel for sure that fiction was something I could exercise some control over. For me, poetry had become a matter of writing like certain other poets whereas, for some reason, I don't know why, prose hadn't. It seemed to allow me some chance of self-determination, even though I'd only written two stories at the time.

Hamilton: Had you shown these early stories to anyone?
McEwan: No, I hadn't shown stuff to anyone. I went to UEA and I had a very good year there. In fact, it was very easy to fulfill the M.A. requirements. It was all in modern fiction, for a start. They were books one would have read anyway: Mailer, Nabokov, and so on, none of whom I'd actually read—and there was little comparative literature. So for most of the year I sat tight and wrote stories, about twenty-five.

Hamilton: Had you become at all involved in politics?

McEwan: At Sussex a bit, yes—I assume you mean student politics—I'd taken part, but not in an active way. I remember there was a great issue at Sussex over the accessibility of files on students. I got fairly involved in that. But as soon as I went to Norwich, to UEA, I found myself right in the centre of an occupation of a building which lasted two weeks. The occupation was very successful, in a sense. It was a model of anarchist government or non-government. Anarchist administration. Students ran their own seminars and the place came alive.

Hamilton: What happened in the end?

McEwan: Well, the thing fizzled out, the way these things do. It was a very good year, though. For the first time, I was sleeping with lots of girls—instead of one at time. It was a second adolescence. I stopped reading books, stopped listening to classical music. I suppose I felt I could write books, so there was no need to read them any more.

Hamilton: Were you at all "into" the drug, hippy business by this stage?

McEwan: Well, I was in it, but I did feel slightly separate from it. I knew myself to be conditioned by another intensely rational tradition. And hippydom was calculatedly anti-rational, a non-verbal world which provided a holiday of the senses, great freedom. But I could never quite leave behind things which I felt were important. I became interested in science in my years at Sussex, and in the philosophy of science. I valued scientific method. And yet here I was sitting around in rooms, cross-legged, with people who were—I don't know what they were really: they had conspiracy theories about the world, they were fundamentally hedonistic, and in fact politically fairly conservative. In this country at least, the political aspect of all that sixties turmoil was separate from this other fun, dope-smoking aspect. Many hippies talked about getting out to cottages and communes in the country. Their values were effectively conservative ones—self-preserving and escapist. For them political analysis smacked too much of rational, linear thought. For me it was a great release from a studious, cautious way of proceeding: suddenly nothing mattered whereas things up to then had always mattered in a way that had been inhibiting.

Hamilton: You'd begun to publish stories by this time?

McEwan: Yes, I'd sold "Homemade" to the *New American Review* and another story to the *Transatlantic Review*. And Secker and Warburg had asked me to turn "Homemade" into the first chapter of a novel. So after Norwich, I had a period in Cambridge trying to write a second chapter. I wasted two months on that, even though I knew all along that it wasn't going to work. Then one day some friends phoned up and said they had bought a bus and were going on the hippy trail to Afghanistan. The offer coincided with the money arriving from America for "Homemade," so I thought, well, this is the kind of call no writer ignores.

Hamilton: So by now you were "a writer"?

McEwan: Well, it was still an aspiration. I don't think I would have described myself unambiguously as a writer—probably because I wanted to be one so much by that point and I didn't dare say it.

Hamilton: The going off to Afghanistan. Was there a touch of the theatrical in that?

McEwan: It didn't seem so at the time. Looking back, the whole thing has shrunk into being something I was glad I did and actually didn't much enjoy. I was with friends I liked very much, but we were always waiting around in Teheran or Munich for money to come through. Long, long weeks of waiting. Boredom and smoking hash in huge quantities without any real point. I mean, I far prefer drugs when they are a subsidiary feature. If you have a drink with a friend and there's no conversation it's a little pointless. In the same way if you're smoking and you're just hanging around, it's pointless. I was much relieved to get back to Norwich. All I wanted was to have a room somewhere with silence and get on with some work.

Hamilton: Did you write anything during the Afghanistan trip?

McEwan: No, I just went off and didn't think about writing. Well, I thought about it but I didn't do anything about it. And when I came back I was rather unsettled and I spent the autumn of 1972 writing notes and teaching English as a second language. Then I sold "Disguises" to the *American Review.* "Disguises" is between twelve and fifteen thousand words long and they gave me $600 for it. This was Christmas 1972 and I was so excited by that that I instantly wrote three stories on the trot. I wrote "Last Day of Summer" and "Butterflies" and "Solid Geometry" on a wave of confidence.

Hamilton: "Solid Geometry" was the first story of yours that we published. It's very ingeniously put together, rather more planned out than some of your other stories of the same period.

McEwan: I suppose it's the most anecdotal. It had different sources. I'd been reading Bertrand Russell's diaries, which had just come out in paperback and I suddenly wished that I had a grandfather or a great-grandfather who had been as interesting or as literate, who had written about his own life in the way that Bertrand Russell had—those were the origins of the narrator obsessed by his great-grandfather's diaries. I had had some lengthy and fascinating conversations with an Argentinian mathematician. I also wanted to write about the kind of people I'd gone to Afghanistan with. So I wrote in a woman, or a girl, in that world, a kind of hippy girl. The narrator is rather a nasty person, cold, sexless, self-obsessed and yet the girl he has married, whatever her warmth and obvious sexuality, is sadly self-deceiving. The story is really about the kind of confusions I felt about where I stood. I was coming down from being someone who'd spent long months in that girl's world and yet I had some wistful nostalgia for it too.

Hamilton: Did you have any view of the "kind of story" you wanted to write, in the way that poets often have very defined ideas about the kind of poem that's "needed" at a given time?
McEwan: No, I don't think I ever had any really clear concept of what I was up to. I think I had an idea that each story I wrote was a kind of pastiche of a certain style and even if after a page or two into the story I began to take it seriously, its origins were always slightly parodic.

Hamilton: Of what, what sort of thing?
McEwan: Either a particular writer or a particular style. "Homemade" when I started it was, I thought, an elaborate send-up of Henry Miller. But then I got into it and felt that this was at least going to be an amusing story. But still by the time I finished it I still felt it was about the absurdities of adolescent male dignity.

Hamilton: The narrator in "Homemade" is looking back on his first sexual experience. How old is he now, at the time of telling the story?
McEwan: Well, I suppose he's meant to be a sort of Henry Miller-ish age, a wizened sixty. It's really about sexual self-aggrandisement. I mean, I had noticed that people, men especially, when they recount episodes of sexual failure, are frequently indulging a form of self-regard—in other words, so successful they can afford to admit failure. And I wanted to write a story about *total* sexual failure. I know it's fairly common for writers to write "my first fuck" stories but I wanted to write a first fuck story where the actual

fuck would be abysmally useless and yet its narrator would foolishly still derive huge satisfaction from it. The bleak satisfaction being simply that he'd got his cock into a cunt and come.

Hamilton: The narrator, though, has in the fullness of time become a rather poised, knowing man of the world.
McEwan: Yes, that poise is integral to the self-regard I mentioned. I suppose that tone came mostly from Miller and a little bit from Mailer, both of whom I enjoyed but thought were totally bogus, and I wanted to send them up.

Hamilton: What other stories started as pastiche?
McEwan: Well, I very much admired *The Collector*. I still do, I think it's Fowles's best book. And in "Conversation with a Cupboard Man" I wanted to do the kind of voice of the man in *The Collector*: that kind of wheedling, self-pitying lower middle-class voice. That was the starting point for the story. What tended to come out in the end was some mixture of what I'd read and my own experience. It was just that at that stage I was a bit of a counter-puncher and material from my own life didn't suggest itself imme-diately. Pastiche seemed a short cut, the line of least resistance.

Hamilton: I sometimes find in those early stories that the first person nar-rator is a lot more literate, if not literary, than you'd imagine him to be if you had a third person account of how he actually behaves.
McEwan: I think that's a legitimate criticism. But then, those stories are not dramatic monologues inside a naturalistic framework. The problem is, as an author you want it both ways. You want your narrator to carry lines which are *your* best lines. If you have a first person narrator, who else can you give your best lines to? Irony will only take you so far. You end up giv-ing them to a person who's meant to be morally discredited. In this sense there is a problem with those early stories; there is a confusion about them. The narrators are fools, and yet at the same time you want them to be fairly perceptive people.

Hamilton: Your first book, *First Love, Last Rites* was accepted for publica-tion by Cape in 1974, wasn't it? What happened to the arrangement with Secker and Warburg?
McEwan: There wasn't any formal arrangement. Tom Rosenthal of Secker wanted to arrange a deal whereby he would give me £1000 to write a novel and then only when the novel was published would he publish my short

stories. But I still felt a long way from writing a novel and I didn't want to sign any contract that would tie up my stories. At that point Tom Maschler of Jonathan Cape came in and said he would publish my stories straight away.

Hamilton: How did you feel about the reception of that first book?
McEwan: Well, I was rather innocently surprised. For example, when I wrote the stories in *First Love, Last Rites* I had no idea that they amounted to a sequence of salacious plots. I was astonished to read the plot summaries in the reviews.

Hamilton: What, were they wrong?
McEwan: No, they were perfectly accurate in a limited way . . . Each story seemed to me a fresh departure. I didn't think I'd put together eight stories whose content was exclusively sexual. I could see immediately, as soon as I read the reviews, that of course that's how they would appear. It was like eavesdropping on a conversation about oneself between fairly intelligent strangers—not malicious people. It was just the odd experience of having your fiction described back to you in ways that you wouldn't describe it yourself. I was astonished to find myself characterised as someone obsessed by certain forms of sexuality. Nevertheless I could not afford to be inhibited by that when I began the stories that made up the second collection. And yet I suppose it bred a certain self-consciousness. "Reflections of a Kept Ape" and "To and Fro" for example are self-reflecting stories.

Hamilton: Both of those appeared in *The New Review*, I'm glad to say, and the "Ape" story in particular is one I'm often asked about. In fact, I'm often asked quite simply: "What's it about?"
McEwan: It's meant to be a funny story really. I had a lot of fun writing it. It's a story I suppose about writerly alter-egos, the pressures writers generate for themselves. The fear of repeating oneself. And it's also about a rejected lover, an insistent, rejected lover peering over one's shoulder.

Hamilton: You held out against writing a novel for quite a time. Were you consciously determined to, as it were, keep faith with the idea of the short story?
McEwan: I didn't want to be talked out of it by other people. And also there's something self-perpetuating about stories. Once you've done one, or half a dozen or thirty, almost any idea will automatically suggest itself in those

terms. Even though I did start five or six novels between 1973 and 1976, I felt that this was a strategic wish, not one that was based round genuine material. The wish to write a novel preceded the wish to write at all. Frequently, when I started writing, I had an immediate impulse to pare the idea down, to reduce it to its most minimal aspect and so it would be a short story or a half hour television play. It wasn't until I'd written "Psychopolis" after I'd come back from the States in '76 that I felt some confidence about length. That story was about 12,000 words and practically wrote itself. Suddenly one afternoon I sat down and wrote up some notes that I'd written earlier; and I wrote them up as the plot of a novel, definitely a novel this time and not a short story. I felt I could now go ahead, that the material was there and I wasn't simply submitting to the idea of the form.

Hamilton: Meanwhile *In Between the Sheets*, your second collection of stories, was appearing and reviewers continued to note your odd obsessions. Do you in fact have obsessions you'd own up to?

McEwan: I'm not a particularly obsessive person, but that's a different matter. One simply cannot account for everything one does as a writer. And as a writer I have a number of obsessions—some writers are allowed to call their obsessions "themes." Oedipal situations recur constantly in my work, for example. I think an awful lot of adult maneuvering and adult sexuality is related to some version of how women related to their fathers and how men related to their mothers. And I think there's a projected sense of evil in my stories which is of the kind whereby one tries to imagine the worst thing possible in order to get hold of the good. I used to play this game as a kid, and in some ways I still play it, trying to conjecture the worst. "Butterflies," for instance, was one of the worst things I could think of. Yet in a nightmarish way I could indulge in it, in the idea of it. I frightened myself with "Butterflies." I still feel vulnerable, though, when people say: what is it with you that makes up these kind of stories? It's very difficult to describe the relation between one's self and one's material. I feel ultimately that there is no other explanation beyond the stories themselves.

Hamilton: Well there is plenty of oedipal activity in your novel, *The Cement Garden*, in which a family of children try to hide the fact that their mother is dead, so that they won't be split up, or taken into care. They bury her in the cellar, and then try to fend for themselves as if nothing had happened. I had the feeling when I first read it that I'd come across this same situation somewhere else, in some other book—or maybe book review. Did you have a source?

McEwan: It didn't have a specific source although since I've written it I've discovered there are plots very similar to mine. There's a novel which I have not read by Julian Gloag called *Our Mother's House* in which a band of kids bury their mother in the garden rather than be separated. And funnily enough I've just had one of those Kirkus Reviews which go round the libraries and review circuits, and it refers to this "familiar" plot. So maybe I've absorbed it. But its origins for me personally are to do with my childhood fascination with large families. As an only child I was struck by the degree of interesting neglect that was possible with large families. The children weren't *always* being loved, always being tended to. When I went to stay with friends from large families, there was always this heady sense that anything could happen, and the parents were remote. An only child is a fixed point in a triangle; I was struck by a sense of animal freedom when I went to stay with a family of five or six children.

Hamilton: Even so, their parents weren't buried in a cellar. In your novel, the girl Julie assumes a semi-parental role, but ends up performing incest with her brother, the narrator Jack . . .

McEwan: Well, yes, but I didn't want a situation in which, because the parents have died, the children just assumed roles which were identical to those of parents. I had an idea that in the nuclear family the kind of forces that are being suppressed—the oedipal, incestuous forces—are also paradoxically the very forces which keep the family together. So if you remove the controls, you have a ripe anarchy in which the oedipal and the incestuous are the definitive emotions. From Jack's point of view Julie becomes something that he aspires to sexually, even though she is his sister and also, in the circumstances, acting as mother to his younger brother and to some extent to Jack himself. I suppose I'm suggesting a situation in which the oedipal and the incestuous are identical.

Hamilton: It certainly strikes one that you are more interested in this aspect of the situation than in the suspense element—will the mother's corpse be found or not?—though the suspense is certainly there.

McEwan: Yes, I wanted the situation to develop. I didn't want the children glancing over their shoulders all the time. I wanted the mother's death to be a point of departure, not a constant presence.

Hamilton: What, if any, different demands did you encounter with the novel, compared to the short story?

McEwan: Well, I was fairly confident because I knew that my material, even when pared down, as it was, could only take the shape of a novel. There are certain strengths of the short story form which I tried to build into the novel. I wanted it to be a short novel, a novel you could read in one go. I wanted it to hold the reader's attention for two or three hours in the way that a short story writer would expect to hold the reader's attention for half an hour or forty minutes. I quite deliberately chose a fairly closed off situation, partly out of a sense of nervousness about having to deal with too much too soon all at once. There's a limited number of characters and the drama ends when the outside world intervenes. So it's a formal compromise and, I hope, a fairly effective one. I think within the limits I set myself I've worked efficiently and honestly. But all the same, it is a very small canvas, and this could be my novel's weakness.

Hamilton: What will happen next, do you think?

McEwan: I'd like what I do next to be larger, more complex, taking into account the adult world, adultly observed. I've recently finished a TV film about the role of women in the Second World War. I'd like to preserve some intensity in my fiction. "Psychopolis" seems to me the kind of direction I'm trying to find. In a way it's like suddenly aspiring to very conventional models. I don't know. What I do know is that there's very little space left for me now in the fishpond I've made, in the stories. Writing the novel was a satisfying experience, but it's almost as if something is now all wrapped up, the material has been recapitulated and condensed. Adolescent narrators have been for me a very useful rhetorical device. Now I'll just have to push on. I've no particular brief on adolescence.

Adolescence and After

Christopher Ricks/1979

From *Listener*, 12 April 1979: 526–27. Reprinted by permission of author.

Ian McEwan was born in 1948; his father was in the army, so they saw the world—Germany, Tripoli, Singapore—until, at eleven, he was sent to a London Educational Authority boarding-school in Suffolk. A dark time, apparently. Things brightened when he went to the University of Sussex, and got brighter still at the University of East Anglia, where he could submit as part of his MA degree three short stories. Then *The New American Review* published his story, "Homemade."

There's a hard sheen to everything he does, a combination of fire and ice which chills some people and scorches others, but which, at its best, has the hiss of steel being tempered. With a gaze that is levelled, he looks at cruelty and hardness of heart, and there is to be no flinching. Lately, though—and this is a crucial time for him, as he turns away from his known territory, adolescence, to what is now closer to him and so more difficult to see with perspective—McEwan has turned his sharp eye on tenderness, on the pains of gentleness and of strange love. Near the end of his latest novel, *The Cement Garden,* the love of Jack and his sister Julie is seen with truth and as truth.

Christopher Ricks: A lot of people have thought that the world of your stories is a very nasty world. I mean, horrible things are being imagined, and some pretty horrible things are being done. What do you think about the complaint that that's just voguish nastiness?
Ian McEwan: I always find this rather difficult to answer. I suppose if you talk about it in the simplest way possible—and that is if I'm sitting down facing an empty sheet of paper—what is going to compel me into writing fiction is not what is nice and easy and pleasant and somehow affirming, but somehow what is bad and difficult and unsettling. That's the kind of tension I need to start me writing. Beyond that, I suppose, I've always been trying to assert some kind of slender optimism in my stories, and I don't think I can really do that unless I can do it in a world that seems to me to be fundamen-

tally threatening, so what I really worry about is gratuitous optimism, not gratuitous violence.

Ricks: Your own life has been fairly settled. I was wondering about your childhood, for example. Given the horrifying imaginings about childhood in the stories and in *The Cement Garden*, what was your childhood like?

McEwan: Well, I have a brother and a sister, but they're much older than I am, so in effect I'm an only child. Certainly that stretch of my childhood up to about eleven or twelve was a very secure one, and very happy. I spent a lot of my childhood in North Africa—a very easy, outdoor kind of life. Yes, I think it's true, fundamentally, I was and I think still am a fairly secure person in that sense, and I can let things go when I sit down and enter the rather closed-off special world of trying to make a fiction. I don't feel threatened by my fiction. For example, if I spend a day writing a piece of prose which is ultimately going to be part of a story, and it's going to be something violent or something terrible, at the end of that day what I will feel, if I think I've achieved what I set out to achieve, will be elation and pleasure. It won't have much to do with the content of what I've done.

Ricks: You write a lot about adolescence, don't you? I know you wouldn't want to be typed as the adolescence man, but you write a lot about that particular hallucinatory clarity of one's physical self, and about masturbation and so on.

McEwan: I write about adolescence, or I have written about adolescence, because it does provide me with a fairly unique rhetorical standpoint. That is, adolescents are an extraordinary, special case of people; they're close to childhood, and yet they are constantly baffled and irritated by the initiations into what's on the other side—the shadow line, as it were. They are perfect outsiders, in a sense, and fiction—especially short stories, and especially first-person narratives—can thrive on a point of view which is somehow dislocated, removed.

Ricks: So do you think as you become more a novelist and less a short story writer—am I right in supposing that that's a move you might make, heralded by *The Cement Garden*—are you likely then to move away from adolescence for something like a technical reason?

McEwan: Yes, partly a technical reason. For sure, I think *The Cement Garden* is the last time, certainly in the near future, that I will spend months and months occupying the mind, living inside the mind of a fifteen-year-old. I was trying to set up a situation where suddenly there were no social controls. Suddenly, children find themselves in the house—there are no teachers, no parents, no figures of authority, they have total freedom—and yet they are completely paralysed. The narrator is at first almost catatonic with freedom—can't move at all. Yes, I would like to broaden out this scope. There's something about why we do have a certain kind of rhetorical freedom by having adolescents as narrators—you do also lock yourself into a fairly small space. That, maybe, is the problem with *The Cement Garden.* There is something of a challenge trying to have the adult world adultly observed, which I think must be faced.

Ricks: You were abroad a lot, weren't you, as a child? And also, I gather, you used the money from the success of your first story to travel to Afghanistan, and you spent some time in America. What about the freedom of those literally other airs? Do you feel that's affected you a lot?

McEwan: Yes it has, travel has been very important to me, especially the travel I've done in the last four or five years. I rather like to travel alone, and I suppose that the travel is a way of not doing anything else. I mean, I don't write when I'm travelling. I don't even think about writing. Travelling rather puts you in the role of author—you're passing constantly through situations without any real responsibility towards them. I do find that very exhilarating.

Ricks: What sort of responsibility do you feel to the places? I think "Psychopolis" is one of your very best stories, and it clearly is about travelling and the particular way in which you're in but not of, without that being irresponsible.

McEwan: I felt quite free of the responsibility of getting Los Angeles right because I thought it would be better to do it in terms of a series of meetings and then very artificially to bring all the people that your narrator has met into one place to have a conversation and in that way to try to represent a city. Somehow I felt so excited about having been in America for the first time, I found myself getting up very early in the morning and itching to write something. I knew that it would have to be about Los Angeles, and I think it was very fortunate that I was only there a couple of days. I'm not a very observant traveller. I don't sort of keep at the back of my mind all kinds of local details, local colour. It made it much easier for me to reconstruct

Los Angeles in terms of a city of relations and relationships, rather than as a place that you might describe in the way that Reyner Banham might describe it.

Ricks: When you write about Los Angeles, one can't help thinking about films, and one of the things that struck me in "Psychopolis" was the way in which the simultaneity of the argument is something which you can do in prose which you couldn't do in a film. That is to say, you know one person is saying this, meanwhile somebody else is competing with him, arguing over it. In a film you wouldn't be able to hear what they were saying.

'Wait a minute,' he was saying, 'you can't impose all that Women's Lib stuff on to the societies of thousands of years ago. Christianity expressed itself through available . . .'

At roughly the same time Terrence said, 'Another objection to Christianity is that it leads to passive acceptance of social inequities because the real rewards are in . . .'

And Mary cut in across George in protest. 'Christianity has provided an ideology for sexism now, and capitalism . . .'

'Are you a communist?' George demanded angrily, although I was not sure who he was talking to. Terence was pressing on loudly with his own speech. I heard him mention the Crusades, and the Inquisition.

'This has nothing to do with Christianity,' George was almost shouting. His face was flushed.

'More evil perpetrated in the name of Christ than . . . this has nothing to do with . . . to the persecution of women herbalists as witches . . . Bullshit. It's irrelevant . . . corruption, graft, propping up tyrants, accumulating wealth at the altars . . . fertility goddess . . . bullshit . . . phallic worship . . . look at Galileo . . . this has nothing to . . .' I heard little else because now I was shouting my own piece about Christianity.

It's a wonderful conversation, partly because it's such an extraordinarily vital argument.

McEwan: Yes, I am quite unashamedly proud of those last ten pages of "Psychopolis."

Ricks: One of the things that was in my mind was the question of endings. For example, it's evident to me, and I hope to everybody who reads you, that

you've put a tremendous lot of thought into how endings will be—neither smack of firm government, conclusive in a brisk, wrong way, nor, on the other hand, open-minded and vacant and please-make-of-it-what-you-will.
McEwan: I find endings difficult. I think they are objectively very difficult. Some endings in my stories I know have just not worked. I feel very uneasy about them. It is walking a kind of tightrope—as you say, you want to avoid a piece of short fiction ending with a great sort of crash like a pianist bringing his elbows down on a piano, and, at the same time, you also want to avoid that feyness of the hanging moment or ending on a hanging participle. You have got to deserve your ending in terms of content, and it has to be worked for. I think, in "Psychopolis," the ending does come off. I spend a lot of time on endings, and I don't write the ending till the end, because I don't usually know the endings till the end. That's another reason why they take up so much time for me—I have to find out what they are.

Ricks: I take it your first moment of knowing you'd succeeded was when *The New American Review* took the story, "Homemade." Do you think there is some special relation between your writing and American writing? Are you much influenced by American writers?
McEwan: I have certainly read all the contemporary major American writers, and there are certainly passages in lots of their books and certain single books that I have liked a great deal. But they do seem quite remote to me in terms of my own work. I suppose writing one does admire is work that you think, well, God, I couldn't have done that—you know, that's something way beyond my own experience or what I could synthesise. Early on, when I first started writing, it was much easier to get going if one moved off with a certain kind of pastiche of what one had read. Both Mailer and Miller provided a taking-off point for "Homemade," a certain kind of voice in Henry Miller, with a cynical, long-winded, rather pompous and yet very funny narrator, which I liked and I hated and wanted to do myself and make it even more pompous.

Ricks: There's one of your stories, though, that is very different from the others. I'm thinking of "To and Fro." I have to admit it didn't grip me, at first. I now think that was wrong but I still feel that it's a special case. Do you want to say something about that story?
McEwan: Yes, I do, because, in a way, it's my favourite. I don't think it got more than one mention in any review of the collection in which it appeared.

Normally I've been pre-occupied with writing a very accessible, clean kind of prose that anyone could read—I tried to avoid writing anything mandarin or pompously difficult. But "To and Fro" is a fifty-five-page story condensed into about eight pages, it seems the only way to solve a particular problem, it's more like a poem. It does require two or three readings. I think I like it most because I know it better than anybody.

Ricks: Can I ask you about circumstances which I think you might not much like—it has to do with shock in your work. "To and Fro" has a certain experimentalism but is by no means shocking; whereas a lot of your other work, though not shockingly experimental, clearly is, in some way, wishing people to be shocked—shocked by some truth about, at least, their own fantasies and perhaps their own obsession.

McEwan: If we're talking about shock, I'm slightly shocked at all this shock, I haven't really met anybody who has told me that they were shocked by my stories. I've met plenty of people who didn't like them; I've yet to meet somebody who said: "Your stories are so revolting I couldn't read them." And yet in print what is set out constantly is a reaction of sort of horror and shock, and this is something to do with someone reacting in print, I think, in a public medium like a newspaper, reacting in print to something that's in print, there's a certain kind of artifice about the shock—I mean as artificial as fiction itself. One of my stories has appeared in a lurid pornographic magazine.

Ricks: It's an anti-pornographic story . . .
McEwan: Yes, it was, and the story really had some rather pure intentions.

Ricks: What about contemporary fiction? Do you see yourself occupying a position in this sort of order of monuments, living monuments?
McEwan: Well, no, I don't—it's very hard to. I don't know if this is a very good time for English fiction. It certainly seems to me that it's a very good time for the theatre, and has been for some years. I know lots of writers and I like them as people, and there are certain of their works, their novels, stories, that I like, but I certainly can't locate myself inside any shared, any sort of community taste, aesthetic ambition or critical position or anything else. I don't really feel part of anything at all.

Ricks: What about the tradition? I want to pick you up bodily and probably against your will, and put you in a tradition of which the greatest writer is

Kipling, and that is short stories of exceptional imagination, of cruelty, humiliation, and very traditional moral values. What would you feel about that sort of tradition?

McEwan: Well I haven't read Kipling—I read *If* when I was sixteen—so I would say if you wanted to pick me up bodily and do that, that was your prerogative. I'm not sure I would share with you the sense that my fiction has been quite as moral as you would suggest. There are certainly rather frail kinds of statements embodied in them, a rather fragile kind of optimism about life. I hope to avoid any programmatic moral manipulation of the stories, and of the novel, too—I try to keep that sense of the story that is going to be moral in some kind of abeyance, and hope that, through restraint, one will generate a degree of compassion for the right people, even if the right people are in some other sense the wrong people. That is why, in *The Cement Garden*, there is no authorial voice that will tell you that incest is a bad show, don't do it, but neither does it say the other, neither does it recommend that everyone should try, and therefore liberate themselves. I'm not really dealing on that level at all. If I can come back one step: when I'm working, when I'm writing, I do feel extraordinarily free. Even when I'm trying to put together the most unfree situations, I do feel colossal freedom myself. There's nothing more exhilarating than to be writing again—your food tastes better, your step has more spring, the air that fills your lungs seems that much cleaner.

Ian McEwan

John Haffenden/1983

From *Novelists in Interview*. London: Methuen, 1985: 168–90. Interview conducted in 1983. Reprinted by permission of author.

Born in 1948, Ian McEwan started writing short stories in 1970, after studying at the University of Sussex and at the University of East Anglia, where he gained an MA. His first collection, *First Love, Last Rites* (1975), won enormous praise and the Somerset Maugham Award 1976 for its sophisticated depiction of sensuality and depravity. A second collection, *In Between the Sheets* (1978) has been followed by two brilliantly executed novels, menacing and exact in their psychological penetration, *The Cement Garden* (1978) and *The Comfort of Strangers* (1981). His play for television, *The Imitation Game* (directed by Richard Eyre)—which Clive James applauded as "a 'Play for Today' of rare distinction"—earned him a wider audience and even hotter critical attention. So, sadly, did "Solid Geometry," a television play adapted from one of his short stories, which the BBC aborted just before it went into production. The three television plays he has written to date are available in *The Imitation Game* (1981).

A man for all media, McEwan has also written a deeply felt oratorio about the nuclear threat, *Or Shall We Die?*, set by Michael Berkeley and performed in February 1983 by the London Symphony Orchestra and Chorus, conducted by Richard Hickox, and a feature film about contemporary England and the tragedy of forgotten history, *The Ploughman's Lunch*—also directed by Richard Eyre, and starring Jonathan Pryce, Rosemary Harris, and Frank Finlay. Most recently he has been at work on the filmscript of a novel by Alberto Moravia to be produced by Bernardo Bertolucci, and he has started another novel.

I talked with him in 1983 at his home in south London, where he lives with his wife Penny Allen, and her two children by a former marriage.

John Haffenden: You established your reputation as a writer of short stories; then you wrote two novels and a television play, and most recently a feature film and an oratorio. I think there is a sense in which you've maintained continuity in so far as much of your earlier work concerns diseased minds and your more recent writing deals with diseased and unsettling societies.

Ian McEwan: Yes, but it is all after the event. It turns out that what I've written is unsettling, but I don't sit down to think about what will unsettle people next.

Haffenden: You are on record as saying that you were surprised when critics chose to emphasize the shocking and the macabre aspects of your early stories, their concern with degenerate or dislocated behaviour.

McEwan: I honestly was very surprised. My friends, most of whom had had a literary education, seemed to take for granted the field of play in the stories; they had read Burroughs, Celine, Genet, and Kafka, so that lurid physical detail and a sense of cold dissociation did not stun them. I was not aware of any pattern, and each story seemed to me at the time of writing to be a fresh departure, often with very trivial rhetorical ambitions like writing a story in the present tense ("Last Day of Summer"). They often proceeded out of doodles that had a certain kind of automatic quality.

I was quite surprised, for example, when the BBC banned "Solid Geometry," but then TV is so safe and dull. It doesn't put on anything funny about sex. I've never seen good sexual jokes on TV.

Haffenden: What was the especial significance for you of the bottled penis that figures in "Solid Geometry"?

McEwan: On the most basic level it was playful, to show a man working on his great-grandfather's diaries with a preserved penis on his desk. It had to be an erect penis, because that's apparently how they're preserved. By extension, the fact that he won't make love to his wife suggests that his own penis is bottled up, as it were, and it provides her with a splendid opportunity (which would have been great fun to do) to bust it open: it's an appropriation, since she quite reasonably wants his cock. But once the penis is out of the jar he goes and buries it and carries on with his work. There's no stopping him.

Haffenden: Since you've mentioned rhetorical ambitions, have you ever felt tempted to be dishonest in writing, when you recognize a trick you know you can get away with?

McEwan: Yes, all the time; it's amazing how many bad ideas you get on bad days. But when you finish a piece of work you rapidly forget all the confused alternatives that existed along the way, and you imbue it with intention. Writing *The Comfort of Strangers*, for example, helped me to articulate ideas and notions for myself. But *The Comfort of Strangers* got written in the most lugubrious way possible, because I would finish one chapter and have no idea what to do with the next. I felt that I would never finish, because the novel was giving me so much personal pain. I had a rough idea of what to do in the first half, but no ideas in advance for the second.

Haffenden: Can you tell me how you set about writing *The Cement Garden*?

McEwan: It has a definite genesis in one paragraph of my notes, at the doodling stage, where I suddenly had a whole novel unfold about a family living "like burrowing animals . . . after mother dies the house seems to fall asleep." Then I saw the four children: "the initial spread of power . . . the girls steal youngest to babyfy . . . gives narrator more space." I remember writing that paragraph and then lying on the bed and falling into a deep sleep for an hour in the afternoon. When I came back to work I made a false start, and later I realized that the beginning really belonged with the father. I also wondered for a time whether I shouldn't have each of the children recounting the novel. And then for a long time I thought it would turn out that the second sister would be the true narrator, since she was keeping a notebook. I kept thinking the narrator was going to go completely crazy: "His imbalance becoming an issue and the household cannot contain him." I thought for a while that Jack would just go under. [Quotations are from Ian McEwan's notebook drafts.]

Haffenden: I think that one character in *The Cement Garden* who really authenticates the fantasy, as it were, is the outsider, Derek, who envies the world of the children: he wants both to enter their world and to break it.

McEwan: Yes, I sympathize with Derek, because I was a sort of only child, and when I went to stay with friends who had brothers and sisters I would fantasize that my own parents had dematerialized to enable me to join a large family. *The Cement Garden* has a source in my childhood wish to have sisters. The other incestuous stories have rather similar tenuous roots. Another source of the novel was my wife's childhood.

Haffenden: In "In Between the Sheets," the title story of your second collection, the reader is tempted to share the erotic fantasies of a father towards his daughter. You place the reader very close to his consciousness, especially when at night he overhears what he takes to be her erotic restlessness, to the point where one is convinced that incest will take place. But then she appears as just an unsettled child. The reader is agog with a sort of shared excitement, but the tact of the story returns both father and reader to decent normality.

McEwan: I'm glad you see it in terms of his *imagination* of her erotic behaviour, when he hears sounds and has such violent and confused ideas towards his daughter. I was uneasy about the way I had him pursuing his writing in a way that takes him away from any real relationship to a point when he is deeply fearful of women and their pleasure: that's reflected in the rather arid way he sets about his day's work, filing things, writing in a ledger, counting the number of words. Perhaps the connection is too simple. But then, I do think short stories demand simple and incisive sets of oppositions. You make a choice of where your complexity lies, and you must concentrate and pursue it.

Haffenden: "In Between the Sheets" ends with the image of "a field of dazzling white snow which he, a small boy of eight, had not dared scar with footprints." It is a marvellous metaphor for refusing to desecrate something pure.

McEwan: Yes, I do think that last paragraph saves the story. I remember an incredibly heavy snow as a child when we were living in Kent, going out in my gumboots and being enchanted. The field was so pure I didn't want to walk on it.

Haffenden: You've said elsewhere that "To and Fro" is one of your favourite stories, perhaps because it's rather personal. Could you say something about it, because many readers do find it a bit obscure?

McEwan: It's fairly simple really. A man lying in bed beside his lover, imagining himself at work pursued by a colleague who seems to crowd in on his identity. Celebrating the sleeping lover, dreading the obtrusive colleague—these are the simple oppositions.

Haffenden: Was "First Love, Last Rites" in any way written as an allegory of your own experience? It is perhaps your most heavily symbolic story; it's about a relationship and pregnancy, and it includes fishing for eels, which you have at some time done.

McEwan: Oddly enough I had no sense of its symbols when I was writing it, none at all. I certainly wasn't inserting symbols into the story. I was remembering and changing certain events in my own life. I think the story is about pregnancy. The narrator has a sure sense of the girl's power as she kneels by a dead rat. I've always thought it was an affirmative and tender story, as I do "In Between the Sheets," and that was part of the source of my astonishment at the sensational copy reviewers made out of the stories. Reviewers seemed to be fixated by things that weren't central.

Haffenden: I agree with you there: "First Love, Last Rites" seems to me to concern the characters purging themselves of false images of an as yet unsatisfactory relationship. Whatever is macabre in the story works towards a positive resolution.

McEwan: I also had a simple-silly desire to end a story with the word "Yes." I was dazzled by the end of *Ulysses*. My problem was how to get to this "Yes." The problem almost preceded the content, and when you concentrate on that sort of trivial puzzle you find yourself drawing quite freely and unconsciously on surprising material: you come upon an eel in a bucket and it's not a symbol—it's a *memory*. When the eel is set free, I was not thinking of it as a thinly disguised phallus, nor did I think of eel traps as vaginas. One doesn't think about symbols, though there comes a time when one can't deny that they are there.

Haffenden: But another story, "Butterflies," concerns a man abusing and finally killing a child, and that is an appalling subject.

McEwan: Yes, "Butterflies" is appalling; it's a story written by someone who had nothing to do with children. I couldn't possibly write that story now, it would frighten me too much. As children come more into your life the possibility of their death is not something you can play with lightly.

Haffenden: Since your more recent work has made a change of gear into greater social and political awareness, can you say something about what caused this shift?

McEwan: It was something I intended, because I had begun to feel rather trapped by the kinds of things I had been writing. I had been labelled as the chronicler of comically exaggerated psychopathic states of mind or of adolescent anxiety, snot, and pimples. My relationship with Penny Allen, who is now my wife, was a rich source of ideas and I had wanted to give them shape. In writing *The Imitation Game* I stepped out into the world—consciously to find out about a certain time in the past and to re-create it—and at that point I felt I had made a very distinct change. But when I came back to *The Comfort of Strangers* I found myself immediately being drawn again into a very private world, without quite intending it, where psychological states once more become more important than relationships between, for example, individuals and their societies. These things are not entirely within one's control, and I don't think they should be. I am aware of the danger that in trying to write more politically, in the broadest sense—trying to go out more into the world, because it is a world that distresses me and makes me anxious—I could take up moral positions that might pre-empt or exclude that rather mysterious and unreflective element that is so important in fiction. I also think the changes I've been through are quite possibly related to form itself: it's when I have to collaborate with other people that I find myself writing about a larger world.

Haffenden: Do you mean that in writing for film or television you don't have the space to invest in detailed expositions of psychological states?
McEwan: Film seems to suggest a large canvas to me, the novel a smaller one. That is how the forms have affected me so far. Of course other writers have found the novel the ideal form for describing a whole society, and there are film-makers like Tarkosky, who have successfully used their chosen form to make inner journeys. I would like to write a less claustrophobic novel. It may be something to do with confidence.

Haffenden: And yet there is an allegorical dimension to your novels which does suggest a larger frame of reference beyond the psychologically hermetic.
McEwan: Yes. I am just daydreaming my way into a novel now, and I write all sorts of messages to myself about what I would like to do. I can already feel that something is emerging, and it is not what I intended. So I hope that moral concerns will be balanced, or even undermined, by the fact that I still don't have complete control. Some element of mystery must remain. I know novelists who talk quite freely about the novel they're going to write next. I envy them to some extent, because I can get depressed between writing things. But I know that for me there has to be some silence, and that silence often means getting very fed up.

Haffenden: I know that you now have some reservations about *The Imitation Game*, your film for television. Do you think with hindsight that it was oversimplified?

McEwan: It was a first film both for Richard Eyre and for me, and it has longueurs and a certain kind of linearity: it pushed forward along one front all the time. But this was its strength too.

Haffenden: You feel it was pace rather than content that was wrong? The plot is straightforward, being the story of a young woman in wartime England in 1940 who tries to challenge and enter the man's world . . .
McEwan: And more broadly it is an allegory of a person against the system. The problem I encountered in the writing was that as soon as you had a woman at the centre she stands there as a representative of her *sex*; a central male character, on the other hand, is understood to be talking for humankind. The play wasn't only about the way in which men oppress women, it was also about the way systems exclude individuals. I think that got lost, and if it were to be done again I would try to make the heroine representative of things that men understood. I wasn't only concerned with why women see themselves as a repressed class, but the way it turned out it does have a one-dimensional feel.

Haffenden: Given that the play is set in 1940 the figure of Cathy Raine does come over as a unique example of rebelliousness and confrontation. What *The Imitation Game* didn't appear to offer was a context for her thoughts and actions as a feminist.
McEwan: Virginia Woolf's *Three Guineas*, from which *The Imitation Game* draws something, was published in 1938 and went through three reprints during the war. As feminist scholars have pointed out, women's experiences have constantly to be rediscovered—there's no tradition. A lot of women were discontented then, but they would not have articulated their discontent in terms of being a woman or sharing their experiences with other women at the time. I think that element should have been in the film, because otherwise it does suggest a kind of anachronism, and I did wince when people said I had put a 1978 heroine into a 1940 drama. I felt it was untrue, but I do feel I should have given it a little more context. I went to see a number of women who had been in the ATS, and they certainly had strong things to say. These were now very conventional ladies living polished suburban lives—rather lonely, with children grown up, houses sterilely clean—and they felt a strange wistfulness for that time when they had paradoxically more freedom because they had their own careers and an interesting lack of security. I think Cathy Raine should have been more related to other women, rather than being just a rather bolshy middle-class girl not getting

a big enough slice of the action. I am being rather crude and dismissive of the play's procedures, but I think the same points could have been made in a more complex way. It was my first crack at a film. But I still think it is moving.

Haffenden: You would have no doubts about the polemicism of the play?
McEwan: No, I would hold by that.

Haffenden: Do you have any misgivings about the way you portrayed the men as stereotypes or caricatures?
McEwan: The men certainly were stereotypes in *The Imitation Game.* I think people objected to the idea that it was possible to make stereotypes out of male behaviour. We have accepted for a long time that women can be made into dramatic stereotypes, and I felt it was possible to have a solid, rounded female character moving against a cardboard background of very familiar but nevertheless stereotypical forms of male behaviour. Men's behaviour is somehow invisible; we don't see ourselves as having a behaviour that is identifiably male—we're just *human.* So the cry goes up that you cannot caricature men like this, and that men are more complicated, and my reply is that of course I have a polemical purpose.

While I was writing *The Imitation Game* two women were thrown out of a pub in Camden Town for knitting. The publican said knitting was what his customers had come to get away from. The next day, in a way that was silly but right, thirty women turned up at the pub with their knitting, and the publican was well within his legal rights to call the police and have them ejected. That confirmed my view that male behaviour can reach incredibly comic and stereotypical limits. It was farcical and delightful that the power of the state had to be invoked to remove these women.

Haffenden: Women's liberation, I think, properly requires not only social changes but also radical psychological and emotional alterations in men's attitudes and behaviour, and I think that would be an area that would continue to involve you as a writer.
McEwan: The problem is, what do you do about it once you've said it? There are ways in which you clearly have to address your own behaviour in private life, but after writing *The Imitation Game*—having escaped the label of being the chronicler of adolescence—I was then suddenly the male feminist, which really made me shrink. I found myself being co-opted into attending various types of convocation on "Sexism in the Media" or "Writers against

Sexism." It was very gratifying to see the enormous amount of attention *The Imitation Game* received, but I found I wanted to back off the subject. I didn't want to be used as a spokesman for women's affairs. I didn't want to be a man appropriating women's voices.

Haffenden: Were you happy about the way you treated the crisis in *The Imitation Game*, where Turner, the intellectual mathematician, fails to make it in bed with Cathy. He feels betrayed and hates the woman, and he avenges himself. It struck me as very brave of you to have come so close to delivering a piece of melodrama and yet to have brought off the real truth of the situation and its nightmare consequences. The danger seemed to lie in relating Turner's impotence to his intellectuality.

McEwan: I hadn't thought of the polarity as being to do with intellectuality and impotence. It had more to do with his sense of total competence in the outer world, and therefore his fear of failure in the inner world. What blurred the issue was that in an earlier scene a dispatch-rider tells Cathy that Bletchley is full of homosexuals, and there is also Turner's description of his dominating mother, so that some gays thought I was saying he couldn't make it and was vicious because he was homosexual. This was a false trail I had made here, one that was not relevant to the argument of the play.

There is among men a fear of women and of their power. What is meant to be clear in the scene is that once Cathy is sexually excited she becomes very demanding, which is very frightening for Turner, and so his anger seemed to be dramatically in order. Once she had made the journey to the centre of official secrets, the other secret—the secret in the private world—creates the same response: she meets the masculine defensiveness that won't admit weakness. I see this defensiveness as a burden for men, and not just as the thing men do to women. I would not like to say who is unhappier in that scene, but it is quite clear who is the more powerful.

Haffenden: Did you move straight on to *The Comfort of Strangers* after finishing *The Imitation Game*?

McEwan: Yes. It sounds easy, but in fact there was a break in time: it was a good year later.

Haffenden: To what extent did Nicholas Roeg's film *Don't Look Now* influence you in writing *The Comfort of Strangers*?

McEwan: I was aware of the film but I hadn't seen it. Nor had I read the book on which it was based. I felt sensitive about it, but then I saw it on TV a couple of years ago, and I thought no sweat.

Penny Allen and I spent a week in Venice in 1978, at the height of the tourist season, and something of our visit found its way into the book. I can't really describe the book as setting out with any clear intention. After being to Venice I came back and wrote some notes about it, which I lost, and then I found them a good one-and-a-half years later; it seemed to me that I had already been describing two characters who were not quite like either myself or Penny, and already it seemed to be describing the city in terms of a state of mind, and vice versa. So the novel took off from the notes. Those notes contain the phrase "self-fulfilling accusation," as well as the first sentence, so I must have been thinking about a novel even then.

I found it terribly difficult to write, and it is a book I find very hard to understand or talk about. It seemed to be saying something either true or so true that it was banal. It was an elaboration of an argument in *The Imitation Game*. This again brings up the question of form, since it wasn't enough to talk about men and women in social terms, I had to address myself to the nature of the unconscious, and how the unconscious is shaped. It wasn't enough to be rational, since there might be desires—masochism in women, sadism in men—which act out the oppression of women or patriarchal societies but which have actually become related to sources of pleasure. Now this is a very difficult argument to make.

I recently attended a *Marxism Today* conference about eroticism and the left, and I made an *extempore* speech—very clumsily—about eroticism not being totally amenable to rationalism, that it wasn't just a matter of talking out a programme of the feminist left. The conference was a broad coalition of socialists and feminists, and I got on to incredibly dangerous ground when I suggested that many women probably have masochistic fantasies and that many men probably have sadistic fantasies, which are acted out in private but never spoken about in any kind of public debate. And then I said that it would be far better in a relationship to embrace this than to deny it, and that true freedom would be for such women to recognize their masochism and to understand how it had become related to sexual pleasure. The same was no less true for male masochists. I was talking here of sexual fantasy. The whole room exploded, and I came away feeling terribly bruised because I had been very inarticulate, as one is when speaking against such hostility. But I was attacked for providing a "rapist's charter" and for poaching on forbidden territory—women's experience.

Haffenden: That goes a long way to explain the characters of Robert and Caroline in *The Comfort of Strangers*. Robert obtrusively recounts his intimate childhood experiences to Colin and Mary, who are strangers to him. What he tells them amounts to a threat, and yet the young couple retreat to their hotel and curiously do not speak about their extraordinary encounter. But they do respond to it unconsciously, in their behaviour towards one another. You mention their "conspiracy of silence" and—in chapter 7—the way they start to "invent themselves anew" and to make up sexual fantasies.

McEwan: I felt they had become mesmerized by Robert and Caroline in ways they could not speak about. Robert and Caroline were for me simply a sort of comic drawing of a relationship of domination, and when this decently liberal and slightly tired couple, Colin and Mary, come in contact with that relationship they find it has a sway over their unconscious life, and they begin to act out—or rather speak to each other—these incredible masochistic and sadistic fantasies while they are making love. By example, as it were, their very carefully constructed rational view—he being a mild feminist, she a rather stronger one, and their sort of balance—becomes undone, because they haven't ever addressed the matter at a deeper level of themselves; they've always seen it as a social matter.

What I was trying to say at the conference was that there is a certain sort of silliness attached to talking about eroticism if you are just talking about it in terms of domestic relationships. There is something intractable about the sexual imagination, and what you desire is not very amenable to programmes of change. You might well have grown up deciding that you accept certain intellectual points of view, and you might also change the way you behave as a man or as a woman, but there are also other things—vulnerabilities, desires—within you that might well have been irreversibly shaped in childhood. People of our generation, who grew up in the 1950s, grew up in the time of the fathers, and I made the point that there are many women for whom the figure of the father lies very deeply and powerfully within their sexuality. I got into incredibly hot water, but I still think I was right. I came away thinking that the left was actually bristling with taboos, almost as many taboos as there would have been at a synod of clergy in the late nineteenth century. Everyone was so used to a kind of likemindedness, that it was stirring for them to see me as an enemy in their midst.

Haffenden: In *The Comfort of Strangers* Colin and Mary take unconscious refuge in indulgent self-involvement, what you call a "rhetorical mode, a means of proceeding," and it's as if they can agree on the politics of sex because they avoid discussing the social confrontation which drove them into collusion.

McEwan: Yes, the one thing they don't talk about is Robert and Caroline, and they interiorize it instead. In order to collude they mustn't talk about Robert and Caroline, and so they become Robert and Caroline.

I think of it as an old-fashioned novel about the head and the heart: two creatures of the head meet two creatures of the heart, and the head goes a bit haywire as a consequence. Robert is a sort of cartoon figure of extreme patriarchal domination, and he cannot tolerate the existence of Colin, who represents a threat to him. Colin becomes useful grist to Robert's ultimate fantasies of cruelty, wherein Robert can exercise his full sadism and Caroline can identify with it.

Haffenden: One of the interesting scenes on the way is where Mary goes swimming. Colin thinks she is drowning and he exhaustingly swims out to rescue her. When he reaches her he finds that she is in fact quite safe and happy, but his care for her is never communicated . . .

McEwan: There is also another current involved there, as it were, in the sense that if you are so wrong about something you have to question whether your desires aren't involved in your judgement, and maybe Colin wants Mary to be drowned and sees her in that way. But for me the dominant feature of that scene is the notion of swimming out too far, which is what they are about to do.

Haffenden: Christopher Ricks wrote a very interesting review of the novel (*London Review of Books*, 4:1, 21 January–3 February 1982), in which he talks about the incorrigibility of certain manifestations of evil, that they just cannot be explained. Yet it is the case that Robert enters very full evidence about the aetiology of his perversion. He explains the source of his sadism in a way which is not otherwise questioned in the novel, and I found that because of that unquestioned ratiocination apropos of Robert I was much more taken up by the subtle and exploratory treatment of Colin and Mary.

McEwan: I think of Robert more as a cipher than as a character. People either buy Robert or they don't. He is part of the premise of the novel rather than an entirely convincing character.

Haffenden: But still you chose not to leave him as an unaccountable figure; you wanted to show how much he understands his sadism.

McEwan: Yes, the violence that Robert does to Colin, which is a violence that is in the air—people do murder each other, wars do break out—has a lot to do with people's perceptions of their own exercise of power, and the pleasures they find in exercising power. What is interesting is the extent to which people will collude in their own subjection, which is true not only of Caroline in relation to Robert but also of Colin. There is something about Colin's behaviour which suggests from the beginning that he is a victim; he goes along with Robert and is easily manipulated, which suggests an unconscious contractual agreement. I think such an agreement can exist between oppressor and victim.

Haffenden: Ricks interprets *The Comfort of Strangers* as a tragedy.

McEwan: I didn't think of it in those terms, but I did think there was a sense in which Colin and Mary had agreed about what was going to happen to them. The city, and their relationship to it, was littered with notions of possible death. In the first chapter I posit a *stranger* for whom they're getting dressed, so that they conjure him up, and that was long before I had a title for the book. So it had a fatalistic element in it from the start which I suppose tragedy shares. A lot of readers were so infuriated by Colin and Mary that they couldn't enjoy the book, and I think there has to be an act of recognition: the ideal reader has to recognize within himself or herself that area of lack of freedom in a relationship.

Haffenden: I wonder if the development in your writing towards greater political awareness was fostered by reading and seeing the plays of David Hare?

McEwan: I certainly feel that David interests me more than most of my contemporaries.

Haffenden: Is that because he relates the private life to the political life?

McEwan: I think that message—the necessity of relating private and personal behaviour with what you do in broader relationships—has come to me through the women's movement. David Hare has an ambivalence towards his subject matter which I find very interesting, and in a way I've been dogging his footsteps. Long after David has written about the state of England now and a certain sense of betrayal, I'm still toiling away in that particular field in *The Ploughman's Lunch*. I went to see *Licking Hitler* before I wrote

The Imitation Game; they're linked, but there's no direct influence, and they come from very different viewpoints. I like *Licking Hitler* enormously, and I engage with David's work.

Haffenden: You have written that before you came to write the oratorio *Or Shall We Die?* you had tried a novel and a filmscript on the same theme.
McEwan: The novel hardly got off the ground, it seemed too programmatic. It had something to do with family relationships which were being soured by things happening outside. The film was much more apocalyptic, a survival fantasy with a cast of millions, but it had too many elements: disaster, thriller, love story . . . and no mystery.

Haffenden: In *Or Shall We Die?* you rather simply oppose the male world and the female world.
McEwan: The male and female in the oratorio were really principles rather than genders: the elements of the feminine and the elements of the masculine, and how our civilization is heavily weighted towards the latter. Male and female should exist in balance within individuals and within society. The oratorio makes a point about tendencies of behaviour. It was in one sense an ethereal polarity, but in another sense the mother and child seemed to me the most powerful and central image of what civilization has to protect—children are its major resource, which nuclear war threatens.

The development of nuclear weapons shows the dissociation of science from feelings, science run amok: this can be usefully described in terms of the male principle, active and aggressive, without the compassion or a sense of nurture. Newtonian physics seems to encapsulate a certain male principle of detached observation. But within the New Physics there are theories like the Uncertainty Principle where the observer cannot exclude himself and faces the limits of what can be known. And just as Newtonian physics slowly found its moral correlative, I think there is hope that various forms of holism, for example, are very tentative expressions of the New Physics moving into moral positions.

I am emphatically a unilateralist; I think this country makes itself a target by having nuclear weapons, and we pervert our economy and our democracy. The position is different for the U.S. and Russia, who clearly have to negotiate between themselves. My view is not idealistic but practical; I want to survive, and I feel great sadness and anger that we devote so much of our national resources and half our scientists to projects of destruction. We have made no democratic decisions about these weapons; the first Labour government after the war took a decision on them without consulting Parliament. All kinds of democratic principles have been subverted by the apparent necessity of having nuclear weapons. I believe quite passionately in the democratic procedures.

Haffenden: Did you have any hesitation about using an oratorio to serve your political—what some critics have felt to be tendentious—arguments?
McEwan: I think I'm one very small part of a massive sense of revulsion. There is a vast anxiety which inevitably finds its way into works of art. It's impossible to keep this preoccupation out, because it is so personal.

Haffenden: Some years ago, in an interview with Christopher Ricks (*The Listener*, 12 April 1979), you said that you felt elated by your work, and that you did not feel threatened or disturbed by the content of what you wrote . . .
McEwan: There is always that paradox about any work of art: it will finally have something optimistic in it because it is an expression of desire or will or energy. I was walking on air the day I finished the oratorio, although I had brought together terrible things. I found it very painful while I was writing *The Comfort of Strangers*, but I did feel terribly happy when I had written a good page.

Haffenden: What sort of pain did you feel in writing *The Comfort of Strangers*?
McEwan: I felt very strongly identified with Colin, as if I was writing my own death in some strange way. I felt terribly sickened by it. Part of me did not want to go on, and another part of me was ambitious . . . and delighted by the writing.

Haffenden: You achieve a terrible coolness in both *The Comfort of Strangers* and *The Ploughman's Lunch*.
McEwan: I get pleasure from the feeling that I have found more truth in detachment than if I had written self-directed or passionate prose.

Haffenden: *The Ploughman's Lunch* is a film which builds up a large number of layers and perspectives. Did you begin with that idea of making a panorama of England roughly a year ago?
McEwan: Yes, but it started in March 1981. I had the idea of writing a film that was set in contemporary England, but I had no idea who was going to

be in it. For a long time I thought it was going to be about royalty. It was the year of the royal wedding, and as that intensified I realized just how everyone was transfixed, even the dissenters: there was no way out of it. Even indifference had to be furiously cultivated. I thought maybe one could look at this fixation through the eyes of an inebriated pressman; and for a long time I thought along those lines, but I got sick of it. I thought you could look at it like an anthropologist, and see it in terms of the powerful myths of kings and queens and princes. After a while I began to wonder if it was so relevant.

But all the time I had the title, *The Ploughman's Lunch*—an invented meal which had been incorporated as a fake past—and so the metaphor was always there. Then I drifted around to what turned out to be the different locations. At the Labour Party conference I met some women who had just set up a peace camp, so I went to visit them at Greenham Common, when they were still struggling to get it together. I also spent some time in Norfolk, thinking that this harsh and beautiful area of England was never represented on film, and I went to Poland. Then I saw how it might all fit together.

Haffenden: It sounds as though you were taking samplings of places rather than of contemporary attitudes.

McEwan: The two were really indistinguishable. Going to Greenham Common, for example, was to visit people who had a very clear sense of value and attitude.

Haffenden: In this process of moving around, were you actually taking the measure of your own commitments and attitudes?

McEwan: Yes. I became very fascinated by the two women at Brighton. They were clearly dedicated to a set of ideas. I had to measure the extent to which I had ideas and the extent to which I would live them out, and I felt great admiration for the women at Greenham Common. At the other end of the scale, I witnessed the law-and-order debate at the Tory Party conference in Blackpool in 1981, and I came to understand something of the real violent hatred that exists among the people who now predominate in the Tory Party. I was with a number of journalists, who see it every year and talk about it remotely and funnily, since the law-and-order debate is always a high point of the circus. But it was extraordinary how people, delegates, were so animated by negative ideas: a political party whose members were brought to their feet by the idea of punishment—longer prison sentences, arming the police, thrashing vandals. The negative passions whipping people into such a frenzy really did shake me. Strangely enough, though, I wanted a film in which people would move quite cynically and calmly among all this, people who would take it for granted the way a lot of journalists did.

Haffenden: The conference scene in *The Ploughman's Lunch* certainly does bring home the eerie reality.

McEwan: Yes, we sneaked in under the auspices of another organization. The Tory Press Office, who had asked to see the script, were initially friendly and said we could film there, but a few months later so many hard-news teams had applied that our permissions were revoked—but not for reasons of ideology. We eventually got in another way, quite legitimately. Our crew had technical passes and our actors had press passes, so we were virtually invisible among all the journalists and camera crews. We also had quite strenuously to avoid getting two other film teams into frame. I was amazed at how easily we could insinuate our actors. Jonathan Pryce was very bold in walking under the platform when Heseltine was speaking (no one recognized him as an actor), and doing it about six or seven times, since we had to do several takes.

Haffenden: It's a very dispiriting film. In the beginning we may be beguiled by the character of James (Jonathan Pryce), but we soon realize that he is selfish and self-deceiving. You seem to have gone out of your way not to provide any character the audience can identify with, and I wonder if that policy of alienation was with you from the start?

McEwan: Yes, there is a great tradition of having sympathetic characters in films, whereas in novels anti-heroes are acceptable: you travel with them. In films you stand outside characters. I suppose it *is* a pessimistic film; it was meant to be addressed to something of the spirit of the age, and to the way in which private deceptions and national deceptions are not entirely disconnected. James's rewriting of the history of the Suez crisis is constantly linked with his deceits in the pursuit of Susan. I do feel we live in dispiriting times, but I also hoped the film would give narrative pleasure and be funny, even though the humour is meant to be rather awkward.

Haffenden: In your interview with Ricks you mentioned that you were wary of putting "gratuitous optimism" into your stories. Did the film medium solve a certain problem for you, in that you could be sincerely pessimistic?

McEwan: Films generally end optimistically, don't they? I think people often don't have the courage of their pessimism. But I thought of the Greenham Common women as a kind of measure of moral certainty. When I researched for the film the women constantly complained about not getting enough publicity, so people will have to remember that they're watching an historical film. The ground has been rather pulled from under our feet since making the film, but Greenham Common was not in the news during the Falklands crisis.

Haffenden: The purity of the peace-camp women in the film seems to go along with a kind of innocence, an apparent unawareness that people could shrug off their appeal in the way the character James does.

McEwan: Yes, by travelling with James you assume his urban and urbane values, so that people camping out in a field can look silly, just as earnest people at a poetry reading can look silly. I wanted not simply to watch James with distaste but to enter his world.

Haffenden: And yet the scene at a poetry reading might appear to be rather gratuitous. It helps the audience to reckon a little more with the extent of James's cynicism, and how he can casually condescend to his decent friend, the poet, but unfortunately the cinema audience will laugh along with James.

McEwan: Yes, the scene is a sort of dog-leg, but we found in cutting that virtually every scene is relentlessly pushing ahead with Suez or the pursuit of the girl. I was very fond of the scene. It is a digression, but I also wanted to keep the sense of a diverse world, and the scene has the effect of getting you on the side of James and Jeremy, his friend, in a horrible and invidious way, to make you giggle at your friend's poetry reading. When you can afford to be so *louche* and cynical, then everyone around you seems too earnest, damned by their earnestness; it is a seductive and lazy viewpoint, one that can prevail in literary or journalistic London, and it's fuelled by drink too. I wanted people both to be sucked in and to be left cold . . .

Haffenden: With a nasty taste?

McEwan: Yes, because England under Mrs Thatcher leaves me with a nasty taste.

Haffenden: James comes over finally as a ruthless character. We see him seizing all his opportunities, and yet he doesn't seem to show much self-awareness, so that he is portrayed as both opportunistic and naive.
McEwan: He is obtuse, I think. He is quite aware of professional self-promotion.

Haffenden: But his obtuseness extends to not understanding the even more worldly characters of Susan and Jeremy. It comes as a shock to him that they are also self-serving.
McEwan: Yes, there is a kind of horrible innocence about him, which does perhaps fit uneasily. But then I wanted so many things: I wanted somebody practising deception and being deceived at the same time, and also the other people being deceived. One point is that the unholy alliance between Britain, France and Israel over the Suez affair is matched in the characters of the film. One fortuitous point of colour matching occurs, for example, when Richard Eyre dissolves through James's map of Suez into a Norfolk field. Similarly, at the end, Jeremy says about Susie and himself, "We're old allies." Everybody is taking pleasure in taking each other for a ride. At the centre of all that it does need a certain gullibility on James's side. But I don't think it's implausible because when you want something a lot you tend to think it must be clear to everyone else why you want it.

Haffenden: What sort of metaphor or parallel did you see between Suez and the Falklands crisis?
McEwan: The Falklands business blew up when I had finished the first draft, so I let it bubble along in the background of the second draft, knowing full well that when we got to Brighton to film the Conservative Party conference they would be talking about the Falklands. While there are clear differences between Suez and the Falklands crisis, I still think they have their roots in the same illusion: a Churchillian dimension, and also war as serving a certain rallying function for the right. It's another form of self-delusion. I can see the case for taking back the Falklands, but I think the case was not really the point; there were more marginal and emotional reasons for sending out the fleet.

Haffenden: I find the historian, Ann Barrington, a complex and sympathetic character in *The Ploughman's Lunch*. She is treated ambiguously, of course, as a compromised character who is emotionally wounded and has thrown in her lot with a commercial film-maker. She looks for private consolation, and yet her political beliefs are still vital and creditable.

McEwan: I always thought of her as very sympathetic. It's only lately that I've begun to feel that she's slightly less than totally sympathetic. For me she expresses something very honourable about the educated English middle class, which doesn't go to Tory Party conferences and bray for more punishment. She does have a sense of history, but she can no longer make an opposition to this prevailing spirit because she herself is tired; the time, she says, is past, so there's no hope to be had. She has a great deal of decency and compassion, but no position of strength.

Haffenden: What about her efforts to act vicariously through James's writing about Suez?

McEwan: That is a monstrous piece of self-delusion. I gave her all the things that many people would desire—a beautiful house, and access to what I think of as a magnificent piece of English countryside—and who could resist her compromises at a certain age? I don't want to make a cruel point against her, simply a human one—that very few of us could occupy a position of total radical opposition without becoming bitter. If you spend your whole life in opposition it must shape your character; you are giving so much of your energy to what you think is bad or evil that you become almost in league with it. I think there is a time in your life when you have the energy to do that, and then you hope another generation will come along to take up the task. What is important is history and memory. So I do still see Ann Barrington as a sympathetic character, one based loosely in her ideas around E. P. Thompson, but with the great difference that E. P. Thompson has in fact moved in the opposite direction, from theory into practice.

Haffenden: The final impression one has of Ann is that she is rather pitiable, both psychologically hurt and yet still believing that James actually shares her ideological integrity.

McEwan: Yes, I wanted to give her a motive for being taken in by James. I've always been fascinated by the way in which people like James who don't say much are often considered to be profound, and can go a long way by being silent.

Haffenden: When he is asked to articulate a defence of socialism and property owning he comes up with a platitude.

McEwan: Ludicrous, yes. I like that scene . . . partly because similar things happened to me when I was about twenty and first began to meet people who had intellectual parents. I would visit their houses in the role of the boyfriend who had to be tested for my opinions. Everybody had a debating-society style, coming up with things like "As Macaulay says . . . ," and I used to find it absolutely terrifying. It was as if the size of your penis were being measured just because you had come in the door. At least, that was my paranoia about it. My parents were always very kind to people I took home, and they certainly weren't interested in gauging the megawatts of their intellects.

Haffenden: Do you think there is much of that sort of thing in your work: I mean, not exactly getting chips off your shoulder but in a way shriving early occasions of embarrassment?
McEwan: Only in terms of tiny bits of oneself going into unsympathetic characters.

Haffenden: Is there now a sense in which you think of your early stories as a kind of apprentice work?
McEwan: I like to think that I can come back to writing short stories, but I do have a feeling that I might not be able to write them as well as I did when I was younger. I don't know. The form itself is a good laboratory. I took the stories very seriously and worked on them very slowly, and I would always want to stand by them. I wouldn't want to lose the concentrated exploration of the short stories, nor to feel as I grow older that my sole duty is to address the nation on public themes: that would be arid and arrogant. I would always want to keep the excitement and mystery of writing, but I would find it harder to achieve that young man's easy swipe at life. A lot of the early stories concern initiation, things to do with becoming an adult.

If you are going to write a novel the subject has to be very appealing: it really has to be something that draws you, even if it is painful, because you are going to have to live with it so long. I have no idea what my next subject is going to be, but I feel very free in doodling at the moment.

Writers Talk: Ideas of Our Time

Martin Amis/1987

From *Guardian Conversations*, no. 69, Institute of Contemporary Arts, London: ICA Video, 1989. Recorded in 1987. Reprinted by permission of Institute of Contemporary Arts.

Martin Amis: It seems to me that *The Child in Time* combines your interest in childhood, your interest in politics, but also your cosmic interests in that it's about time and how we can't know it. Did you feel as you were writing the book that things were coming together? That you were taking on everything at once, instead of singly?

Ian McEwan: Yes, I'd been waiting for some time for the right kind of material that would make that possible. It was less the idea of childhood and children, so much as the vast literature on childcare that made that possible for me. The immediate prompt was a book by Christina Hardyment, which was a review of three hundred years of childcare called *Dream Babies: Child Care from Locke to Spock*. It was quite clear that if you wanted to look at any age, any generation, any particular time, you could do worse than to look at the kinds of advice that people were being given to raise their children. Behind that advice lay an idea of forming the kind of person we want, and in the person we want lay the aspirations of a particular time.

It was clear, too, looking at this and other related books, that the pendulum swings. There is, in the late eighteenth-century and early nineteenth-century, a rather Rousseau dominated, quite libertarian view on raising children. The Victorians we all know about. Edwardians were very sentimental in their approach—a much softer touch. The twenties and thirties, which I think would be the worst time to be subjected to the realized advice, was dominated by breezy confidence in social sciences. So there were slide rules issued to mothers to calculate when to breastfeed, and stern advice not to fondle or cuddle your babies because it over-stimulated them and distorted their brain development. Then came Spock and child-centered childcare, which seemed to be related to a post-war, liberal consensus, and one that has now, I think in England certainly, begun to decline—a time of moral relativism. I thought I had this opportunity in writing, as it were, the next chapter, a fictional swing of the pendulum.

Amis: The book is set in the future, in an indeterminate future.
McEwan: Yes. There is a passage that deals with the possibility of having the public world of moral advice overlap with the intimate nature of childcare. Stephen is a writer of children's books. He didn't actually mean to be, but he's ended up as one, and he finds himself on a government committee that is writing the definitive new book . . .

Amis: On how to raise children . . .
McEwan: Yes, it's called *The Authorized Child-care Handbook.*

Amis: The changing fashion is more than just a history of taste, isn't it? How we raise our children is very much tied up with how we raise ourselves.
McEwan: That's right. I'd found a subject that encompassed the intimate and the social. I had been looking for a long time to bring these two threads in my writing together.

Amis: And the cosmological or the cosmic in this? You say at one point that we just don't know what time *is*. Different kinds of time are dealt with in your book—the speeded up time of childhood, the slowed time of committee life, and so on. In fact, your hero goes back in time, or is allowed a glimpse of an earlier time. There's this sort of post-relativity, this new uncertainty about time. We now know that time isn't just the succession of moments, that it is in fact a dimension, can be altered.
McEwan: It seems as if science is catching up with what everyone always knew, what mystics and visionaries have written about, which is that time certainly isn't sequential, or linear. There are those moments described by William James in his *Varieties of Religious Experience,* rare moments when we sense that all time exists all at once. Of course, novelists have always played tricks with time. Although you read a novel sequentially page after page, when you come to reflect on it, you have to think of it as a structure, as architecture—and that's a strange trick with time, too. Since I *was* talking about children, and childhood is clearly something that occurs in time, I was keen to try and embody as many of these subjective experiences of time and yet place them within both a scientific and almost mystical frame.

Amis: Many novelists are catching on to this, because science has suddenly revealed itself in the last years. We're used to abstract art, but abstract science is what we're having to get used to now. The Newtonian world breaking down into a sort of *hippie* world, down on the level of matter—things can be two places at once, things can't be looked at.

McEwan: This scientific revolution is more than half a century old, but it's only just beginning to trickle down to us liberal arts know-nothings and possibly beginning to project some sort of ethical dimension for us. The certainties of *The Authorized Child-care Handbook* run absolutely against the much more fractured, and I think much more interesting, world view proposed by quantum mechanics.

Amis: In this indeterminate present, the Prime Minister in your novel, whose sex is never specified directly with a pronoun, is clearly some sort of Thatcher ghost or specter. So the old witch is still with us in whatever it might be—twelve years' time. The child raising handbook is a reflection of a sort of Thatcherite ideal with great stress on punctuality, self-interest, getting the job done, and so on. Now, we know that novels, even novels that are set in the future, are really about the present, but did you think that going into the future was sort of technically forced on you because you're writing about time? Do you think it's also to do with the fact that for the first time in history, or for the last couple of generations, the future is no longer a given? It's something that has to be achieved—by good luck mainly—but that gave you a desire to visit it?

McEwan: Yes, recently there have been a number of novels set in the near future, and I wonder whether this is related to an insecurity that we even have one and that it would be better at least to visit it in the mind, just in case we never actually turn up there ourselves bodily. But I never really thought of it as a novel set in the future. I simply thought that I was writing in a satirically distorted present. But I do have a novel that I abandoned in the early seventies which was set in the 1990s, a little fragment of which survived in *In Between the Sheets*. I think, without realizing it, I was returning to that idea. We used to want to reclaim the past, and now it's the future we need to nail down and make certain for ourselves, even if it is in the form of a dystopia.

Amis: There's also the sense that to get any sense of proportion about the present, we have to go into the future and become, as it were, the historians of the future, since they might not exist. We have to wonder, scratching our heads, what on earth we thought we were doing here in 1987 with the sort of status quo we have. As I said, in your book, various times or textures of time are dealt with. You've written a passage about the ways time slows down during a car crash—a familiar feeling, I think, for anyone who's ever been involved in one.

McEwan: It might be a good moment to mention that the head of each chapter contains an extract from *The Authorized Child-care Handbook*, HMSO. One reviewer apparently phoned Cape to ask where they could lay their hands on this book . . . [audience laughs] . . . and I'm engineering a vast advance to complete it. [Reads heading of chapter six and car crash passage from chapter five.]

Amis: The scene with the prying loose of Joey ties up, as indeed everything ties up in this very intensely made book, with the birth in the closing pages. It's a metallic birth contrasted with a warm and human one. It's well known that writing about happiness, writing about rapture and joy, is a much more difficult business than writing about . . . even something as beautifully done as the loss of the child in the first chapter. Montherlant said, "Happiness writes white. It does not show up on the page." Tolstoy perhaps is one of the few writers who made happiness exciting on the page. Did you find it presented a special difficulty to have a happy ending, a joyful ending? It's not something you've been famed for in the past. I think there's a fear of sentimentality that clouds sentiment.

McEwan: On this count, there's been great difficulty this century for writers. But to be at a birth and to experience such uncomplicated pleasure and joy made me feel that in the weeks afterwards there was, even aesthetically, a responsibility to face up to the challenge of writing about happiness. And, yes, it is a lot more difficult. It was while writing this scene that I realized that I was in fact making a dry run for the birth. I think of this as a happy scene, and it's a pre-figurative scene. It's the first sign in the book that things are going to work out well, that the man is delivered, as it were, by Stephen, just as Stephen will deliver a child.

I think you do cross a line. You grow older, you have children, and you want the world to go on, and you want it more and more passionately. You can indulge all kinds of recklessness in your twenties, but as you get older you do begin to reckon up what you love in the world. It begins to shape itself into—can we call it an aesthetic?—I suppose so. At least a sense of responsibility.

Audience: Why are both of you so persuaded that the future is insecure and more insecure now than it has been for the last thirty or forty years?

McEwan: Well, simply because we've acquired and stockpiled the capability to destroy the whole fabric of life on earth—more so than thirty years ago when we could merely have destroyed societies with the available A-bombs. We now have somewhere between forty and sixty thousand warheads, which would simply be the end for the whole enterprise, the whole biological, evolutionary enterprise. I guess Martin and I—I think I speak for us both—feel those to whom it falls to make political decisions in this area don't inspire a great deal of confidence in their sagacity and restraint.

Amis: You feel that in fact it's got a lot safer recently?

Audience: No I don't, no. I feel for many years it's been insecure, but I don't feel it's any *more* insecure now than it has been for some time. I can sense you feel it's now a very dangerous time to live and are being rather pessimistic about it.

Amis: It's more an awakening from seeing the status quo for what it is and saying, I think irrefutably, that this can't go on forever, that the present arrangement and the time—the second thought period which would intervene between deciding to press a button and actually pressing it—is getting tinier all the time. We're now on the brink of the militarization of space, which is, like the H-bomb, another water break, another waterfall that we're tumbling down. And the time to deal with a nuclear missile is when it's on the ground and not when it's coming toward you at four miles per second. Again, time is being contracted . . .

McEwan: By expertise . . .

Amis: Yes, by computers . . .

McEwan: By active management of the will—political and industrial will. It's not just happening to us, that's the odd thing about it. We're doing it.

Amis: I think it has taken a generation for this to become a subject for writers—took a long time, in fact. But since the evolutionary peak of this ability to destroy all life is clearly the most important thing that's ever happened to our species, then you wouldn't expect writers to be talking about it the next day. These things do mysteriously draw in some sort of cycle and then emerge all together. It may sound as if suddenly we're all saying the obvious, but I think that it's not obvious enough, is it?

Audience: Is it creatively rather stultifying if you write in the shadow of this likelihood of being blown up?

McEwan: Well, it's certainly *emotionally* stultifying. And it's frightening and it represents, obviously, a challenge. People used to say at the outbreak of the Second World War that things looked clearer, more vivid—I'm talking about actual perception. I read the diary of a young woman written in September 1939, and she wrote that the postbox was glowing the most extraordinary red. I think perhaps you might find in writing and in other art forms an intensification in response to this.

Audience: Can I ask you about the Charles Darke character? Isn't he the author of your child handbook?
McEwan: Yes.

Audience: The end of the book focuses on this beautifully described birth. I wondered whether the anti-story of that is the regression you build in for Charles Darke going backwards through time and living in the tree hut and becoming a child? Is that for you, on second thought, an admission that the political *is* in fact regressive and is disappearing into some dark backward abysm, whereas the individual, the isolated specific, is the only hope? Is that where the politics and the personal come apart in your own structure? That we see that politics is in fact undoing itself and disappearing and erasing and thus leaving *only* the person?
McEwan: There's a problem here, because I never thought there was much in the way of politics in the book. These were moral rather than political issues. In fact, that Charles Darke was a government minister slightly queered my pitch I see in retrospect. Charles was someone who could always join either party—he was not someone who held consciously political beliefs. He was an ambitious man. I was more concerned with the contradictions of public and private life, the dangers of keeping them in separate compartments. I think the moral and political consequences of that are dire. Stephen thinks to himself that, unless there's an unbroken line between private public values, something goes seriously amiss, and you get the absurdity of licensed beggars. Charles, I think, is a nasty character, simply because he has this private obsession and yet for the sake of his own ambition will write a childcare book which contradicts his private life. I didn't really intend to suggest that right wing politics in particular are regressive. But I think I led myself into that trap because he's a government minister.

Audience: You said that children are all we've got now. Do you mean *your* children or children in general? Because surely there's rather a large difference. When you talk about your own child—having a child which is your own—it's certainly more egocentric than a social and political notion of children in the world and their future.

McEwan: I mean children in general. Our only link with the future is our children. The only people who are going to be around in a hundred years' time are our children's children. I certainly wasn't talking out of some private pleasure in my own children. If I thought the fate of the planet lay exclusively in the hands of William and Gregory McEwan, I would fear for the future [laughs].

Amis: Mine would help. I think we'd better finish now and thank Ian . . .

The Pleasure of Prose Writing vs. Pornographic Violence: An Interview with Ian McEwan

Rosa González Casademont/1989

From *BELLS: Barcelona English Language and Literature Studies* 1.3 (1989): 55–62. Rpt. in *European English Messenger* 1.3 (Autumn 1992): 40–45. Reprinted by permission of author.

Rosa González: You started as a writer of short stories, but you haven't published any more since your two collections of the seventies, and in fact your novels are getting longer. Doesn't the short form interest you any more?

Ian McEwan: I'm writing a short novel at the moment, but no, I haven't written short stories since the seventies. They belong to another stage of my life. They were a kind of laboratory for me. They allowed me to try out different things, to discover myself as a writer. They were really the means by which I kick-started myself into writing. One day I'll start writing short stories again, but at the moment the novel is what I find myself doing.

González: But even though your novels are more discursive than your short fiction, they are nevertheless very tightly constructed and they are written in a very precise and controlled prose. Those seem to me to be the essential qualities of the short story. Would you say your style has been shaped by your training as a short story writer?

McEwan: My first two novels were extended short stories, and some of the habits of short story writing carried over into them. But I've always felt the most important aspect of the actual business of writing is at the level of sentence construction, of shaping sentences and shaping paragraphs, and shaping parts of characters and making chapters. And in that hierarchic sense, to take pleasure in sifting language itself.

González: So the length doesn't matter . . .

McEwan: No, I rather dislike that tradition in English novel writing of throwing anything down. People feel, well it's four hundred pages, no particular sentence matters, or only certain scenes matter. And everything else is spoken, as it were, onto the page, with no pleasure taken in language.

González: Do you have any literary model? For example, you have been considered as an inheritor of Kafka . . .
McEwan: I would not presume to be Kafka's inheritor. All kinds of foolish and flattering things are written about writers. They constantly get overpraised; it's a hazard of the profession, and you have to learn to live with it. Kafka has been very important to me though. He was the writer who enabled me to begin writing. His work—and this is paradoxal given the claustrophobic labyrinthine nature of his imagination—offered a fantastic freedom; a freedom from the English novel really, with its obsessive social documentation, its historical specificity, and interest in many things that I had no interest in and knew nothing about, like class nuance and mobility, furniture, what kind of clothes characters were wearing and so on.

The English novel seemed to me like a very dusty, dark, overfurnished room, its fabrics all moth-eaten. In Kafka there seemed to me a marvellous clarity, his characters belonged in any time, in any place, and that seemed to me a freedom. I also admired his humour, which I think is not sufficiently acknowledged.

As far as I'm concerned, Kafka is the first modern writer, of a kind that could not have existed in the nineteenth century. I feel that Henry James could have. Conrad straddles both worlds. Even Joyce draws something from the nineteenth century. But there is something irreducibly modern, definitely modern about Kafka. Many writers have one author who opens the door, but they are not necessarily models. I wrote a pastiche of Kafka, after reading his story called "Lecture to an Academy," which is narrated by an ape. I wrote a story told by an ape, an ape who is living with a woman who is so busy trying to write her second book that she no longer is paying any attention to the ape. At the time I was trying to write my second book and perhaps Kafka was my ape. Or perhaps I was his.

González: Even though in a sense you were very lucky because your first book of stories, *First Love, Last Rites* (1975), was an immediate success, it also established you as a controversial writer. Do you feel that this reputation has affected your later work negatively?

McEwan: Yes, I have found it difficult, due to the insistence of certain newspapers to sensationalise what I do, and to portray me as some kind of literary psychopath. Once this set of expectations is set up round my work, people read it in this way. And even when, as in *The Child in Time*, there isn't this element, then *all* people write about is the absence of it. So, yes, I have a problem with my reputation and I give readings to try to oppose it, because I think that my work is not a monochrome of violence and horror. But, I don't know, all writers grumble about their press, and this is my particular grumble.

González: Your last novel, *The Innocent*, was summarized in a *Sunday Times* review (6 May 1990) as "Sex, Death and Hidden Perversions," obviously a most biased judgement, although there is in this novel a latent violence, a mixture of love and horror . . .

McEwan: Well, I don't undertake to write about these troubling things lightly, nor do I do so in the hope that it will get me more readers, in fact I think it has got me fewer. But our society is violent, and writers are bound to reflect this. The important thing is not what is described but why it is described. I'm interested in how a violent impulse grows inside us. In *The Innocent* a rather ordinary man is caught up in a difficult situation and becomes extremely violent. The protagonist's mind is full of images of the Second World War. I wanted to show the brutality man can aspire to by comparing the dismemberment of a corpse to the dismemberment of a city: the bomb-devastated Berlin of the post-war.

González: Why did you choose this particular setting, and what was the point of departure of the novel?

McEwan: I went to the Soviet Union in 1987 with a small delegation of anti-nuclear people called European Nuclear Disarmament. Perestroika was then just a few months old. We were there because we wanted to take advantage of these new developments to persuade the Soviet authorities to stop persecuting members of their own anti-nuclear groups. This all seems ancient history now. We were there to make contact with these groups, the Russians who dared to speak about Russian weapons. The Soviet government only spoke about American weapons. We wanted to talk about both and we were trying to bring these two groups together.

So we met policy makers in the institutes, in particular the Institute of American and Canadian Affairs and we were treated, I think, to a most extraordinary trailer to what was going to happen in Europe in the next two or three years. These people, foreign policy intellectuals who wrote out the policy options for the Kremlin, were talking of the most extraordinary things, one of which was that Eastern Europe would have to go its own way and that the Soviet Union would begin unilaterally to withdraw troops from East Germany. When we asked, in our excitement, where we could read these ideas, we were told nothing was written down because if Mr Gorbachev went and someone else came along, they would lose their jobs. It wasn't until President Gorbachev addressed the UN—I think it was the end of 1988—that the true force of these changes became apparent.

I left Moscow full of thoughts that the Cold War was coming to an end. It so happened that three weeks later I found myself in Berlin, which I hadn't visited in a long time. I did many of the things that tourists used to do: I went to Potsdamer Platz and stood on a wooden platform and looked over what was once a busy thoroughfare and was now just raked sand full of mines and automatic guns, and I began to think that soon this too might disappear. By soon I thought some five to ten years—that seemed pretty soon to me. So, I began to plan a novel about the Cold War, not the end of the Cold War but the height, or the depths of the Cold War, in 1955. I was looking for a story, a true story, and for a long time I thought it was going to be about an escape from the East. Then I read about a tunnel dug by the Americans and the British in collaboration, a very daring project, a tunnel that ran four hundred metres into the Russian sector in order to tap telephone lines, that connected with Moscow.

Two things attracted me about this tunnel: one was that the Russians knew about it even before the Americans had started to dig it and yet didn't do anything about it because they didn't want to endanger the position of the spy who had told them. I thought what a curiously useless thing spying is, what an oddly circular, self-contained, self-referential system it is. I began to read more, and I began to see that you had to look very hard for a country that had ever changed its foreign policy on the basis of information acquired through spying. Spying is simply move and countermove within this closed system. In some ways it is analogous to forms of literary modernism.

The year 1955 threw up some interesting things too for an Englishman. By that time it was quite clear to at least half, and I'd say the better half, the more intelligent half, of the British population, that the British Empire's days were now over—this was one year before the Suez crisis, which was a watershed in British self-perception. The baton of empire was being self-consciously handed over to the USA. The consoling myth for many Britons was that we were Greece to their Rome, that we were the older mature empire, the Americans were the brasher, more powerful empire, that what we lacked in economic and military power we made up for in a certain kind of wisdom. 1955 was perhaps the first flowering of the Pax Americana. As empires go, I'd say, the American empire was the less vicious in some respects because its power and its influence extended not, in the first instance at least, through the sword but through other means: pop music, movies, fast food—the word *teenager* was invented in 1953. So the young man who is at the centre of *The Innocent*, Leonard Marnham, goes abroad for the first time in his life and is rather unconfident, rather in the way his country is so recently unconfident. In a previous generation an Englishman abroad, the Englishmen of Evelyn Waugh's *The Loved One*, would've felt he belonged to a superior race. Evelyn Waugh's hero could afford to look down his nose at the Americans; their habits appear extravagant but fundamentally empty and vulgar. For Leonard Marnham, on the other hand, the Americans offer a world he'd rather like to enter. Much of the novel is concerned with Leonard overcoming his distaste for rock and roll and beginning to like freezing cold Coca-Cola, and accepting that grown men might drink chocolate milk, accepting the paradox that this very powerful nation seems also to have a culture of the nursery: the food, the drink, the music, all seem somewhat very childish at first to a serious Englishman. But Leonard is won over to it.

González: One of the recurrent themes in your work is gender identity and the ambivalent attitude of men towards women, a mixture of fear and at the same time envy, as reflected for example in the many instances of transvestism in your books. Could you elaborate on this idea?

McEwan: I don't know if I can. I mean, my novels, the work, is the elaboration. Yes, the difficulty of understanding between men and women has always interested me. There are both comic and tragic possibilities in this difficulty that men and women have in satisfying themselves in relationships, of feeling free in them, of being honest . . .

González: You have referred to men as being afraid of women. Recently you mentioned it in front of a Spanish audience, and there was a lot of head shaking and frowning from the male side.

McEwan: I think, men's insistence on power, in relationships or in society, is based on fear; fear maybe of being engulfed, fear that might have its roots in childhood dependency on a woman. I can't see what else could produce so many rapes, so much violence, if there wasn't something in women that men identify as a threat to their existence. The head shaking and the frowning are inevitable. I think you have to look quite deep inside yourself for this fear; superficially it manifests itself as irritation or aggression.

González: Another recurrent theme in your work is the sexually confused world of adolescents, which is not a subject that has been much explored in British fiction. Why do you think this is so, and why are you so interested in it?

McEwan: Well, I suppose it is because when I began writing I was twenty-two and the material that forced itself upon me was my own recent past. Adolescence is a difficult transitional time, a rite of passage. It involves fantastic confusion: economic dependence, coupled with an adult wish to explore the world. There is an outsiderly quality to adolescents too, a heightened degree of self-consciousness. They make, in fictional terms, perfect narrators: they stand outside and yet they long to take part. My adolescence was painful for its rather empty quality. I felt the world was passing me by, and I think something of that quality worked itself into my fiction.

González: Your last two novels have moved from the claustrophobic world of private trauma to the wider world of public and political matters. Is this because of your own personal engagement with such public issues as anti-nuclear campaigns, or the pressure-group *Charter 88*?

McEwan: I've always been interested in politics to some extent. I never found before an adequate means to accommodate this interest in my work. I wrote an oratorio because I felt the novel was an unsuitable form for such pressing moral concerns. But it's a mine field, politics and the novel. If you set about writing fiction with a clear intention of persuading people of a certain point of view, you cramp your field, you deny yourself the possibility of opening up an investigation or free inquiry, which I think is the great redeeming quality of this.

González: Nevertheless, whereas your early work offers a rather bleak vision of the human condition, your last two novels end on a much more hopeful note. How would you account for this shift in outlook?

McEwan: Well, I've obviously changed over the years. When you are young you can easily afford pessimism. I think as you get older you find yourself searching for meaning. When you are young, you've got infinite time. We were happy to see that revolution on the street; as you get older you begin to doubt what will come of it, and also you might own a bit of the street by then, and you don't want it broken. Also, children force upon you a search for value. You have a stake in the world, you want it to continue, and you look hard for what will help it continue; and that is bound to make you fantasise, about things like trust and good honest communication between people. This inevitably comes through in your fiction.

Profile Writing: Ian McEwan

Patrick McGrath/1990

From *BOMB Magazine* 33 (1990): 14–16. Reprinted by permission of publisher.

Patrick McGrath: Cold War Berlin is a plausible and familiar setting for an espionage novel, but at the same time it's a zoned, sectored, occupied city, littered with ruins and haunted by memories of violence. Was this the attraction of Berlin as a setting?

Ian McEwan: Not really. The attraction originally was to Berlin in the present. I was there in 1987, when I had already decided to write a novel set in the Cold War; but at that time I hadn't any clear idea of the exact period. What attracted me then was the reification of the Cold War in terms of the Wall, and the absurdity of it, the banality of it, the fact that everybody steered their lives around it quite efficiently, and yet there were the dogs, the raked sand, the guns—the most incredible investment of technology, deadly technology, to prevent people from simply crossing from one street to the other. It wasn't until much later that I chose the period, the mid-Fifties, and that came after I saw a reference in Peter Wright's *Spycatcher* to the tunnel. The idea was then lodged in my mind that I could write a novel set in the Cold War which would conclude with the beginning of the *end* of the Cold War, and that this would be mirrored in some personal reconciliation.

McGrath: You've said elsewhere that the Venice of *The Comfort of Strangers* was a state of mind as much as a physical locale. I wonder if the Berlin of *The Innocent* became for you a state of mind also, an analogue of postwar consciousness?

McEwan: Berlin was like a fridge in a way, a deep freeze, in that the postures of the combatants in World War II were frozen in place in Berlin. So it was like history held in limbo. The period in which the novel is set was a time when the British Empire was dissolving: the war had made us virtually penniless, and the Empire was coming apart for internal reasons too, and the mantle was passing to the Americans, who had strengthened their economy enormously through the war. So I was interested in writing a novel that was about this moment of crossover, just a year before the Suez Crisis, a moment when an Englishman could no longer afford that sort of cool and easy superiority towards Americans expressed by, say, the hero of *The Loved One*. Suddenly, the Americans seemed to have the style, they seemed to have the confidence, to be taking larger strides around the place.

McGrath: One facet of the Americans in the novel is their ability to suppress the past, in the form of Leonard's suitcases.
McEwan: Well, forgetfulness, I think, is an important ingredient in sustaining the myth of innocence, and I think innocence is a very double-edged matter. Terrible things have been committed in its name. I often invoke the memory of President Carter giving a speech after the Iranians had taken the American hostages, in which he said that "now America has lost its innocence." It intrigued me to hear that myth again summoned up, of this country that's been involved in two world wars, and the Vietnam War, and the Korean War, and has its fingers in millions of pies around the globe—how it can call up this genie of innocence; and I think it requires a quite determined rewriting of history or *erasure* of history, to do so. In many ways, I think this is also true of the British, although I don't think that myths of innocence are quite so powerful in Britain. Probably an older civilization can't sustain such an idea. But yes, I think innocence is a very loaded and poisoned word when one's talking about nations. I think it was de Gaulle who said that "nations and governments have no morals, therefore no innocence." They act out of self-interest.

McGrath: You mention a reconciliation at the end of the novel, yet your character, Leonard, never actually gets to America for a reunion with Maria, the woman he loved in Berlin back in 1955.
McEwan: Well, I've left it open to the reader to decide if Leonard is not actually about to die. At the end of the novel he's sixty-seven, has a heart condition, and is left with his eyes closed slumped on a bench in the shade of a tree. I'm not sure anyway that Leonard in any sense deserves Maria. He's a man who goes on protesting his innocence without ever really examining his guilt: having been involved in at least a manslaughter, and having betrayed his country, and by an act of extraordinary paranoia rejected the woman he loves, because he suspects her of having an affair, he still manages to leave Berlin with an idea of his innocence intact. He's a worrying instance of a man who makes no use of history. There is a degree of reconciliation, but it's a reconciliation very much against the background of wasted time. I

went over to Berlin as soon as the Wall started to come down, in November of last year; I'd finished the novel in June, and to my amazement I found myself at Potsdammerplatz, which is where Leonard imagines his reunion with Maria. I found myself at Potsdammerplatz at six o'clock on a Sunday morning, the 12th of November, watching a crane lift up a huge chunk of the Wall, and then I was going through the breach in the Wall with my wife and ten thousand other people. Perhaps because of that moment I rather cling to, or exaggerate, the sense of reconciliation that lies at the end of the novel. Certainly as I went through and crossed into No-Man's-Land, crossed the raked sand that had been cleared of mines, I had a very ambivalent sense of the moment: it was joyful, it was extraordinary, it was cause for celebration, but also, if the Wall had come down so easily and we could come through like this, then what on earth was it doing there for so long? And a sense of waste was very, very strong. I hope the novel catches that sense, which is why I couldn't grant Leonard a simple reunion with Maria. I wanted the novel to have this double-edged feeling, this bittersweet feeling, that at last he'd seen his way through, that he'd been wrong to mistrust her, that there was a certain kind of truth and a lesson learned. But also his life had gone by, he was sixty-seven. That, for me, was the Wall coming down too, it was not a simple matter of unalloyed joy, it was a moment in which you get the sense that a whole generation, or two generations, had lost time, had lost opportunity.

McGrath: Would you talk about the relationship Leonard has with Otto, Maria's ex-husband, who is killed in her apartment and whose corpse then gives Leonard such trouble?

McEwan: I had the idea of Leonard as an ordinary kind of a guy carrying within himself the very destructiveness that was there in Otto. In many ways Otto is kind of doppelganger; he's that demon writ large that is also in Leonard, and, I would argue, in all of us. When Otto's discovered asleep in the wardrobe, there's a moment when Leonard leaves off arguing with Maria and goes to contemplate this man, and he thinks to himself: "She chose him, and then she chose me. Our fates are somehow bound together. She's bound me to this man." Then when the fatal fight starts in the apartment, Leonard finds himself in the middle of a marital row, and it's described purely in terms of warfare, a gun battle. This is carried on later when Leonard is facing the terrible act of dismembering Otto and sees Otto from the point of view of a bomber aiming at a target. In all these indications of violence, in the fight, in the dismemberment scene, what I'm trying to suggest is that we stand at the end of the European century and in its social memory are extraordinary feats of violence in the slaughter of two world wars and the associated genocides.

McGrath: One is very powerfully engaged by the dismemberment scene.
McEwan: If you're trying to invoke a sense of ordinary people caught up in terrible acts of violence, you have to do it in a way that *actually generates moral dread*. Stylized or mannered violence, like the kind you see on television, where people jackknife conveniently over their gunfights, would simply be a kind of pornography.

McGrath: Then there's the long-drawn-out sequence in which Leonard attempts to dispose of the suitcases containing the dismembered parts of Otto's corpse.
McEwan: Leonard with the suitcases is a man burdened not just literally but metaphorically with a memory. Europeans carry these suitcases; there's hardly a life, still, in Europe that isn't massively transformed by the war, or the displacements surrounding the war. These are the suitcases that arrive finally in the other bit of the plot, the Cold War bit of the plot, back in the tunnel. That's meant to close a circle, to suggest that the freezing of postures absorbs back into itself the violence which was held in. Those suitcases are taken back into the tunnel like something being absorbed back into itself, so that what preceded the Cold War, the hot war, in which 50, 60, 70 million people died, not only in combat or in the Final Solution, but also in genocides all up and down the century—somehow it was important to take this back into the Cold War, to see that the Cold War was like violence frozen in the act. Now that the Cold War is over, you will really see, I think, that that European demon, that "Otto," will stalk the place once more. I don't think it's a matter of simple jubilation. Anti-Semitism, for example, has emerged quite spectacularly in France, but there have been other attacks, swastikas being daubed on walls in north London, graves being desecrated in the Soviet Union. There are old ethnic hatreds and rivalries emerging in Central Europe. We do have this fantastic destructive capacity, which stands in stark contrast to the great triumphs of European civilization. So I think the novel is trying to say, well, here's a love affair, the very best of what we can achieve, and here's this terrible act of violence, which is the very worst. Europeans live this intense double life. They created, for example, the political culture of individuality, and yet they practice genocide on a scale that is unequaled in any other time or place. It's that two-faced nature of European civilization

I was trying to hint at in a person, and maybe we can only understand these things if we bring them to a personal level.

McGrath: Unless that happens, do you suspect that Europe is doomed to repeat its mistakes?
McEwan: Well, I'm staggered when I see pictures in newspapers of swastikas on pavements. I think, where's history? Where is a sense of history? I think I then get a sense of other human beings as automatons—it strikes such a chill in my heart, that we might have to run through all that again. And knowing too that it was always there, that the Cold War simply imposed a rigid false order that suppressed all these possibilities—not only the possibilities of free expression, but also the possibilities of free hatred. No, I think the European twenty-first century is going to be very difficult. I don't see it simply as democracy extending everywhere, all peace and prosperity, because there is this human problem of ancient hatreds. The Cold War prevented us from confronting this. We never had the chance to face up to what World War II unleashed, and the loss wasn't only in the East, it was in the West too.

McGrath: In what sense? Because the West was contaminated by paranoia?
McEwan: Well, I think that thought was the contaminant in a way. The Cold War made sophisticated positions difficult. If you were in the peace movement in the West, for example, you were clearly aiding the Kremlin. If you were a dissident working for the extension of political rights in the Soviet Union, then you were clearly acting in the interest of the CIA. It was this sort of simple vision and thought that robbed intellectual life of its richness. It put a lot of people in a false opposition. It's very hard to think clearly when the world gets divided up.

McGrath: The concept of innocence seems finally to acquire its complexity in the novel because two sets of opposition are invoked: one is innocence as against experience, the other, innocence as against guilt. Leonard moves through questions of sexual innocence, political innocence, moral innocence, legal innocence—all spliced together so that a tremendous richness and density accumulates around the idea.
McEwan: It's curious, because I wrote the novel with no clear sense of the title, and I often wonder if I hadn't called it *The Innocent* whether we would be talking about it in this way. Titles become very powerful, controlling

metaphors, and unless you have a title in the beginning which is helping you write the book it's very difficult, retrospectively, to name a book, because it involves deciding what it's about. Even with *The Innocent* I never felt completely at ease.

McGrath: Is that still true?

McEwan: It is still true because I find that we're talking only of innocence, whereas for a long time I wanted to call it *The Special Relationship*, for example. For a long time I wanted to call it, rather flatly, *The Letter in Berlin*.

An Interview with Ian McEwan

Liliane Louvel, Gilles Ménégaldo, and Anne-Laure Fortin/1995

From *Études britanniques contemporaines* 8 (1995): 1–12. Reprinted by permission of publisher.

Gilles Ménégaldo: Mr McEwan, you seem to privilege, in your short stories in particular, the perspective of children and/or adolescents or adults who are immature and sometimes have a limited approach of the world—why this constant and renewed interest in children's perspective and discourse?

Ian McEwan: Well, I should answer the question in terms of my own situation at the time these stories were written, in the early seventies, when I was in my early twenties and looking for both a voice and a subject.

I was very much in reaction against a certain kind of English writing which took the form of social documentary, and which was principally interested in the nuances of English class. To me it seemed like a stuffy, over-furnished room. Round about that time, when I was twenty-one, I began to read Freud and Kafka, and also Thomas Mann, and they seemed to offer freedom. In retrospect, I can't quite understand how I saw Mann as someone detached from a definable social world, but I certainly thought Kafka was. My point of departure was to look for de-socialised, distorted versions of my own existence. Many of those early stories were like dreams about my own situation: they carried only a little biographical content, but they bore the same structural relationship to my own existence that a dream might. Often I understood this only long after a particular story was written.

I found in the voices of adolescence a detachment, which was useful rhetorically. I had read stories in the literary tradition of "crossing the shadow line," of emerging into young adulthood, and since I'd emerged recently into young adulthood myself, it was a natural subject. Adolescents were a useful presence in the short story form, because they were full of adult desire, and childish incapability, a useful tension fictionally, and one I probably felt in my own life. The eye of the child gave me somewhere else to stand, a different way—a colder regard, perhaps—a way of looking at the adult world, of describing it as though one came from another planet.

So *First Love, Last Rites* and to a lesser extent the second collection of stories, *In Between the Sheets*, were a dream-like recapitulation, as it were, of my life up to then. All kinds of conflicts, all kinds of frustrations were enriched with fantastical, rather outrageous situations. By choosing the short story form, and having the stories narrated in the first person, I opted for an intense and enclosed fictional universeworld—and that way took my first tentative steps as a writer.

Ménégaldo: Could you specify the kinds of problems that were raised by this attempt to identify with the point of view and the discourse of a child? I noticed, for instance, that the adolescent in "Homemade" is much more literate than the one in "First Love, Last Rites"; you obviously try different kinds of adolescent language, according to the social background but also the mental frame-up of your characters.

McEwan: Yes, I tried out a lot of different voices with these stories. Many of the stories in *First Love, Last Rites* were written in one year, when I was a student at the University of East Anglia. I was immersed in post-war American fiction at the time which was all new to me. I used the short story form as a way of trying on different clothes—writing pastiche. The form is particularly useful for a writer at the beginning of a career. You can spend five or six weeks pretending to be Philip Roth, and if it's a disaster, then you know, you can move off and go and pretend to be Nabokov.

So my head was filled with other people's voices and I didn't find it a problem. Pastiche was my own way of finding my own voice. "Homemade," for example, was a rather flamboyant story, written after reading *Tropic of Capricorn*. I wanted both to honour Miller and make fun of him by describing a rather foolish, miserable, and hilarious episode of lovemaking, rather than a triumphant sexual conquest. That story also borrowed something of Philip Roth's *Portnoy's Complaint*. "Disguises" owed a little to Angus Wilson's "Raspberry Jam," a strange and quite vicious story of his early writing. I don't remember now all the literary sources of those stories, but I certainly patrolled other people's territory in order to come back with something that I could start to call my own.

Ménégaldo: A related aspect is that a number of these stories deal with specific situations and with characters who are marginal, alienated, and excluded from society in other ways. You attempt to express another kind of restricted universe, that of people who have some kind of psychological problem for instance, such as in "Butterflies," or "Conversation with a Cupboard Man"—in other words, you express the point of view of otherness, and of course there are very often provocative subject matters, dealt with in an unusual way (I'm thinking, for instance, of "Butterflies"). Could you comment on that?

McEwan: Well, these narrators were alienated figures, outsiders, sociopaths. They must all, I have to admit, bear some relationship to myself. I think they were dramatisations of my sense not only of exclusion, but of ignorance, profound ignorance about the world. I had no clear idea of where I stood in relation to British society generally. Nor did I have an artistically worked up romance about myself as an outsider; in fact, I wanted to join in. But my own background was rather *déclassé*: both my parents came from working-class backgrounds—hard-working, very poor. My father became commissioned as an officer when I was fairly young, and that involved the whole family in a certain kind of strange displacement. My father became an officer in the British Army, but not an officer of the middle class. He was what was called a "ranker." That gave us a curious kind of dislocated existence. Then I went to a boarding-school which was itself an experiment in social mobility: most of the kids were working-class, very bright, from the Inner London area, exported to the countryside to see if they could improve themselves with a state-funded English public school education. So that too was a kind of vacuum. Then straight into a newly constructed university, having spent a pretty alienated year myself, doing the most appalling kinds of jobs—I worked mostly as a dustman.

So I really didn't know where I fitted in. As I said earlier, when I read the fiction of Angus Wilson or Kingsley Amis or John Wain or Iris Murdoch—figures who were central to English writing at the time—I could find no way in for me there. I didn't really understand the middle-class world they described. Nor did I recognise the working-class world described by David Storey or Alan Sillitoe. I had to find a fictional world that was socially, and even historically, disembodied. So these characters carry with them something of my loneliness, as it was, and something of my ignorance of social texture, and something also of my longing for social texture, social connection. That's why they've come out in this strange way.

At the same time I wanted to give these stories a surprising quality—I mean, I was often accused, later, when these stories were published in volume form, of writing to shock, and although I've always denied it, it is the case that I did want them to be vivid. I was struck by the uniform greyness of

English writing at the time. Kafka could have a man wake up to find himself transformed into a giant bug. He takes it for granted, worries about how he's going to get to work, worries about what his parents might think, but isn't worried by the fact that he *is* a giant bug. I loved that mixture of fantasy mediated by emotional realism. That was what I was looking for, and that was what I wanted to write.

Anne-Laure Fortin: Do you intend the reader to have a moral response to your works?

McEwan: Well, that's a very difficult question. I don't really know how to begin to answer this.

Fortin: In an interview, you said: "Through restraint one will generate a degree of compassion for the right people."

McEwan: Generally the question of morality and writing is difficult for writers to answer, unless they write with a specific sense of moral purpose, which in turn of course poses problems of imaginative freedom. One could take the view that writing is drenched in morality, that language is a repository of moral values and there's no escape from it. Well, that's true, but it doesn't seem to me very significant, it doesn't say anything. Slowly I've come to the view that what underlies morality is the imagination itself. We are innately moral beings, at the most basic, wired-in neurological level. We've evolved in society. During the seven million years since we branched away from the chimpanzees, our evolution has taken place in each other's company. We have shaped each other. We've probably become clever because we've had in part to try and outwit each other or to cooperate with each other or seduce each other. Social behaviour is an instinct with us, coloured of course by local cultural conditions. Our imagination permits us to understand what it is like to be someone else. I don't think you could have even the beginnings of a morality unless you had the imaginative capacity to understand what it would be like to be the person whom you're considering beating round the head with a stick. An act of cruelty is ultimately a failure of the imagination. Fiction is a deeply moral form in that it is the perfect medium for entering the mind of another. I think it is at the level of empathy that moral questions begin in fiction.

Liliane Louvel: A set of stories and novels are concerned with the notion of passage and thresholds, in the broad sense, not in the restrictive one. So could you comment on that, when we look at the emphasis on ritual which is in your work, and perhaps we could see a sort of homology between the itineraries of characters and some recurrent spatial structures, such as mazes or labyrinths or the tunnel or maybe the tree in *The Child in Time*. So could you speak about that and the use of space?

McEwan: Well, I'm often asked about rites of passage in my work, and labyrinths, tunnels, mazes. It's difficult for me to respond. I don't consciously set out to write rites of passage. I don't ponder the metaphorical possibilities of labyrinths or tunnels. Perhaps therefore I am the true innocent of my novel *The Innocent*.

Ménégaldo: What is also very perceptible in your work is the problematic identity of characters in search of their own self, in search of a new, different self. That is an enduring topic, I think, not only in the short stories but in the novels as well. There is a certain emphasis on the notion of mask, disguise, shift of identity, of sexual identity as well. Maybe this could be paralleled with your fiction, that may also in a way borrow different disguises and be subjected to different readings. In other words, in the same way as you raise problems of identity in your fiction, you also raise the problem of the identity of your novels, of the type of novel—there are gender problems or identity problems in the same way as there are genre problems. For instance, some critics refer to the neo-gothic element in your work, for instance in *The Comfort of Strangers*, or the way in which you use the spy-novel model in *The Innocent*, etc. Would you like to comment on that?

McEwan: Yes, different kinds of *genres* become a kind of resource. I am not an enthusiastic reader of spy-novels. Nor have I ever been remotely interested in the Gothic tradition. And yet I've been described as a writer who draws on these traditions, or is part of them. I've been toying for some years now with writing science fiction. If I could just find the right way in, I'd be happy to do it. But again, I don't read science fiction. They say you can be most profoundly influenced by the books you haven't read. Perhaps in the same way you are swayed by the literary *genres* which you are too impatient to read.

There are notable exceptions of course, but genre writing is so passionately committed to bad prose. By convention the detective novel sets itself free from considerations of originality. Well, that's not the kind of fiction I'm interested in, but I am intrigued by the detective novel. I don't want to read one. I want to write one. It interests me because I've been thinking a great deal recently about the scientific as opposed to the mystical or religious world-view. Or, put another way, the head and the heart—a familiar polarity in Western literature. I think we all sense that the polarity is useful but also artificial. Our everyday reasoning is drenched in emotionality and yet we feel there is a tension. The detective-hero embodies these tensions. As a problem solver he is an arch-rationalist, and as a man who follows hunches and contemplates motivation he is a creature of the heart. I've got a feeling I could turn this to my own purposes. And this is what would lead me to poach on the genre.

Louvel: You show a lot of interest in science, especially in *The Child in Time.* We are now living at the end of a century where there are new ways of conceiving the world, new "episteme," new theories in the field of mathematics and physics, the theory of chaos, fractals and all that . . . Is science a source of inspiration for you and do you think it might lead to new forms of literature?

McEwan: I've always been interested in science. I've often regretted I didn't do a science degree. I don't share the general suspicion, nourished partly by our Romantic tradition, and sustained even now, particularly in Britain, by a liberal arts education, that science crushes the human soul or the imagination. I believe the contrary. I think it's a route to wonder. The world as presently conceived by the cosmologies of physicists seems far more extraordinary, far more exciting, far more of a challenge and stimulus to the imagination than a world depicted as, say, being propped up by two elephants. The last twenty or thirty years have seen extraordinary times in science. The rediscovery, or the renewal rather, of Darwinian thinking by way of genetics and the discovery of the structure of DNA has been particularly interesting. In the biological sciences generally there's been something of a renaissance. The first three decades of this century encompassed the great classical era of modern physics; quantum mechanics and relativity theory offered two entirely distinct and contradictory ways of understanding the world. The mighty project of unifying them is beginning to be fulfilled. Perhaps an even more significant task will be to generate an ethics from these emerging syntheses. Philosophy is increasingly informed by neuroscience. Evolutionary psychology is beginning to offer a bridge between biology and the social sciences. Who knows, we might yet arrive at a radical synthesis of the humanities and the sciences.

Where this leaves fiction, I don't know, but a writer is bound to be interested in the possible consequences of such things. That is why I've been interested in reading more science and thinking more about our distrust of it. In *Black Dogs*, my heart was really with the character Bernard, the rationalist. But I gave the best lines to June, the mystic. At some point, I'd like to redress the balance. I'd like to write a novel in praise of rationalism—rationalism as I understand it, mediated by emotional wisdom—and beyond that, in praise of what I think is probably the most splendid and most effective intellectual tool we've ever given ourselves—scientific method. In the world of letters there is something vaguely perverse about this because the dominant assumption is still that numbers, scientific measurements, scientific endeavour is somehow cold and profoundly inimical to the soaring human spirit. But I just don't buy that.

Louvel: So maybe new shapes and new forms will come out of that?

McEwan: Yes, I think they will evolve, but not in the hands of any one writer.

Ménégaldo: To come back to another recurrent motive in your books, the theme of loss and deprivation, absence and what is called in French "le travail du deuil": a number of protagonists are deprived of parents, often fatherless, for instance the protagonist in *Black Dogs*, looking for a substitute father and mother, and the counterpart of that is another central motive of appropriation and possession. These two motives seem to be constantly interwoven in all your work. Could you comment on that, and has there been an evolution on that level, from the situation you describe in *The Comfort of Strangers* to the one you describe in *Black Dogs*?

McEwan: Well, I never really understood it myself, but it's been pointed out to me at various times. There is a great deal of loss in my work and it was only in my mid-thirties that I began to understand the source of this sense of deprivation. In the story, "The Last Day of Summer," a boy of eleven is involved in a rowing accident in which a mother figure and a small baby are drowned. This is the "last day" of summer because the next day the boy's boat is going to be put away. It's September and he's going to go off to his new school. It wasn't until I was well into my thirties that I understood that the story is really about my being sent away to boarding-school at the age of eleven. The woman in the boat is clearly my mother, the baby in the boat is clearly myself, as is the boy. Their drowning is the "death" of my mother, and the end of childhood. In those days boarding-schools were much harsher places than they are now. Being sent away as a child produced in me the sense of loss that has seeped into my fiction.

The other matter, possession, invasion. Well, like many writers, I suppose I have a sponge-like quality, an emotional neutrality. I absorb things from other people without being fully aware of it. This has obvious advantages for a writer, but if I'm not careful, people can invade my space all too easily. I've had to learn to put up barriers. *The Comfort of Strangers* expresses something of that anxiety—if you open yourself up too much, you can be taken over. There are always people who want to take you over. I believe that there's a small indefensible core of your own selfhood which you have to hang on to at all costs.

Ménégaldo: Another aspect that could be related in a way to the previous one is the emphasis on family relationships, and conflicting family relationships, at various levels, for instance the complex and ambivalent relation there is to the father figure or father substitute in some of your works, for instance the ironic father figure in "Solid Geometry," the sadistic father in *The Comfort of Strangers*, and at times on the contrary a rather positive view of the father-son relationship as in *The Child in Time*, for instance, or to another degree, the substitute relationship between the narrator in *Black Dogs* and the figure of Bernard. Why again this ambivalent attitude to the father figure?

McEwan: Well, I think a writer can only answer such a question in biographical rather than thematic terms. The father figures you mention come unbidden, they push at the door, which means I have to talk about my own father. He is presently very ill and weak, but he was once a powerful, domineering, slightly bullying man who was extremely loving towards me, passionate about me in ways that were both supportive and oppressive. I inherited my mother's shy nature. He was precisely one of those figures from my fiction who seemed to want to take me over. He was the regimental sergeant-major, feared and hated by the men below him because he was so strong, such a stickler for the rules, such a disciplinarian. You'd have to say he was a very effective soldier. He wasn't tough like that with me at home, but he was frightening. He didn't have—and I think he would agree himself—he didn't have an easy way of talking to children. He was a loving man who did not have the means to express his love. I remember once when he came to stay in my house and my seven-year-old son climbed on my lap while we were talking and put his arms around my neck. I hardly noticed; one of the joys of having children is that you simply inhabit this terrain of love. We went on with the conversation. And then my father pointed at little Gregory and said, "That's amazing, that would never have happened between us. You were too frightened of me." And I nodded, rather sadly.

One recurring nightmare scene from my childhood: my father would seize hold of me in a playful way and, ignoring my struggles, pretend that I was a baby and cradle me and make a shushing noise. He would do this in front of people. I felt that he was ridiculing my relationship with my mother. He thought that I was too close to her. It was an intense drama he enacted behind the mask of a joke. So I had very powerful and confused feelings about him. I loved him and I feared him. I enjoyed doing exciting things with him—climbing the ropes of the Army assault courses, going out into the North African Desert with him. But I also shrank from his loud presence.

Perhaps this was another reason why Kafka interested me. He addressed his father in a long letter. I ended up addressing mine with stories and novels. In *The Cement Garden*, I killed him off early on. He's there in *The Comfort of Strangers*, and he pops up in other places. In the later fiction, I've tried to redeem him by becoming the father, by trying to take his strengths, his huge capacity for love and giving it expression.

Ménégaldo: I'd like to ask you a question concerning the broadening of your scope in literature, the growing part that is played by history and historical facts, and also by a reflection on the state of society. You've written, for instance, a reflection on the institutional discourse and power in *The Child in Time*, and more specifically on ideology and commitment in *Black Dogs*. Could you comment on that evolution from a rather restricted world in a way to broader social and historical issues, which were sometimes broached upon in your previous stories, but more definitely in the recent works?

McEwan: Well, I said at the beginning of this conversation that one source of the closed-off quality of my short stories was my ignorance of the wider world. At the same time, I did describe relationships, often in fairly bizarre terms. A couple makes for a kind of society, and for a while the couple was my world. As I understood more I began to take courage and wanted to incorporate what I had understood.

An important moment of transition was writing for television. Dialogue without narrative gave me a moral freedom which I'd felt I didn't have in the stories. Or perhaps I mean it gave me a moral purpose which I thought would inhibit the stories. I wrote a television film called *The Imitation Game*, which is about a young woman's attempt to find interesting work during the war. It was heavily influenced by feminist thought. It certainly made a society, that of England in 1940, and although it wasn't completely successful, I began to understand what people meant when they talked of writers playing God.

The Comfort of Strangers edged into a slightly larger world, and by the time I'd written an oratorio about the threat of nuclear war and came to start *The Child in Time*, I thought I could find ways of bridging the earlier, small canvases of intense psychological states with a broader public reality—oddly enough, through the idea of child-care manuals. In them one had an unconscious expression of the spirit of the age, of what people really wanted their children to be—projections of their ideal selves.

From then on, I've never really been interested in anything other than trying to find connections between the public and the private, and exploring how the two are in conflict, how they sometimes reflect each other, how the political invades the private world.

Fortin: In 1979, you said: "I don't know if this is a very good time for English fiction." I wonder what you meant then and if you've changed your mind now.

McEwan: Well, I think things have improved. The eighties were a reasonably good time for British fiction. Things opened out and we shook off our provincialism. All kinds of new people came along. We had writers from the Commonwealth or ex-Empire bringing all kinds of Englishes into British fiction. A lot of good women writers came onto the scene. Literary fiction itself seemed to occupy more space in the public mind: new lists were started, and there was the success of the Waterstone's book chain which by the end of the eighties had almost a hundred shops. The Booker Prize, for all its idiocies, helped bring literary fiction to a wider readership. Then there was a spate of takeovers in the publishing world in the mid to late eighties, which led to writers being paid vast sums of money which I personally did not abhor. There was an interesting mix of formal experimentation with a commitment to remaining connected and relevant to a readership. There was a fairly general kind of audience that was ready to fork out money for hardback books. So I think we've had something of a silver age, certainly in quantity; only time will tell about the quality.

Ménégaldo: In your last novel, *The Daydreamer*, which is a children's book, in a way, you tread a new path. However, you revert to the short story form you seemed to have given up. What part will the short story play in your forthcoming works? A second aspect of the question is that this book seemingly addresses a different readership. Yet, a number of stories concern the adult reader as well, and one is able to recognise familiar motifs and images that you used in other stories and novels—for instance the doll motif that you used in *In Between the Sheets*, or the dismemberment motif that you used in various other stories and in *The Innocent*. Why did you choose to rewrite these motifs differently? It also seems that you identify at last with the fictional writer of *The Child in Time*, who also wrote children's books.

McEwan: Well, *The Daydreamer* is a series of stories with a central character linking them all. It also has a kind of shape. So in a sense it's a hybrid, a mating of novel with a collection of stories. There is a degree of development: by the end the boy-hero's final daydream takes the form of a humorous version of Kafka's *Metamorphosis*. He has a deep foreboding that the adult world he is soon to join is profoundly dull. Grown-ups seem to do little else in life beyond sitting around talking, snoozing, or worrying. He goes to bed with these thoughts on his mind, and the following morning wakes to find himself transformed—into a giant person, an adult. But then he tastes some of the pleasures of the grown-up life: he kisses a girl, he stays up late, he has interesting work, he's invented an anti-gravity machine. The future is redeemed.

When I wrote *The Daydreamer* I wasn't really thinking about short stories. I was writing for children, and I wanted self-enclosed, bedtime tales that would take twenty-five minutes to read, that would have strong plots, be surprising, and contain not a hint of moral instruction. I ended up with a collection of stories, but I thought at the time I was doing something else. And that's the only way I'll write stories now. They can't be means to experimentation or pastiche. Perhaps I'll find some other way in the future (to try and answer your question) of fooling myself again into writing them.

As for the recurrence of themes, I can only say—well, this is the furniture of my mind. I don't choose these things, they're there because I wrote as seriously as I would for adults. I wrote carefully, I put the stories together over a period of three years, I only wrote one when I really *had* one to write. *The Daydreamer* was written while I was working on *Black Dogs* and the screenplay of *The Innocent*. I'd like to think that *The Daydreamer* is a book for adults written in a language children can understand. In Italy it had an exclusively adult readership because of the way it was presented. Because it's a celebration of daydreaming, and therefore of the imagination, the Italians took it to be in the tradition of Calvino, of *Cosmicomics* and so on.

A book about daydreaming is bound to be, by extension, a book about writing. I have to say that over the last twenty-five years my pleasure in writing has steadily increased, to the point of delight. It used to be a source of pleasure-pain, a kind of compulsive self-torture. But now I know that the crucial ingredient of writing-pleasure is *surprise*. Surprising oneself with a thought, or a formulation. Making something that seems to come from a mind that is better than your own. On a good day, writing offers itself up as pure mental freedom, and as one of the greatest single pleasures in life— right up there with sex and skiing and mountain walking.

Ménégaldo: What will be the next pleasure of writing? Do you have any plans?

McEwan: I have all the usual superstitions about speaking of the next thing, but it's there, embedded in the conversation we've just had.

Interview with Ian McEwan

Jonathan Noakes/2001

From *Ian McEwan: The Essential Guide* by Margaret Reynolds and Jonathan Noakes, published by Vintage (London, 2002), 10–23. Reprinted by permission of The Random House Group Ltd. Interview was conducted in Oxford on September 21, 2001.

The Child in Time

Jonathan Noakes: How did you begin *The Child in Time*?

Ian McEwan: *The Child in Time* was one of those novels that didn't really begin with any clear route map. It had its origins in a number of little scraps, pieces, ideas, enthusiasms. One of them was a recurrent dream, the sort of dream that you only remember that you've had before when it comes again—finally I remembered it and wrote it down. And I should say that dreams have very rarely been a source of inspiration to me, nor am I a great believer in them, despite the plot of the novel. This dream was of myself on a drizzly day walking along a country footpath and coming to a bend in the road and pausing there, with a very powerful premonition that if I walked off to my left I would come to a place . . . a pub or a meeting place of some sort, and I would find out something very important about my origins. And it was actually rather a scary dream, and it made me begin to think about how I might write about a character, not quite myself, and what he was doing on this road, and what would happen when he got to this place. So that was one part of it.

Quite separately from that, and at the time I didn't know that these were at all connected, I was reading a rather remarkable book called *Dream Babies* by Christina Hardyment. It's a sort of history of childcare manuals—a most unlikely book. I think I was reading it because someone had given it to me for my birthday, that was about the only reason. I hadn't gone looking for it, it was a piece of complete serendipity, and its subtitle was "Childcare from Locke to Spock." What Hardyment was suggesting, among many other things, was that childcare manuals are an extraordinarily accurate way into the spirit of an age. You have the intense regulation of the Victorian notion

79

of breaking a child's will, followed by a rather sentimental child-centred Edwardian view, followed by the rather grisly pseudoscientific notion of childcare that predominated in the 1920s and '30s, with a lot of input from behaviourists, and then in 1948 . . . Spock.

And this was the early '80s, with what would turn out to be a rather radical and successful government taking control, and we, the children of Spock, were rather surprised by the popularity of this government—not so popular in 1981, but certainly by 1984—and I thought, "Well, maybe it's time for another childcare manual." And I did in fact think of a rather satirical and Swiftian childcare manual that I might write, and I thought, "No, this is going to be too long and the joke's going to be too sustained." But I kept little fragments of this.

Then I began to see how these things might fold together. There was my interest in science, which I'd had since my teens, always rather regretting that I hadn't done a science degree at university, fascinated by what I could understand of quantum mechanics and relativity theory, interested generally too in Newtonian mechanics and the history of science, and slowly these things began to fall together.

I had begun the book thinking I was writing a social comedy. Sometime halfway through I began to revise that notion, went back to the beginning, wrote the chapter in which the little girl is lost, and really started again; and by then—because I was anticipating the birth of my first child—I began to have a clear sense that this was a novel that was going to end with a birth, and in fact it ended with a descriptive scene drawn from the birth of two children. By the time I finished in 1986 I had two sons.

Noakes: Why is it that trauma—and, linked to that, the idea that security is a comforting illusion, but only an illusion—is a focus in so much of your work?

McEwan: Well, no one, finally, can feel completely secure in the world. There is always an edge of danger, and we're talking on September 21st, 2001, only ten days after the most dramatic illustration of that [the terrorist attack on the World Trade Centre, New York]. Security is what we find mostly in our relationships, but they can't defend us from the outside world.

And I suppose I have been interested more generally in how private fates and public events collide. *The Child in Time* was very much an attempt to write about something quite intimate, like childcare, and something quite public, like a childcare manual. I think the reason I was excited by *Dream Babies* was that it gave me a way in to just that mix of public and private concern. Love is very fragile and difficult to attain, and hard to keep and all the more precious for it. The novel—all novels, not just mine—is extended and extended through time, and with that comes change, difficulty, and the exploration of conflict. If we want to simply celebrate love, say, then I think we must turn to lyric poetry. A four-hundred-page novel celebrating a love affair that never went wrong could be very demanding on the reader.

Noakes: The novel suggests, especially towards the end, that there's a deeper patterning to time than we're immediately aware of. How did you arrive at that idea?

McEwan: Well, there any many notions played with in *The Child in Time* that I'm not sure I really hold with, but that were attractive and convenient in an exploration, an investigation of childhood and how it sits within us all our lives, and how in some respects, when we contemplate our whole existence, it seems to be in a perpetual present. That's a very subjective sense of time and childhood, of course, but I was rather intrigued by the way that certain quantum-mechanical versions of time seem to completely undo the standard clock-time sense of it, and I thought that I could forge—with a little bit of creaking and groaning from the subject itself—a connection between this mathematically-based notion of time and all sorts of other versions of it: not only the permanent sense of the whole past living inside your head, but also the way time accelerates in a crisis. Remember, too, that the novel more or less unfolds within the gestation period of a pregnancy. The child is conceived in Chapter Three and the novel then is framed by that sense of impending arrival.

Noakes: *The Child in Time* has an elaborate formal structure. How much working out of that formal structure might be done before you begin to write?

McEwan: With a novel like *The Child in Time*, as I said, its beginnings were haphazard. It's impossible to plan the architecture of something unless you know its content, so the structure gets worked out along the way in this kind of novel. I'm very aware of it. It seems to me something that's genuinely operative—that is to say, I think it really does affect the way a reader responds to it. A sense of shape might not be immediately perceived by a reader, but I think the effect on the reader is an added clarity.

I think architecture really makes for clarity, and it's clarity that I'm most interested in in the sentences too—not principally music, but precision and a strong visual clarity. So as I become clearer about what it is I'm going to do, so I make alterations to the shape of what is going to happen in the future. Then of course there is the delicious moment of having your first draft down finally, and then you can go back and make sure that everything conforms to that architectural sense.

Noakes: How much re-drafting might you do typically?

McEwan: Well, everything's changed a great deal with word processing. *The Child in Time* was the first novel I ever wrote on a word processor. Before that I was never quite settled on a way of doing drafts. *The Comfort of Strangers* was written in longhand and sent out to be typed. I found that to be very unsatisfactory. *The Cement Garden* I wrote in longhand and typed up myself—slightly less unsatisfactory, but typewriters I found were a real problem: a machine seemed very much to interpose in the immediacy of writing by hand.

Word processing, I think, delivered me into a wonderful virtual space. The chapter that is in the computer, but not yet printed, has the same—or the equivalent—virtual quality as an idea in your head that you've not committed to paper yet. Since working with a word processor, I've been able to do far more drafts than I otherwise would. So I revise all the time, I'm constantly going back. It's hard for me to say how many drafts there were of *The Child in Time*. I revise the previous day's work first thing in the morning, that's the first combing-through. When I get four or five thousand words together, a chapter, two chapters, I do a second . . . then I don't look at them again until I've got the first draft down. I'm only revising just behind me, as it were, as I go forward.

The Child in Time I suppose had three major drafts, with lots and lots of those sorts of local immediate revisions. I do work fairly slowly. I'm not the kind of writer who, in a second draft, is consigning a hundred and twenty pages to the dustbin and then writing another hundred and twenty or twice that. But my drafts will be printed out in double-space: another pleasure and luxury of word processing. I like working through drafts most at night . . . A pool of light, a black pen, and I really start attacking it with a sort of freedom, knowing that, again, everything I write here is virtual. More coolly the next morning I might say, "Well, yes, I'll leave that," or I might accept that change. That's the chance, though, not only to deal with the sentences locally, read them aloud, taste them, test them, but to look at those larger things that you mentioned, such as the formal structure, which is like architecture.

Novels do resemble buildings. A first chapter, a first line is like an entrance hall, a doorway. The reader has to be drawn in—what first meets the eye is important. So I don't use or accept the term architecture merely as a metaphor, I think, again, it's operable, it's something that works on the reader. You're asking the reader to step inside a mental space which has a shape. That's very like someone stepping inside a modern building, going to look at it and deciding whether they like it or not.

Enduring Love

Noakes: At the beginning of *Enduring Love* you're drawing the reader in. What else are you doing with that opening section?

McEwan: Well, its narrator is a failed scientist and a successful science journalist, with a particular cast of mind—a highly organised mind—and I wanted immediately to suggest this kind of mind. It's a chapter that relies heavily on a very disciplined sense of the visual, and of the relationship of the different figures. There are characters converging across a field . . . Joe's way of describing those is in terms of their distance, their points of the compass, there are lots of precise visual details to suggest someone who has got a fairly confident grip on the world, the sort of grip that I would associate with someone who embraces a strong materialist view of it. So the characterisation of Joe was central to that.

Secondly, I'd read that de Clérambault's syndrome—this strange psychotic delusional state—is often triggered by an intense moment. When I started *Enduring Love* I didn't have that intense moment; this opening chapter that people have liked was not written until—I don't know—halfway through the novel, when I found the sort of thing I wanted. But from the point of view of Jed Parry—a lonely man, very much an outsider with his own deep intrapsychic world—to be plunged suddenly into this community of work was, I thought, a way of triggering his particular delusion that Joe loves him.

More broadly, I suppose that I wanted to—cynically, if you like—hook the reader. Again in that architectural sense, this is the first room I wanted the reader in, and I wanted the door locked behind them. And I suppose too that I wanted to suggest, in Joe's way of analysing and describing what's happening, something out of game theory and evolutionary psychology, a Darwinian way of looking at the world. That is, to talk about who lets go first as something that involves morality, involves instinct, involves an adaptationist account of why we are what we are, quite distinct from the deist account that Jed is going to espouse.

Noakes: And then the third point of view, which you play off against the other two, is Clarissa's as a university teacher who specialises in a Romantic poet, John Keats. Why did you choose that as the third counterpoint?

McEwan: She just sort of grew. I mean, one doesn't map these things out. I wanted Joe's world to be intact and loving and broadly sympathetic, in order for it to seem all the more threatening that Jed moves into it. I wanted someone both sympathetic and wrong. I wanted in Joe someone who was slightly repellent, but right. It's sometimes quite clear in life that it's not the nicest people who are right. Sometimes someone is dead right, but you don't like them.

I'm aware too that there's a tradition in Western literature that celebrates the heart, the intuition, trusting your feelings. Perhaps it derives a great deal from our Romantic tradition. The scientific, the rational, is often cast into the minds of villains, and I think Mary Shelley might have a lot to answer for in this. But I thought I would like to write a novel that rather celebrated the rational. Not necessarily by making my rational hero too sympathetic, but by celebrating his thought processes. So in Clarissa I wanted someone who was very sympathetic, who had her own sort of enduring love, not only for Keats, but for finding or projecting more letters from Keats and Fanny Brawne—one of the greatest love affairs conducted by letter in literature, I think.

And I wanted the reader to side with Clarissa. There are all kinds of false trails in *Enduring Love*. I wanted the reader to toy with the idea that Joe might be going completely crazy, or maybe even that Joe was Jed. These are games one plays, and withholding information is crucial to this kind of novel writing. But I wanted Clarissa to be wrong. I wanted the police to be wrong. I rather like those plots. I once wrote a movie with Macaulay Culkin in it. It had a similar plot, completely different circumstances, where someone has an understanding of the truth, and none of the other characters—including the reader, including the audience—believe them. I'm sure I'll come back to that. I don't know why it's there, but it's something that I haven't yet played through.

Noakes: Like *The Child in Time*, *Enduring Love* plays on the idea that communication between two people can be very difficult, even if those two people are close. Why should this be?

McEwan: I think I can only answer that in terms of the nature of the novel. Clearly misunderstandings occur in life all the time. Not only between people who are very close, but between people who are not close, simply because they don't understand each other. We see this played out at national levels, we see it in sectarian disputes, we see it when marriages come to an end, or love affairs collapse. What is exceptional, I think, about the novel as a form—and here it exerts its superiority over movies, over theatre—is its peculiar ability to get inside minds and to show us the mechanics of misunderstanding, so you can be on both sides of the dispute. You can have unreliable narrators that will draw the reader into the wrong side of a dispute, and then turn it round later. You can be single-minded about it and withhold information, you can be omniscient. But over two or three hundred years we have evolved a literary form that I think is unequalled in its ability to get inside the nature of a misunderstanding. And misunderstandings can stretch from something that is mild and social and comic, to the deepest forms of hatred. Though—and this comes back to the way that three or four or five hundred pages have to take you through a period of time—it cannot really dwell in one moment, so again it can look from all sides at the nature of misunderstanding. So inevitably if you write novels you're going to find yourself writing about—at some level—conflict between people.

Atonement

Noakes: *Atonement* is partly about guilt. You've said that a novel can look at all sides of a question and it can refuse to take sides. Nevertheless we are encouraged in *Atonement* to take sides, partly because the narrator turns out to have been part of the story, and is therefore partial. What's the significance of the possibility that this "atonement," this account—the nearest Briony, as a non-believer, can get to "atonement"—may be inaccurate? Another fantasy?

McEwan: Part of the intention of *Atonement* was to look at storytelling itself. And to examine the relationship between what is imagined and what is true. It's a novel full of other writers—not only Briony of course, who's stalked, haunted by the figures of Virginia Woolf, Elizabeth Bowen, Rosamond Lehmann, but Robbie too has a relationship, a deep relationship with writing and storytelling.

The danger of an imagination that can't quite see the boundaries of what is real and what is unreal, drawn again from Jane Austen—another writer who is crucial to this novel—plays a part in Briony's sense that her atonement has consisted of a lifetime of writing this novel. She's condemned to write it over and over again. Now she's a dying woman, she has vascular dementia, her mind is emptying, and finally she writes a draft which is different from all the others. She fails, as she sees it, to have the courage of her pessimism, and rewrites the love story so that the lovers survive.

What really then is the truth? Well, as she says, when the novel will finally be published, which can only be after she's dead, she herself will become a character, and no one will be much interested in whether she is real or not, she will only exist within the frame of the novel. So I wanted to play, but play seriously, with something rooted in the emotional rather than the intellectual. I wanted to play with the notion of storytelling as a form of self-justification, of how much courage is involved in telling the truth to oneself. What are the distances between what is real and what is imagined? Catherine Morland, the heroine of Jane Austen's *Northanger Abbey*, was a girl so full of the delights of Gothic fiction that she causes havoc around her when she imagines a perfectly innocent man to be capable of the most terrible things. For many, many years I've been thinking how I might devise a hero or heroine who could echo that process in Catherine Morland, but then go a step further and look at, not the crime, but the process of atonement, and do it through writing—do it through storytelling, I should say.

Noakes: So Briony's a writer. Joe is a writer. Stephen is a writer. What do you think about being a writer, writing about writers?

McEwan: I think it could be immensely sterile if that's all it was. I think that I'm always drawn to some kind of balance between a fiction that is self-reflective on its own processes, and one that has a forward impetus too, that will completely accept the given terms of the illusion of fiction. I've never been interested in that kind of fiction that triumphantly declares that art is not life. Only novelists ever think that art is life. Readers never have any problem with it. But I do have an interest in something self-reflective along the way.

Noakes: A number of novelists born just after the Second World War have written about the experiences of their parents' generation. What are the reverberations of the violence of the Second World War to the generation that grew up in its shadow?

McEwan: Well, I was born in 1948 and my father was a professional soldier. The war shaped our family life. It was the war that brought my parents together. It was the war that killed my mother's first husband. I grew up in army camps in places in the world in which, again, our presence was to some extent determined by the recent war. And then, more importantly, I suppose, it was the war that set in place the alignments of countries that brought us into the Cold War. It was such a constant presence in my child-hood. My father and his friends, as soon as they had a beer in their hand in the evenings, which was every evening, would talk about the war. Wherever they started in their conversation, that's where it would always end. It was a constant presence, and geopolitically it remained a presence.

So as we reached the end of the twentieth century our generation, fifty-ish, looked back. The Berlin Wall came down in 1989, and with it came a momentary optimism about a new world order, which rapidly foundered as of last week, so it seemed natural always to return, to focus one's attention on this defining time. Especially when it pushed a contrast on us between our parents' lives and our own. My parents' lives were shaped by the great Depression and the Second World War. I was born in 1948, the beginning of the welfare state. I don't come from either a literary or a wealthy family, but I had access to the most extraordinary education that someone in my social position, thirty years before, would not have been able to take advantage of. It was an unprecedented period of prosperity and relative stability, and there were enormous differences between those generations. As great, I think, actually greater than the kinds of differences that Virginia Woolf and her contemporaries dramatised between themselves and their late-Victorian parents.

Noakes: You include some highly graphic scenes of violence. We're used to seeing violence in popular culture. What are the differences between artistic and exploitative representations of violence, do you think?
McEwan: If violence is simply there to excite, then it's merely pornographic. I think treating it seriously—which means doing it without sentimentality—you're always going to bring to it a certain quality of investigation, so it's not only the violence you show, you're writing *about* violence. You're showing something that's certainly common in human nature. You're not necessarily taking sides, it's not necessary always to produce a moral attitude, but in the greater scheme of things you are bound to place the reader in some form of critical attitude towards the circumstances. There is always a larger intent.

For example, if you're writing about the retreat to Dunkirk, as I do in *Atonement*, you can't avoid the fact that tens of thousands of people died in that retreat, and yet we have a rather fond memory of it in the national nar-rative, and you want to play off something of the sentimentality of the "mir-acle" of Dunkirk against the reality for ordinary soldiers as they made their way towards the beaches. Many of the images that I used in the Dunkirk episode I drew from the Bosnian conflict. I used photographs from that to remind myself of how soldiers and civilians, hugely intermingled, would suffer the most appalling consequences.

I talked of sentimentality. I think that is the recurring element of popular culture's treatment of violence. There are no consequences. Someone gets hit over the head with a bottle and they fall, the camera moves on, the plot moves on. Anyone who's hit on the head with a bottle is likely to suffer a lifetime of consequences. Blindness might be one of those, because the visual regions are at the back of the head. In other words, you've got to embrace it, and you've got to make your reader do what Conrad did in his famous Preface to *The Nigger of the Narcissus* (1897), you've got to make your reader *see*. So, when people accuse me of being too graphic in my depictions of violence, my response is, "Well, either you *do* violence, or you sentimentalise it." If you're going to have it, you've got to show it in all its horror. It's not worth doing it if you're simply going to add it there as a little bit of spice. I'm not interested in that at all.

Noakes: Do you have a reader in mind as you write?
McEwan: It's always difficult to answer that question. I suppose it's my most crabby, sceptical self. A rather hard-to-please, ungenerous soul, whose most common remark is "Come off it!" But it's always a version of myself. I think there's a danger for writers as they get older, and as they become well established, that no one really will tell them anything they don't want to hear.

Noakes: In what ways do you see your writing developing in the future?
McEwan: I think I've come to the end of a cycle of novels with *Enduring Love*, which began with *The Child in Time*, included *Black Dogs* and *The Innocent*. Those were novels in which *ideas* were dramatised or played out. They are, among other things, novels of ideas. Both *Amsterdam* and *Atonement* are moving off in another direction. I suppose the emotions perhaps will mean more to me. I think I might, in formal terms, be moving backwards for a little while into the nineteenth century. I spent the summer reading Tolstoy and Chekhov. I'm about to read George Eliot's *Middlemarch*. I think the nineteenth-century novel perhaps brought the form to its point of—or one point of—perfection. I think, in the creation of character, the great nineteenth-century novels are unsurpassed, and I think that I might push forward in my own little projects to make my novels more character-led.

When I got to the end of *Atonement* I felt that Briony was the most complete person I'd ever conjured, and I'd like to do that again and take it further.

The Art of Fiction CLXXIII: Ian McEwan

Adam Begley/2002

From *The Paris Review* 44.162 (Summer 2002): 30–60. Reprinted by permission of author.

Begley: In your third novel, *The Child in Time*, we meet the parents of the narrator, and I suspect that they resemble your parents. How true to life is the portrait?

McEwan: Fairly close, though somewhat idealized. My parents had a difficult relationship without ever conceding the fact, and it was hard to write about when they were both still alive. I was born in 1948, on the edge of Aldershot, a rather ugly Victorian garrison town. My father at that time was a sergeant major. He was a Glaswegian who had lied about his age and joined up in 1933 to escape the unemployment along the Clyde.

He makes an appearance in *Atonement*. In 1940 he was a motorbike dispatch rider and he was wounded in the legs. He teamed up with another soldier who'd been shot in the arms, and between them they worked the controls of a motorbike. They pass Robbie on the road into Dunkirk.

David McEwan was very handsome, erect, with a dangerous look about him. A hard-drinking man, quite terrifying. He was a great stickler for all the spit and polish of traditional army life, and at the same time he adored me as I grew older. But my earliest recollections are of weekday idylls with my mother interrupted at weekends by the loud appearance of my father, when our tiny prefabricated bungalow would fill with his cigarette smoke. He didn't have much talent for communicating with small children. He was a man who liked the pub and the sergeants' mess. Both my mother and I were rather frightened of him. She grew up in a small village near Aldershot and left school at fourteen to go into service as a chambermaid. Later she worked in a department store. But for most of her life she was a housewife, with her generation's fierce pride in the orderliness and gleam of the family home.

Begley: There's a scene in *The Child in Time* where the mother is weeping. We don't know quite why—all we get is the vague sense that there's something wrong.

McEwan: My father's drinking was sometimes a problem. And a great deal went unspoken. He was not particularly acute or articulate about the emotions. But he was very affectionate towards me. When I passed exams he was very proud—I was the first one in the family to get any tertiary education.

Begley: What were you like as a kid?

McEwan: Quiet, pale, dreamy, very attached to my mother, shy, average in class. There's something of myself in Peter of *The Daydreamer*. I was an intimate sort of child who never spoke up in groups. I preferred close friends.

Begley: Were you a reader from an early age?

McEwan: My parents were keen for me to have the education they themselves never had. They weren't able to guide me towards particular books, but they encouraged me to read, which I did, randomly and compulsively. At boarding school in my early teens I had more direction. When I was thirteen I was reading Iris Murdoch, John Masters, Nicholas Monsarrat, John Steinbeck. L. P. Hartley's *The Go-Between* made a huge impression on me. I was also reading popular science—Asimov on the blood, Penguin Specials on the brain, and so on. I thought seriously about studying science. When I was sixteen I came under the influence of a very effective English teacher, Neil Clayton, who encouraged wide reading and had the knack of making writers like Herbert, Swift, and Coleridge seem like living presences. I thought of Eliot's *The Wasteland* as a highly accessible rhythmic jazz-age poem. Clayton was something of a Leavisite. I began to think of literature as a kind of priesthood that I would one day enter.

I went to the University of Sussex, one of the new universities. It had a lively, radical sense of what an educated person should be. You were encouraged to read across subjects, in an historical context. Reading Kafka and Freud in my final year made a big impression on me.

Begley: What were you in university for? What did you see yourself becoming?

McEwan: I'd abandoned the priesthood idea after the first year. I simply thought I was getting an education. But I was beginning to feel excited about writing. As is often the case, my wish to be a writer preceded any clear notion of subject matter. After graduation I found out about a new course at the University of East Anglia, which would allow me to write fiction along with the academic work. I phoned the university and amazingly got straight through to Malcolm Bradbury. He said, "Oh, the fiction part has been dropped because nobody has applied." This was the first year of the program. And I said, "Well, what if I apply?" He said, "Come up and talk to us and we'll see."

It was a wonderful stroke of luck. That year—1970—changed my life. I wrote a short story every three of four weeks, and I'd meet Malcolm in a Norwich pub for half an hour. Later on I met Angus Wilson. They were both generally encouraging, but they did not interfere at all, and gave no specific advice. That was perfect for me. Meanwhile, I was expected to write papers on Burroughs, Mailer, Capote, Updike, Roth, Bellow—and they were a revelation. The American novel seemed so vibrant compared to its English counterpart at the time. Such ambition, and power, and barely concealed craziness. I tried to respond to this crazed quality in my own small way, and write against what I saw as the prevailing grayness of English style and subject matter. I looked for extreme situations, deranged narrators, obscenity, and shock—and to set these elements within a careful or disciplined prose. I wrote most of *First Love, Last Rites* that year.

Begley: How did those short stories get from the pub to the publishing house?

McEwan: *Transatlantic Review* published my first story sometime in 1971. But by far the most important editor at the beginning of my career, and the first to take me on seriously, was Ted Solotaroff at *New American Review*. He started publishing my stories in 1972, and he was a very helpful and perceptive editor. His *Review* was a quarterly in the form of a paperback book and every issue contained gems by writers I had not heard of. I think of him as a key figure in American letters. I'm much in his debt. The thrills of publication early on in a writer's life can never really be repeated. Solotaroff once put my name on the cover of the *Review* along with Günter Grass, Susan Sontag, and Philip Roth. I was twenty-three and I felt like an impostor, but I was also very excited. About this time I took off on the hippie trail with two American friends. We bought a Volkswagen bus in Amsterdam and we drove it to Kabul and Pakistan. On the road I often dreamed of being back under undistracting gray skies, writing fiction. After six months I was desperate to get to work. Soon after I returned, Tom Maschler at Cape offered to publish a collection of my stories. In the winter of 1974, I moved to London from Norwich. This was about the time that Ian Hamilton's *New Review* was getting going. He died in December 2001, and all of us who knew him are still in mourning for him. The magazine was also a milieu—the unofficial office was the Pillars of Hercules pub in Greek Street. Ian presided over a lively, chaotic, drink-fueled scene. I met many writers who became lifelong friends and whose work I have followed closely since—James Fenton, Craig Raine, Christopher Reid. I met Martin Amis around that time and Julian Barnes, who was writing a column for the *New Review* under the name of Edward Pygge. All of us were about to publish our first books. It was a delightful entry for me—a kind of literary country mouse—into a metropolitan literary scene that seemed extraordinarily open to newcomers.

Begley: "Homemade" is the first story in your first collection—that's the one with the teenage narrator who tricks his kid sister into incest.
McEwan: It was intended as a parody of a Henry Miller narrator whose sexual boasting would extend in single sentences across whole paragraphs. It was also a genuflection in the direction of Roth's Portnoy.

Begley: "Homemade" introduces some choice topics: coitus, incest, self-abuse. Despoiled virginity. Did you ever regret having started out with such a bang?
McEwan: It was fun at the time. These days it has its occasional drawbacks, this "Ian McAbre" thing. Sometimes I think I'll never quite escape my early reputation. Even a reflective review by Updike of *Atonement* was flagged, tabloid style, by *The New Yorker* as "Lust and Disgust."

Begley: When you published the early stories, did you consider yourself daring?
McEwan: Impatient rather than daring. Among my friends, conversation was so scabrous much of the time anyway. We'd all read Burroughs and Roth and Genet and Joyce, all things were sayable, and had been said. I didn't think of myself as an iconoclast. In fact, I thought I was writing a rather well-mannered, conservative prose. I did think there was a certain self-limiting dullness about English fiction, with its fine nuances of everyday life, and every shade of gray, minutiae of dress, accent, class. The social codes, the way you can manipulate them or be destroyed by them. It's a rich field, of course, but I knew nothing about it, and wanted nothing to do with it.

Begley: Because of your background?

McEwan: There was something curiously dissociated about my background. When my father was commissioned from the ranks, our family entered a no-man's-land of class, no longer at one with the ordinary soldiers, nor proper members of the officer class. And my boarding school was a state-run experiment in propelling working-class boys from central London into the educated middle classes. Then I went to two new universities, which were, in English terms at least, aggressively déclassé. I had no particular place or allegiance in these convoluted strata, and my early fiction was written with complete indifference to the whole business. My fascination with Kafka made me think that the most interesting fiction involved characters who could hang free of historical circumstance. But, of course, nobody hangs free. English reviewers were quick to identify my characters as "lower-middle class." Useful, as Larkin might say, to get that learned.

Begley: How about children? They can hang free of history. There are lots of children in *First Love, Last Rites.*
McEwan: It's true, you don't have to describe their jobs, or their marriages and divorces.

Begley: Did you have other reasons for writing about children?
McEwan: A twenty-one-year-old writer is likely to be inhibited by a lack of usable experience. Childhood and adolescence were something I knew. Many writers at the beginning of their careers go through a kind of imaginative recapitulation. Childhood perceptions are so bright I find them hard to forget. They creep in if you can relax your attention sufficiently—they don't have to be effortfully recalled; they're just available.

Begley: One of the glories of *Atonement* is Briony's point of view in the early chapters, when she's still a precocious little girl with an itch to write and a dangerous taste for melodrama. Did it feel like a return to something to be again imagining the world from a child's perspective?
McEwan: It seemed a far deeper immersion. Not wanting to shock people or indulge the grotesque allows far greater freedom psychologically. It's always a problem doing children in fiction—the restricted viewpoint can become stifling. I wanted to be able to portray a child's mind while drawing on all the resources of a complex adult language—as James does in *What Maisie Knew.* I didn't want the limitations of a childlike vocabulary. Joyce does this in the opening pages of *A Portrait of the Artist as a Young Man.* We've all

tried to imitate it. He holds you there in a little boy's sensory and linguistic universe, and it's a piece of magic that glows—and then it's gone, just like childhood itself. Joyce moves on, the language spreads. My way round the problem was to make Briony my "author" and let her describe her childhood self from the inside, but in the language of the mature novelist.

Begley: How prominent were you before *The Cement Garden* came out?
McEwan: Disproportionately. In the mid-seventies when Amis and I were first published there didn't seem to be that many young novelists around. We got all the attention.

Begley: By that time you had developed regular writing habits?
McEwan: I'd be at work by 9:30 every morning. I inherited my father's work ethic—no matter what he'd been up to the night before, he was always out of bed by 7:00 A.M. He never missed a day's work in forty-eight years in the army.

In the seventies I used to work in the bedroom of my flat at a little table. I worked in longhand with a fountain pen. I'd type out a draft, mark up the typescript, type it out again. Once I paid a professional to type a final draft, but I felt I was missing things I would have changed if I had done it myself. In the mid-eighties I was a grateful convert to computers. Word processing is more intimate, more like thinking itself. In retrospect, the typewriter seems a gross mechanical obstruction. I like the provisional nature of unprinted material held in the computer's memory—like an unspoken thought. I like the way sentences or passages can be endlessly reworked, and the way this faithful machine remembers all your little jottings and messages to yourself. Until, of course, it sulks and crashes.

Begley: What's a good day's output for you?
McEwan: I aim for about six-hundred words a day and hope for at least a thousand when I'm on a roll.

Begley: In the introduction to *A Move Abroad* you write: "There's a degree of self-pleasuring in imaginative writing which is not even remotely assimilated by literary theory." Can you give me an example of that?
McEwan: The joy is in the surprise. It can be as small as a felicitous coupling of noun and adjective. Or a whole new scene, or the sudden emergence of an unplanned character who simply grows out of a phrase. Literary criticism,

which is bound to pursue meaning, can never really encompass the fact that some things are on the page because they gave the writer pleasure. A writer whose morning is going well, whose sentences are forming well, is experiencing a calm and private joy. This joy itself then liberates a richness of thought that can prompt new surprises. Writers crave these moments, these sessions. If I may quote the second page of *Atonement*, this is the project's highest point of fulfillment. Nothing else—cheerful launch party, packed readings, positive reviews—will come near it for satisfaction.

Begley: In the introduction to *The Imitation Game* you write about your envy for busy filmmakers with their urgent meetings, always speeding around in taxis.

McEwan: If week after week you do nothing but commune with ghosts, and move from your desk to your bed and back, you long for some sort of work that involves other people. But as I've grown older, I've become more reconciled to the ghosts, and slightly less interested in working with other people.

Begley: Have you ever written a screenplay with which you were satisfied?

McEwan: I've been happy with quite a few. It's what happens afterwards that can cause the heartache. I was spoiled by my first experience, *The Plough-man's Lunch*, which went without a hitch. Richard Eyre and I decided we'd like to do a movie with a state-of-the-nation atmosphere. Over several months I gathered up odd bits of material—I hung around a BBC newsroom, read books about the Suez crisis, visited the party political conferences, and watched the making of some TV ads. Later I went to Poland at the time of Solidarity, and thought about how a nation dreams itself up.

Graham Greene has a good image for this process: there are moments of inspiration which he calls *pools*. Making a novel consists of digging the trenches between the pools. My pools were nothing so grand as inspirational—they were simply the settings or scenes I wanted. When I'd worked out a way of connecting them all up, I wrote out a plan for the movie on a couple of pages and showed them to Richard one lunchtime at the National Theatre, where he was working. He read them and said instantly that this was the kind of thing he wanted to make.

I wrote the screenplay in six weeks. Richard had some useful suggestions like, "It would be nice if the main figure went home so we could see what his background was like." The Falklands War began and provided some interesting parallels with Suez. But really, those two sheets of paper I showed Richard at the beginning were more or less the movie as it was made. The experience was sweet and simple. Nothing went wrong. I had no idea at the time how unusual this was.

Begley: And what was your experience with the film of *The Innocent?*
McEwan: Protracted, messy, painful. I knew it was a bad idea to adapt my own novel for the screen, but I allowed myself to be talked into it. I was drawn by the opportunity of incorporating the fall of the Berlin Wall, which happened months after I finished the novel in June 1989. All the separate elements were fine—a wonderful cast, with Isabella Rossellini, Anthony Hopkins, Campbell Scott, and with John Schlesinger directing. But there was no chemistry, as they say. It was not a happy set. Only the rushes looked good, which, of course, they always do.

Begley: Where did the idea for *The Cement Garden* come from? I always think it's a book about "infinite municipal sadness"—a line from your "Two Fragments."
McEwan: I'd delayed writing a novel for years. I came back from an exhilarating first visit to the USA in 1976. I was toying with ideas about children trying to survive without adults—this is the setup in any number of children's books, and, of course, it's the essence of *Lord of the Flies.* I was thinking about an urban version I might write of that story, but I had no clear route in. At the time I was living in Stockwell, south London. It was a desolate neighborhood of high-rises and weed-covered wasteland. One afternoon as I was at my desk, these four children, with their distinct identities, suddenly rose before my imagination. I didn't have to build them up—they appeared ready-made. I wrote some quick notes, then fell into a deep sleep. When I woke, I knew that at last I had the novel I wanted to write. I worked obsessively for a year, paring the material back all the time because I wanted the novel to be brief and intense.

Begley: Was it a kind of exorcism?
McEwan: Well, more of a kind of summary. This and my next novel, *The Comfort of Strangers,* brought to an end a ten-year stretch of writing—formally simple and linear short fiction, claustrophobic, desocialized, sexually strange, dark. After that I felt I had written myself into too tight a corner. I turned away from fiction for a while. I wrote a television film set against the

code-breaking operation at Bletchley Park during the war. Then *The Plough-man's Lunch*, and an oratorio for Michael Berkeley. By the time I set out on a new novel in 1983, *The Child in Time*, I was thinking in terms of precise physical locations, and times—even time itself—and of social texture and a degree of formal ambition.

Begley: *The Child in Time* begins with the abduction of a child—one of those moments of life-changing drama that became something of a hall-mark.
McEwan: Yes. I was still interested in writing at the edge of human expe-rience. But now I was beginning to take character more seriously. These moments of crisis were to become a way of exploring and testing charac-ter. How we might withstand, or fail to withstand, an extreme experience, what moral qualities and questions are brought forward, how we live with the consequences of our decisions, how memory torments, what time does, what resources we have to fall back on. At the time this was hardly a con-scious choice or a systematic program; it was simply how it came out in a number of novels, beginning with this one. And of course, these scenes—the stealing of the child, the black dogs, the fall from a helium balloon, and so on—offered attractive fictional possibilities in themselves. They presented challenges of pace, description, a sort of drumbeat of sentences, cadences you can only get from action scenes. They also offered a means of exerting a hold over the reader. And I could have action *and* ideas. I developed a taste for these various elements over a period of time.

In 1986 I was at the Adelaide literary festival where I read the scene from *The Child in Time* in which the little girl is stolen from a supermarket. I had finished a first draft the week before and I wanted to try it out. As soon as I was done, Robert Stone got to his feet and delivered a most passionate speech. It really seemed to come from the heart. He said, "Why do we do this? Why do writers do this, and why do readers want it? Why do we reach into ourselves to find the worst thing that can be thought? Literature, espe-cially contemporary literature, keeps reaching for the worst possible case."

I still don't have a clear answer. I fall back on the notion of the test or in-vestigation of character, and of our moral nature. As James famously asked, What is incident but the illustration of character? Perhaps we use these worst cases to gauge our own moral reach. And perhaps we need to play out our fears within the safe confines of the imaginary, as a form of hopeful exorcism.

Begley: You've talked about the pleasure you took in writing *The Innocent*. Some readers might find that hard to understand, given the novel's bloody reputation—a minute description of a body being carved up limb by limb and packed into a suitcase.

McEwan: That reputation rests on half a dozen pages. For the rest, as far as I was concerned, *The Innocent* was a new departure for me into the historical novel. The transfer of power from the British to the American empire was a long, slow process, and came to completion in the 1950s, culminating painfully for the British in the humiliation of Suez. I've always been drawn to situations in which events on the large scale find a reflection in the private life. An awkward young Englishman, a telephone engineer, coming of age in cold-war Berlin in the mid-fifties, discovering for himself the power of American money and confidence, the reach of its military, the seductions of its food, music, and movies; and a city emerging from its ruins, haunted by the ghouls of its recent past—all this absorbed me completely. I was lost to old maps and photographs. I became a telephone engineer.

I stayed away from Berlin while I was writing the novel, which is mostly set in 1955. However, in the final chapter, set in 1987, the aging hero, Leonard, decides to revisit the city, and I thought I would, as it were, go with him. I arrived with a heavy dose of flu. This brash, opulent Western half of the city was not the ruined place I had come to know so well. I walked about, feeling old and bewildered. I visited the apartment building where Leonard used to stay with his lover, and I felt ridiculous pangs of love for a nonexistent girl. I went out to the southwest corner of Berlin to the site of the spy tunnel. I climbed a fence to get into an abandoned lot. Watched through binoculars by East German border guards in their observation tower, I poked about among the mounds and trenches, finding bits of old telephone cable, pieces of sacking made in Chicago, a bit of old switching gear. And again, I felt nostalgia for a time I never knew. I'd come as far as I possibly could from those short stories and two short novels in which I thought time and place were irrelevant distractions. Now I was in a foreign city, feeling the passing years and tricking myself into thinking I was one of my characters.

Begley: You tricked yourself in the way you hoped to trick your readers.

McEwan: Generally one would like to avoid tricking oneself.

Begley: Did you do medical research for *The Innocent*?

McEwan: I went to have dinner with Michael Dunnill, who was the University Lecturer in Pathology at Merton. I told him I was planning a scene in which an inexpert and frightened man cuts up a body—

Begley: And he said, "Oh, you must be Ian McEwan."

McEwan: He said something even more frightening. When I asked him how long would it take to saw through an arm, he invited me to one of his regular early Monday morning autopsies. "You come along," he said, "and we'll cut an arm off and see." I said, "But what about the relatives?" And he said, "Oh, my assistant will sew it back on and it won't show at all."

I began to have serious doubts about this Monday morning appointment. I felt the writing was going well and I didn't want to be blown off course. At the same time, I felt it was my novelist's duty to go. Then, very fortunately, I had supper with Richard Eyre, who thought I was crazy to go. He said, "You'll invent it much better than you'll describe it." Immediately he said this, I knew he was right. Later, I showed my scene to Michael Dunnill, and he passed it. Had I gone to the autopsy, I would have had to become a journalist and I don't think I'm a good journalist. I can describe accurately the thing that I imagine far better than the thing I remember seeing.

Begley: There are writers who say that their basic unit of thought is the paragraph. And there are writers who say that their basic unit of thought is the sentence. And there are some people who work in scenes.

McEwan: It's hard of course to separate them out, but I suppose I'd opt for the sentence. That's where the work at any moment has to be carried out. I feel that if I don't get the sentences right in the first draft, it's going to be hard to get them right later. Not impossible, naturally, but hard. So I work slowly, as if the first draft is the last. I read aloud completed paragraphs— it's a vital unit too, and I like to hear how the sentences sound against each other. First drafts of whole chapters I read aloud to my wife, Annalena. Or I save two or three of them up to read to her on holiday. I like to think of the chapter as an intact, independent entity with a distinct character of its own, a kind of short story—so that's an important building block. Then there are times when all these distinctions break down, and there's only the scene, and I'll work ten or twelve hours at a stretch to get it down. These are usually the set pieces we were talking about earlier. They go down relatively fast, and need a lot of slow revision.

Begley: Wendy Lesser, at one point in a review of your work, claims that Graham Greene is "the shadowy eminence who colors the plot of *Black Dogs*."

McEwan: Greene's name gets evoked whenever a writer attempts to combine the dramatic in an exotic location with a degree of moral or religious reflection. Tropical lassitude, a gun, a whiskey bottle, an unresolvable dilemma . . . It's a tribute to Greene that he made this territory so very much his own. I read him with interest, and I like the things he says about the nature of fiction itself, but I'm not a great admirer. The prose is a little too flat for my taste.

Begley: Let me quote Wendy Lesser again: "The great novelist (unlike the clever, tricky novelist . . .) does not construct an entirely new fictional world each time he writes a novel. He cannot choose to do that as his inferiors can because the world he visits in his fiction has a reality for him that is not entirely of his own willed making."

McEwan: It seems an odd notion to me, that a great novelist should be less free than a so-called inferior. But I know what she means. I'd leave greatness out of the equation. All novelists, except perhaps the genre writers, are to varying degrees helpless before their subject matter. It chooses you, is the useful cliché. And the personality of the novelist leaves its ineradicable traces. I'm sure this is the case also for sculpture and music and all art forms. But the novel is a special case. As a form it's so rich in explicit meaning, so intimately concerned with other minds, with relationships, and with human nature, and so extended too—tens of thousands of words—that the writer is bound to leave his or her personality behind on the page. There's nothing we can do about it. The form is total in its embrace. I like to think that each book I start is a completely new departure, that *Atonement* and *Amsterdam* are entirely different worlds. But I've learned that whatever you do, readers will have no difficulty assimilating it into what you've done before.

Begley: There's a passage in *Black Dogs* about a photograph of June and Bernard as a young couple. Looking at this snapshot, the narrator realizes that it is "photography itself that creates the illusion of innocence. Its ironies of frozen narrative lend to its subjects an apparent unawareness that they will change or die."

McEwan: When the past is mediated by photography it acquires a spurious innocence. Fiction has this over photography: it doesn't condescend, it doesn't have this in-built posthumous irony—that's Susan Sontag's phrase.

Novels help us to resist the temptation to think of the past as deficient of everything that informs the present. When we read *Pride and Prejudice* or *Middlemarch*, we're not tempted to believe that because the characters wear funny hats, get about by horse and don't talk explicitly about sex that they're innocents. This is because we are allowed full access, or carefully arranged partial access, to their feelings and thoughts, their dilemmas. Assuming we've been carried along by the narrative, they appear before us, these characters, intact, as contemporaries, unscarred by unintended ironies.

Begley: It takes courage to write without irony. To write, for example, about Evil with a capital *E*.

McEwan: Especially when you don't believe in it. Where there's no God, it's difficult to give much intellectual credence to evil as an organizing principle in human affairs, as a vaguely comprehended supernatural force. In *Black Dogs*, June believes in evil in these terms, and her husband Bernard does not. But he knows it's a potent idea. It's a useful way of talking about a side of human nature, and it's metaphorically rich and, for that reason, hard to live without. Harder to live without evil, it would seem, than without God.

Begley: In *Enduring Love*, evil takes the form of mental illness. What part of the novel came first? Was it the attempted assassination in the restaurant, the part excerpted in *The New Yorker*?

McEwan: The first chapters were about a man thumbing through his address book, looking for someone he might know with criminal connections, and then going out to buy a gun from some aging hippies. At that point I had no idea why he wanted the gun, or who he was. But I knew I wanted this scene. It was one of Graham Greene's pools. The first trench I dug led me to the attempted murder in the restaurant. That was how *Enduring Love* began, with random scenes and sketches, whistling in the dark. I wanted to write in celebration of the rational. Since Blake, Keats, and Mary Shelley, the rational impulse has become associated with the loveless, the coldly destructive. In our literature, it's always the characters who fail to trust their hearts who come unstuck. And yet our capacity for rational thought is a wonderful aspect of our natures, and often is all we have to put against social chaos, injustice, and the worst excesses of religious conviction. In writing *Enduring Love*, I was responding to an old friend who once said to me that he thought that Bernard, the rationalist in *Black Dogs*, never gets a proper crack of the whip. It's true, June's spiritual interpretation of her experience dictates the central metaphor of the novel.

Begley: Do you think that science becomes a character in *Enduring Love* in the same way that history becomes a character in *The Innocent* and *Black Dogs*?

McEwan: Not exactly. The boundaries of science have expanded in recent decades in a rather interesting way. Emotion, consciousness, human nature itself, have become legitimate topics for the biological sciences. And these subjects of course are of central interest to the novelist. This invasion of our territory might be fruitful. There was a possibility with this novel of integrating the science more successfully than I could in *The Child in Time*.

There's a moment in *Enduring Love* when Joe is remembering a conversation he had with Clarissa about a baby's smile. Joe quotes E. O. Wilson, who speaks of the smile as a "social releaser," an element in human behavior that has been selected out to gain that baby a greater share of parental love. All perfectly reasonable of Joe, up to a point. It's clearly not learned behavior—even blind babies smile. It's hardwired, as they say. But Clarissa thinks this is hardly an adequate description of a baby's smile. And Joe—this is a flaw in his character—Joe presses on, wearing her down thoughtlessly, insensitively, because even he knows that what they are really talking about is the absence of a baby in their lives.

I wanted to do more than simply raid science for interesting metaphors. Biological thought has made it possible to rub the emotional against the scientific in a small scene like that. It's far more interesting than trying to assimilate a quantum mechanical view or a cosmological view of time into a novel. It's riper; it's on a human scale.

Begley: The appendix to *Enduring Love*, with its clinical case history, fooled some critics in America.

McEwan: I had fun writing that appendix. One critic castigated the novel for adhering too closely to the case study on which it was based.

Begley: Joe is obviously sympathetic to evolutionary biology. To what degree does this reflect your own beliefs?

McEwan: Only religious zealots would want to deny that we are products of biological evolution. The question is how much our evolutionary past explains us to ourselves. My guess is, more than we previously liked to think, and a little less than the exponents of the "just so" stories of evolutionary psychology would want. We can describe a human nature, a set of predispositions, that exists across cultures, and we can make educated guesses at the adaptive pressures that have produced it. But I'm not sure how far, how deep, this can take us into the fine grain of individual behavior. Culture, the social environment, which itself has helped shape our genes, gives out an overwhelming and fascinating signal. It's hard to separate out. Clearly, there's a sense in which our lives make us what we are. But we are not born tabula rasa, and we cannot take on any shape. Our differences do not occur within an infinite range, and the ways people are similar is at least as interesting as the ways in which they vary. This is an area in which novelists and biologists should have a lot to say to one another, and it was one of the reasons I wrote *Enduring Love*.

Begley: What was the genesis of *Amsterdam*?
McEwan: It grew out of a long-running joke I had with my old friend and hiking companion, Ray Dolan. We speculated lightheartedly on an agreement we might have: if one of us began to go under with something like Alzheimer's, rather than let his friend succumb to a humiliating decline, the other would take him off to Amsterdam and have him legally put down. So whenever one of us forgot a vital piece of hiking equipment, or turned up at the airport on the wrong day—you know the sort of thing that starts happening in your mid-forties—the other would say, "Well, it's Amsterdam for you!" We were walking in the Lake District—actually along the route that the character Clive Linley takes—and I thought of two characters who might make such an agreement, then fall out and lure each other to Amsterdam simultaneously for mutual murder. A rather improbable comic plot. I was halfway through *Enduring Love* at the time. I sketched the idea out that night, then put it away for a rainy day. It wasn't until I started writing it that the characters appeared, and then it seemed to take on a life of its own.

Begley: *Amsterdam* is very different from your previous novels.
McEwan: The four novels that preceded it—*The Child in Time*, *The Innocent*, *Black Dogs*, and *Enduring Love*—all grew out of a wish to explore certain ideas. By comparison, *Amsterdam* felt irresponsible and free. I had a simple scheme and I went along with it to see where it might lead. Some readers considered the novel a lighthearted diversion, but for me, even at the time, it seemed as much a turning point as *The Child in Time* had been. I thought I was giving the characters more space. There were certain intellectual ambitions I wanted to wean myself away from. I could not have written *Atonement* without first writing *Amsterdam*.

Begley: To go back to Graham Greene—he used to make a distinction between his serious novels and his "entertainments." Would you put *Amsterdam* in the entertainment category or serious novel category?

McEwan: I think Greene abandoned the distinction by the end, and one can see why. But I catch your drift. I had enormous pleasure writing *Amsterdam*, and I remain pleased with it. It was well received when it came out, but its (as opposed to my) misfortune was to win the Booker Prize, at which point some people began to dismiss it. For that reason alone I'd want it to be judged seriously along with everything else I've written. I certainly wouldn't bracket it off as an entertainment and hope for more lenient treatment.

Begley: How did *Atonement* get started? Was it Briony?

McEwan: Cecilia came first. Like *Enduring Love*, this was a novel that grew out of many months of sketches and doodling. One morning I wrote six-hundred words or so describing a young woman entering a drawing room with some wild flowers in her hand, searching for a vase. She's aware of a young man outside gardening whom she wishes both to see and avoid. For reasons that I couldn't explain to myself, I knew that I had at last started a novel.

Begley: Because that's the hook, the love story?

McEwan: I knew nothing. Slowly I pieced together a chapter—Cecilia and Robbie go to the fountain, the vase breaks, she strips off and plunges into the water to retrieve the pieces, she walks away from him without a word. Then I stopped, and for six weeks or so I pondered. Where is this? When is this? Who are these people? What have I got? Then I started again, and wrote the chapter about Briony attempting to put on a play with her cousins. By the time I had finished, the novel was coming into focus. A whole household was emerging, and I had the vaguest notions that Dunkirk and St. Thomas's Hospital lay far in the future. Crucially, I realized that Briony was the author of both these chapters, that she was going to commit a terrible error, and that writing a series of drafts throughout her life would be her form of atonement. Later, when I had finished part one, I swapped these two chapters round and rewrote them many times.

Begley: What kind of novels do you think Briony wrote when she wasn't writing *Atonement*—when she wasn't doing her atonement?

McEwan: She was a sort of Elizabeth Bowen of *The Heat of the Day*, with a dash of Rosamond Lehmann of *Dusty Answer*, and, in her first attempts, a sprinkling of Virginia Woolf. In an early draft I wrote a biographical note for inclusion at the end of the book. Then I decided against it. But here it is. The point about Greene (he keeps coming up) is that he was always prepared to give a younger writer a kindly puff, however bland. July 2001 was when I made my last changes to the proofs.

About the author: Briony Tallis was born in Surrey in 1922, the daughter of a senior civil servant. She attended Roedean School, and in 1940 trained to become a nurse. Her wartime nursing experience provided the material for her first novel, *Alice Riding*, published in 1948 and winner of that year's Fitzrovia Prize for fiction. Her second novel, *Soho Solstice*, was praised by Elizabeth Bowen as "a dark gem of psychological acuity," while Graham Greene described her as "one of the more interesting talents to have emerged since the war." Other novels and short-story collections consolidated her reputation during the fifties. In 1962 she published *A Barn in Steventon*, a study of domestic theatricals in Jane Austen's childhood. Tallis's sixth novel, *The Ducking Stool*, was a best-seller in 1965 and was made into a successful film starring Julie Christie. Thereafter, Briony Tallis's reputation went into decline, until the Virago imprint made her work available to a younger generation in the late seventies. She died in July 2001.

Begley: Do you think that you possibly let Briony off too easily in giving her long life and literary success?
McEwan: She never acted out of malice, and besides, in her circumstances, with much to reflect on, long life was no great reward. The real villains, Paul and Lola Marshall, had success, happiness, and a long life. Psychological realism demands that sometimes the wicked prosper.

Begley: Did you grow up hearing stories from your father about being evacuated from Dunkirk?
McEwan: Yes. Towards the end of his life (he died in 1996) the retreat to Dunkirk was much on his mind and he went over and over his experiences. I was sorry that I was never able to show him my own version. I suppose his death was unconsciously reflected in the number of absent fathers in the novel. The men who straggled towards Dunkirk would have been aware that their fathers had died or fought in this same stretch of northern France. My

father ended up in the same hospital, the Alder Hey in Liverpool, where his father had been treated in 1918.

Begley: We haven't talked much about *The Daydreamer*. What was it like to switch gears after *Black Dogs* and write for children?
McEwan: It's not very different at all.

Begley: What were your ground rules?
McEwan: No mentions of income tax, no explicit sex scenes. Of course, there's subject matter that one avoids. But there's very little you cannot discuss with a ten-year-old, if you can find the right language. And I've always liked a clear, precise, and simple prose of the kind I think children would enjoy and understand. I avoided any moral heavy breathing—I don't like children's fiction that tells them how to behave. I wrote the chapters as twenty-five-minute bedtime stories and read them to my sons. I incorporated various familiar household details—our cat, the untidy drawer in the kitchen, and so on. The boys helped with suggestions, and later on they saw the proofs, the cover design, the reviews. They saw how a book was made. At the time, I was working on *Black Dogs*, so it was a very agreeable diversion.

Begley: In *The Child in Time*, Stephen talks about the best children's books having a quality of invisibility. Did that come back to you, that phrase, when you sat down to write *The Daydreamer*?
McEwan: I don't remember, but it's certainly something to aim for. Children are not going to sit back and admire the grace and density of your imagery. They want the language to work on them and take them right into the thing itself. They want to know what happens. Perhaps that kind of invisibility belongs to an age of lost innocence, and is therefore all the more appropriate in a children's book.

Begley: You're about the only member of your generation who seems to aspire in that direction. There's Amis's verbal display, Rushdie's exuberance, Barnes's erudition.
McEwan: Well, hang on, we were talking about children's fiction. After a century of modernism, its experiments and fallout, this kind of invisibility we're talking about is impossible in serious writing. My ideal would be a canvas of pale eggshell to which is added a set of vivid strokes. These strokes

would take you right into the prose, and ideally propel you with greater force out the other side, into the thing named, into the thing itself. Having it both ways . . . but that's merely an aspiration.

Begley: How much does this have to do with writerly self-consciousness?
McEwan: I sometimes feel that every sentence contains a ghostly commentary on its own processes. This is not always helpful, but I don't think you can ever quite escape it. At best, you can take it for granted, and not become enslaved to self-reference, and remain faithful also to the sensuous, telepathic capabilities of language as it transfers thoughts and feelings from one person's mind to another's.

Begley: Do you think you will write more books like *The Daydreamer*, for both children and adults?
McEwan: When people ask me that, or whether I'll write a stage play, I always lie and say yes automatically.

Begley: Why?
McEwan: I don't want to close down the possibility. But at the same time, I know that between books I'll simply wait and see what comes up. This is a process you can't have, and don't want, under your full conscious control. Of course I'd like to write a play, or another children's book, or a stunning sonnet sequence. But what does that really mean? What it means is that I'd like to have one already written. This reminds me of a recurring dream I have. I'm at my desk, in my study, feeling particularly well. I open a drawer and see lying before me a novel I finished last summer that I've completely forgotten about because I've been so busy. I take it out and see at once that it's brilliant. A masterpiece! It all comes back to me, how hard I worked on it, then put it away. It's brilliant and I'm so happy to have found it.

Begley: So is there a punch line to that, like the novel is signed *Martin Amis*?
McEwan: No, no. It's a happy dream. It's mine. I don't have to do a thing but put it in the post and try not to wake up.

Zadie Smith Talks with Ian McEwan

Zadie Smith/2005

From *The Believer Book of Writers Talking to Writers*, edited by Vendela Vida (San Francisco: Believer Books, 2005): 207–39. Reprinted by permission of Vendela Vida.

> Aspects of the "English Novel" to avoid:
> *Polite, character-revealing dialogue*
> *Stable, linear narrative*
> *Lightly ironic ethical investigation*
> *Excessive amounts of furniture*

I have often thought Ian McEwan a writer as unlike me as it is possible to be. His prose is controlled, careful, and powerfully concise; he is eloquent on the subjects of sex and sexuality; he has a strong head for the narrative possibilities of science; his novels are no longer than is necessary; he would never write a sentence featuring this many semicolons. When I read him, I am struck by metaphors I would never think to use, plots that don't occur to me, ideas I have never had. I love to read him for these reasons and also because, like his millions of readers, I feel myself to be in safe hands. Picking up a book by McEwan is to know, at the very least, that what you read therein will be beautifully written, well-crafted, and not an embarrassment, either for you or for him. This is a really big deal. Bad books happen less frequently to McEwan than they do to the rest of us. Since leaving the tutelage of Malcolm Bradbury and Angus Wilson on the now famous (because of McEwan) University of East Anglia creative writing course, McEwan has had one of the most consistently celebrated careers in English literature. We haven't got space for it all here, but among the prizes is the Somerset Maugham Award in 1976 for his first collection of short stories, *First Love, Last Rites*; the Whitbread Novel Award (1987) and Prix Fémina Etranger (1993) for *The Child in Time*; he has been shortlisted for the Booker Prize three times, winning the award for *Amsterdam* in 1998. His novel *Atonement* received the WH Smith Literary Award (2002), the National Book Critics Circle Fiction Award (2002), the Los Angeles Times Book Prize for Fiction (2003), and the Santiago Prize for the European Novel (2004). He's written a lot of good books.

Because of the posh university I attended, I first met McEwan many years ago, before I was published myself. I was nineteen, down from Cambridge for the holidays, and a girl I knew from college was going to Ian McEwan's wedding party. This was a fairly normal occurrence for her, coming from the family she did, but I had never clapped eyes on a writer in my life. She invited me along, knowing what it would mean to me. That was an unforgettable evening. I was so delighted to be there and yet so rigid with fear I could barely enjoy it. It was a party full of people from my bookshelves come to life. I can recall being introduced to Martin Amis (whom I was busy plagiarizing at the time) and being shown his new baby. Meeting Martin Amis for me, at nineteen, was like meeting God. I said: "Nice baby." This line, like all conversation, could not be rewritten. I remember feeling, like Joseph K. that the shame of it would outlive me.

I didn't get to speak with McEwan that night—I spent most of the party hiding from him. I assumed he was a little annoyed to find a random undergraduate he did not know at his own wedding party. But I had just read *Black Dogs* (1992)— that brilliant, flinty little novel, bursting with big ideas—and I was fascinated by the idea of an English novelist writing such serious, metaphysical, almost European prose as this. He was not like Amis and he was not like Rushdie or Barnes or Ishiguro or Kureishi or any of the other English and quasi-English men I was reading at the time. He was the odd man out. "Apparently," said my friend knowledgeably, as we watched McEwan swing his new wife around the tile dance floor, "he only writes fifteen words a day." This was an unfortunate piece of information to give an aspiring writer. I was terribly susceptible to the power of example. If I heard Borges ran three miles every morning and did a headstand in a bucket of water before sitting down to write, I felt I must try this myself. The specter of the fifteen-word limit stayed with me a long time. Three years later I remember writing *White Teeth* and thinking that all my problems stemmed from the excess of words I felt compelled to write each day. Fifteen words a day! Why can't *you* write just fifteen words a day?

Ten years later, less gullible and a writer myself, it occurs to me that my friend may have fictionalized the situation a little herself. An interview with McEwan himself, like the one you are about to read, was of course the perfect opportunity to settle the matter, but it's only now, writing the introduction after the fact, that I remember the question. I do not know if Ian McEwan writes fifteen words a day. However, he was forthcoming on many other interesting matters. McEwan is one of those rare novelists who can speak with honest perspicacity about the experience of being a writer; it is a life he openly loves, and talking to him about it felt, to me, like talking with an author at the beginning of their career, not at its pinnacle. The fifteen-word thing may indeed be a red herring, but my friend had intuited a truth about McEwan: he is not a dilettante or even a natural, neither a fabulist nor a show-off. He is rather an artisan, always hard at work; refining, improving, engaged by and interested in every step in the process, like a scientist setting up a lab experiment.

We did this interview in McEwan's house, which is Dr. Henry Perowne's house in the novel *Saturday* (2005). It is a lovely Georgian townhouse that sits in the shadow of London's BT Tower. From the balcony of this house Perowne sees a plane on a crash trajectory, its tail on fire. It is a perfect McEwanesque incident. —Z.S. (Spring 2005)

I. "It had been a malevolent intervention . . . "

Zadie Smith: I'm not good at this. I interviewed Eminem a while ago, and when I got home and transcribed it, it was more like "An interview with Zadie Smith in which Eminem occasionally says yes and uh-huh." I talk too much. I'm going to get straight to my first question, which I guess is also the biggest one. I thought we could start there and maybe get small afterwards. Because I read all the books so close together—
Ian McEwan: What order did you read them in?

Smith: Basically chronological.
McEwan: OK.

Smith: Except *In Between the Sheets*, which I read only a few days ago. Anyway: there is a line in *The Child in Time*, when you discuss the traumatic event in that novel, the abduction of a child: "it had been a malevolent intervention." And much of your past fiction has dealt with that idea, of a malevolent intervention. Then when you read this latest book, *Saturday*, which deals obliquely with 9/11, it becomes clear that something about the nature of what happened on that day was already a McEwanesque incident. Because the burst of the irrational into the rational was your *modus operandi* anyway. And so (this is a strange thing to say to the writer himself) when you see a writer moving into his strongest period, and staying there, or at least not losing his previous strength, then I always figure that either the age has come to meet him or he's come to meet the age. I think it's the previous case with you, and I remember thinking even before I read *Saturday* that if there were to be a 9/11 novel which was integrated and serious and soon—because it is quite soon—it was more likely to be written by you than anybody else. Because your fiction was already *about* the idea of a malevolent intervention. And I wondered whether you knew that consciously or whether you agree with that.

McEwan: The first thing I remember thinking was that it [9/11] was a heroic moment for journalism. That was my first sense. Perhaps it's because Annalena [Annalena McAfee, McEwan's wife] works in a newspaper I take an interest in the sort of *thingyness* of newspapers, but it happened two o'clock our time, London time. So front pages had to be clear and basically twenty-five pages set out, produced, and this much-hated profession had its sudden noble moment.

Smith: But it was a moment. You talked about that in the two articles you wrote about September 11 for the *Guardian*. The moment turns quickly and depressingly.

McEwan: But it was a moment that seemed first to demand accurate journalism before anything else. That was my first feeling. And the best things written about it have been journalism, not fiction. I read a lot of what came out and was impressed by it. Actually I think another instance of this on a much smaller scale was the Dunblane massacre. Hit the wires at about three-thirty in the afternoon. By the time of the London evening papers there were ten, fifteen pages. So my first instinct, my first reaction was that journalists rose to the bar that day, and when I wrote I just wanted to write in that public way, expressing my immediate reaction, the same honorable tide that everyone else was on. Not to write fiction. But even as I was doing that I was thinking the human way into it would take more than journalism, would be more intimate than that. The thought of so many of these people announcing their love down mobile phones . . .

Smith: There was a small paragraph—I think it was in the second article you wrote about it—where you say that if the terrorists had been able to empathize properly with these others, with the very *idea* of otherness, then they couldn't have done what they did. Now, that's something I do believe, and it's a belief I sort of "push" in my fiction—that real empathy makes cruelty an impossibility. But I always assumed when I read your fiction, that that wasn't at all what you believed. Especially in the earlier work, the opposite, much darker truth seems to be being articulated: mainly, that even after empathy people still can and do perform the most terrible acts.

McEwan: I've always thought cruelty is a failure of imagination. And I know that I include within that the possibility that some people do empathize with their victims very much, in fact, that's the reason they harm them—they get some erotic charge out of harming what they love. But that's a special case. That's still about pleasuring the self and not heeding to the true terror of the child that's being tortured or whatever it might be.

At least since the early '80s, it's begun to fill out for me as an idea in fiction, that there's something very entwined about imagination and morals. That one of the great values of fiction was exactly this process of being able to enter other people's minds. Which is why I think cinema is a very inferior, unsophisticated medium.

Smith: Absolutely. Because you get surfaces only.

McEwan: Right. And with the novel we have happened to devise this form, this very elastic, mutable form that can allow us moments of real human investigation. Milan Kundera says very wise things in this context. He lays a lot of stress on the novel as a mode of investigation. It's an open-ended way of looking at our own image, in ways that science can't do, religion's not credible, metaphysics is too intellectually repellent on its surface—this is our best machine, as it were.

Smith: You use that machine quite differently from your peers. Yours are different English novels than the English novel as I was brought up to think about it.

After I read your back catalog I Googled you and I found this website for kids—because a lot of kids are studying you at the moment, you're on the A-Level list. It was a message board of kids freaking out because they didn't know how to read you. It was very interesting. I think the barrier they kept coming across is that they come with their ideas of an English novel, the classic English novel, where character is revealed through dialogue for a greater part of the book, where action is laid out along a basically stable idea of linear time, where the tone is lightly ironic and your job as a reader is to perform a kind of ethical investigation. They particularly rely on a pretty muscular narrator to nudge them in the direction of correct judgement. So Austen never leaves us in any doubt that Mrs. Bennett is not a person to be respected, for example. But your books screw with time, they use very little dialogue, and the narration is ethically ambivalent. It's all a bit metaphysical when you're sixteen and you've got an essay crisis on. They were freaking out.

McEwan: Why are they freaking out? I don't understand. Because they're being told too much?

Smith: Well, let's take one of those aspects. Time in McEwan. Most of your contemporaries dealt with time in a pretty traditional fashion. If Rushdie was interested in it, if Amis was interested in it, if Barnes was, it was usually historical time. And partly politicized historical time in the case of Rushdie and when Amis spins time backwards. Flashbacks and historical jumps are used to cast the present in a new, challenging light. But the idea of what does it really feel to *be* in time, to exist in it—this is not something that English A-Level students have to face up to very often.

McEwan: Well, I don't have any conscious design on time, I don't think—except when I was thinking about it as a specific element of the novel, as with *The Child in Time*. But apart from that, if there's anything going on about time in my novels it's really a spin-off of some other concern. Something to do with the fine print of consciousness itself. I mean, I'm interested in how to represent, obviously in a very stylized way, what it's like to be thinking. Or what it's like to be conscious, or sentient, or, fatally, only half-sentient. And how difficult it is to see everything that's going on and understand everything at one time and how much our recollections can play into what we accept as reality—how much perception is distorted by will. That's something I find very interesting. The ways in which we convince ourselves, persuade ourselves of things, either to settle some notion of our own or an intellectual position. That's why I've liked the evolution of psychology; they talk a lot of about self-persuasion . . . In my fiction I've tried to indicate my sense of how interestingly flawed we are in the ways in which we represent ourselves and "what we know" to each other. So if time gets fractured or refracted along the way, that's an offshoot. I don't do that consciously.

Smith: Maybe it's "the malevolent intervention" that messes with time. Like the car crash in *The Child in Time*, where a four-second moment seems to last forever. I thought when I read *Saturday* that your audience, through 9/11, now has a mass experience to mirror exactly that strange sensation, when time elongates. The towers fell in slow motion. Time was warped by this insane event, and we all felt that communally. Prior to that my only experience of time trauma was when I was fifteen and fell out of my bedroom window—timewise, that was a deeply surreal experience. I knew that privately but to share it with anybody was a bit—

McEwan: You fell out of your bedroom window?

Smith: Yeah.
McEwan: Sleepwalking?

Smith: No, no, no, trying to smoke a fag.

McEwan: Oh my God.

Smith: Yeah, comedy story. I almost died, but the point is, that fall and the slowness of it, literally the *days* of it—I couldn't find a way to talk about it without sounding a little loopy. But several times in your fiction that feeling is expressed, very accurately I think.

McEwan: Yeah, but isn't it also something to do with demands of narrative—so let's say we're looking at a fifteen-year-old, balancing a buttock on a window ledge, doesn't want to breathe smoke back into the bedroom—

Smith: Yeah, that was it.

McEwan: Suddenly you're dividing the moment with much more intensity. Even in describing it you're slowing the movement. Because you think this is high-value, rich experience, therefore only two seconds are 1,200 words. And you've done it for the reader, already, without having any notion of time, you would have conveyed this slowing instinctively. And probably, one mistake I regret in *The Child in Time* was the way I harangue the reader, telling everybody that "TIME IS SLOW." You don't need to say that. The prose slows it down.

Smith: But I think in the car incident the two are quite well meshed, the description and the feeling, it's a pretty amazing passage.

McEwan: Yeah, all I need to do is cut away from the bits where it says "time slowed."

Smith: Now, what about repudiating previous work? I've been trying not to read the reviews of *Saturday* because I want to have my own feelings about it, but I presume a few people picked up on *The Child in Time* reference and also the magic realism references in the book. You satirize that kind of writing, and also the magic realism in your earlier work. And actually, reading your back catalog, I realized there's quite a lot of it. More than I remembered.

McEwan: Yeah. I wouldn't do it now, I must say. And although I never really trusted any magic realist literature, very far, I was at least able to—you know how it is, you give characters views you can't or wouldn't condone.

Smith: Yes, exactly. It's fun to do that. It makes you brave.

McEwan: Yes. But I suppose I do have a sneaking sympathy with the view that the real, the actual, is so demanding and rich, that magical realism is really a tedious evasion of some artistic responsibility.

Smith: Because the magic is *in* the real. I was trying to pick out some of my very favorite lines in *The Child in Time*—and there's the one about the neck. Do you remember this?
McEwan: No. Neck?

Smith: Yeah, it's a lady's neck: Emma Carew.
McEwan: Oh, right. "The fan of tendons round the neck of Emma Carew, a cheerful, anorexic headmistress, tightened like umbrella struts when her name was remembered and spoken aloud."

Smith: Exactly. Now for me, that brings wonder already, there is no need for the rest. But was there a switch in your mind, a point where you decided to stop writing stories about women in relationships with monkeys, for example?
McEwan: Well, as I say, I never had much time for it.

Smith: The short stories have quite a bit of it, though.
McEwan: There's some.

Smith: There's a lot of different approaches: there's hyper-realism, there's allegory, there's the supernatural, the grotesque—there's a whole raft of techniques used to introduce the incredible.
McEwan: Yes, but those were short stories and I think they're great to try, to "put on," like trying on your parents' clothes. When people ask, "Is there any advice you'd give a young writer?," I say write short stories. They afford lots of failure. Pastiche is a great way to start. But I was never really a great one for that kind of extreme Angela Carter magic realist stuff . . . although actually I got to know her and admire her and was kind of a neighbor in Clapham.

Smith: Oh, really?
McEwan: I liked her really on the basis of those stories she wrote in Japan. But then the further she got into fairy tales and then into *Nights at the Circus*—that wasn't for me.

It seemed to me such a narrowing down of all the possibilities. The real, the actual, they place heavy demands on a writer—how to invent it, how to confront it or pass it through the sieve of your own consciousness. So I was never a great Márquez person, I admired the *Tin Drum* but never really admired it the way I did Kundera, say. And it seems to me now that that style has become a bit like the international style in furniture, this sort of lingua franca that really defies the central notion of the novel which is that the novel is local. It's regional, it's a bottom-up process, and somehow these international styles seem to have a top-down process. They are too similar to each other.

Smith: They have trademarks. One of their trademarks is a kind of kinetic energy. Energy at the expense of everything else.
McEwan: Yeah. It's tennis without the net. There's no fun.

Smith: Nothing at stake.
McEwan: Yes. But then I thought if I'm taking a sideswipe here at that kind of fiction [in *Saturday*], I'd better include myself!

> **II. "Someone once asked me, 'If your life could be extended to 150 and you could start another career, would you?' and I said, 'No, thanks, I think I'll stick at this.'"**

Smith: I still feel this technical difference between you and the generation you came up with, not just in quality but in kind. I found a quote of yours: "What drove me was an impatience with the English fiction I read. It seemed like a polite talking shop of which I was no part" and I wanted to think about that in reference to dialogue, because I do think your dialogue is different and serves different purposes than, say, Amis's. There's a lot less of it, for starters.
McEwan: Well, Martin would have his roots more in Dickens, in a love of the absurd and caricature.

Smith: And dialect plays a more serious role with Amis, as it does for me. Less so with you.
McEwan: Yeah.

Smith: Only, recently there's more dialect in yours than there was before.

McEwan: Yeah. Martin used to sit around with his dad and take a lot of pleasure in looking, with some kind of hilarious scorn, at the way people spoke and how these phrases passed into the language, and he would come back with a fresh nugget and say, "Yeah, Kingsley and I were talking about the way people say"—whatever it was—and he'd be able to impersonate it exactly.

Smith: He still does that?

McEwan: Yeah. Wonderfully accurate, but there is some distancing going on there, too.

Smith: Well, there will always be a little difference in someone like Martin's comfort in the language, his kind of flippant freedom with it, and your own, possibly more hesitant, approach. You spoke a little bit about that in "Mother Tongue," and linked it with class.

McEwan: There is all that. My mother's hesitancy in language was a crucial element of my English class position. But like anything to do with English class, my exact position was complicated. My parents were working class but when I was fourteen my father was commissioned as an officer . . . He was one of the British army officers who've come up through the ranks; they're not Sandhurst, they don't have university degrees and they're not posh, and all his friends were similar people. And I know looking back that all the other officers sort of looked down on them. They respected them, too, because they knew an awful lot about the army. And when my father became an officer, we were immediately posted somewhere else, so we went from being part of the sergeants' mess world to the officers' mess world. And that was a kind of rootlessness right there, which was partly about language, the way we spoke and the way we did things.

Smith: It's like you had a kind of impersonality thrust upon you—and of course there's a lot of English criticism about that idea. That the less rigidly placed you are in this society the more conceptual space you have to write.

McEwan: It's the business of class but also, for me, a question of rootlessness in terms of location. I spent my first three years of life in Aldershot in a garrison town and then it was the Far East and then it was North Africa, so I know, even when people say where do you come from, well, I can say Aldershot, but I know that I'm not rooted in any particular place. And then I went to a strange boarding school, a state boarding school where the kids were largely working-class kids from central London from broken homes, they'd take a few kids from lower-middle-class parents like myself, an officer but not grand, not Sandhurst. The idea was to take those kids from central London, working-class kids, give them the kind of education they would have got at a public school and send them to university. And that's what they did. It was an old-fashioned, ameliorative view which is now long out of fashion. So that was another kind of rootlessness, I was with all these boys, there were three hundred of us in what was once a stately home on the Essex-Suffolk border, beautiful countryside. It was hilarious, a wonderful school in many ways. Everyone stayed in the sixth form, they sent a third of the sixth form to Oxbridge—

Smith: That's pretty impressive.
McEwan: Yeah, everyone went to university. And then I went to sort of a bright, plateglass type university in Sussex and then another one in East Anglia.

Smith: Were you conscious of wanting to be a writer or of taking it seriously from that early stage? Your first stories are so unerringly confident.
McEwan: I think I was making a strength out of a kind of ignorance. I had no roots in anything and it was almost as if I had to invent a literature.

Smith: One of the other striking things about your stories is the absence of—I don't know what to call it—let's say a "judging consciousness." The narrator who guides your judgement as you read—that idea is completely evaporated. The reader is absolutely out on a limb. There's no help given, and English readers, like those kids on the internet, are used to at least being pointed in the direction of what they should disapprove of. And that's not there.
McEwan: I wanted to write without supports. I was very impressed by a quote from Flaubert:

> What seems beautiful to me, what I should like to write, is a book about nothing, a book dependent on nothing external, which would be held together by the strength of its style, just as the earth, suspended in the void, depends on nothing external for its support.

Smith: Christ. You need ambition for that.
McEwan: But I was writing tiny little stories, certainly not novels. Those kind of remarks impressed me, I liked them and there still is an element

of that remaining. At the beginning of *Saturday* it's there in the idea of the character getting naked out of bed and standing unencumbered in the dark. It's as if he's just being born.

Smith: It does have that form, of the whole day being made with nothing taken for granted, no quick flashes into the past, every single block of it is built, as if by hand. You go through the day with Henry. That's an enormous amount of work, I would think, to write.
McEwan: Yeah. But to go back to this business of roots and stories and what I didn't like in fiction—

Smith: Right, because I thought you meant Iris Murdoch at first and that kind of conversational fiction, "chattering classes" or Hampstead fiction, or whatever.
McEwan: There are many of them still alive, like Margaret Drabble, and I actually was inclined to change my view later, because there's good stuff there . . . but at the time, in describing a world about which I knew nothing and had no interest, I was impatient. I thought writers ought to be hippies. I did have a rather romantic sense of what it should be. I got a bit hot under the collar about all the politeness and the overstuffed quality.

Smith: Furniture everywhere.
McEwan: Furniture. All of it described, you know, the names of everything. But it was exactly this: too much already taken for granted. It was a world and the reader was meant to have already filled in a lot of the colors, assuming a bond between writer and reader—a class bond, often—and I didn't share it. Whereas with people like Roth there seemed to be an energy about the prose. It had this wonderful self-invented, handmade, watermark quality, and that's why I liked both Roth and Updike. They've loomed over my writing life, even though nothing in my stories reveals that.

Smith: That intrigued me, too, these influences of yours that can't quite be detected, or at least not directly.
McEwan: But it's about reading something while you're working and your heart is just longing for your project, and the joy of reading this book by somebody else is actually what makes you turn up at the desk the next day in the broader sense, you see. If I can just generate the same feeling in the reader that this writer generated in me then I'll have succeeded. And that is probably the biggest influence.

Smith: What about some of the things that have been said about your progression as a writer? Usually the story is from good to bad to worse, but you've moved forward and consistently got stronger and stronger and I've heard a lot of quite lame dinner party suggestions as to why that might be so. But I wondered how you felt about it yourself. My feeling is that being slightly outside a privileged literary class tends to make you more artisan-minded, the way Keats was, the idea of working and working and working until it's right.

McEwan: I had a long apprenticeship. I started writing in about 1970. It was 1978 before I published a novel and even that was just sort of an extended short story. As was my second one.

Smith: But you have always been a writer—I mean, you're working life has been a writing one. And this is a subject which honestly concerns me, not a little, because it's my life and it's likely to be my life for a really long time. And I'm terrified by the stultifying effects of being a writer and staying a writer. But you don't seem to feel it, or not as strongly as I do.

McEwan: No, not at all. Someone once asked me, "If your life could be extended to 150 and you could start another career, would you?" And I said, "No, thanks, I think I'll stick at this." And the reason I gave, I quoted Henry James on fiction. He said that the concern of the novelist, the subject material, is all of it, all of experience. And you don't run out of experience by being a writer.

Smith: That's true. Sometimes it feels endless. But to me I have other days where I feel like it's a corrupt, intellectually finite, and stupid way to live, with nothing real in it—I can feel myself cannibalizing my own life and I think "how long can this go on for?" There is a lot in *Saturday* of the details of your own existence.

McEwan: It is the first time I've really cannibalized my life.

Smith: It is the first time. And I wondered what happens next.

McEwan: Next, I will almost certainly have an entirely invented set of circumstances.

Smith: There's always a difference, though. Certainly I find the more I carry on at this lark the less I have time for imagined, physical detail. I just don't do it. If I need a sofa, I look across the room and there's a sofa. If I need a lamppost, there's a lamppost in the street. I can't conjure lampposts out of nothing. Maybe when I was fourteen. That's completely beyond me now. **McEwan:** No, quite. And also how much furniture does one need any more? In answer to your question, having cannibalized my life for this novel, it makes the next one easier. I'm left with everything that's not *this* [*points around the room*], and that's a hell of a lot. I have no idea what it will be. There's also all the past which I've never really borrowed—my childhood. But I don't know. Naturally when people say, "You've got better" I get a bit pissed off and say, "Well, what was wrong with the others? What was I doing wrong before?"

Smith: Well, it's not that the earlier stuff was worse, but it's that the tools and machinery of this one work so very smoothly, one feels completely confident as a reader. You've no problem at all anymore with "making a novel." When I think of both my novels the second halves of both are rubbish because of basic, technical inability. When you're younger, every page is still a struggle. And when I read *Saturday* I just felt: well, "making a novel" is the least of your bloody problems, mate. Same with Roth. There are other things that are being developed—ideas, themes, larger ambitions to do with a canon of work—but the "making a novel" bit feels like it's done effortlessly. Maybe that's not how it is at all. But I wondered whether the autobiographical stuff makes the composition process a slightly smoother process. **McEwan:** I have to say I thought it would be. I made this decision, "OK, I will blatantly use my life in this next novel so that will save me an awful lot of time." Actually it didn't. It was just as much a struggle. Even when I was actually using the internal layout of this house for the scenes, it rarely occurred to me as I walked about this house that this was the same house in the book. It's somehow a map of a parallel house.

Smith: Talking of parallels, there's a paragraph in *Saturday* about surgery, apparently, but it seems to me to be about writing. **McEwan:** Oh, well done.

Smith: I read it and thought it can't be about anything else. You know the paragraph I mean? "For the past two hours he's been in a dream of absorption"—it's such an exact description of what it's like to write when it's going well. And my favorite line is when you talk about him feeling "calm and spacious, fully qualified to exist. It's a feeling of clarified emptiness, of deep, muted joy." The events you put next to it, as comparative experiences—the lovemaking and listening to Theo's song—are two human states which are often advertised as bringing similar pleasure: basically, personal relations and art. But the book seems to suggests that there is a deeper happiness that one can only find in work, or at least, creative work. And I felt that joy coming off the book in every direction. Joy at being a writer!

McEwan: I'm glad that you found that paragraph. I knew I wanted to write a major operation at the end but it would really be about writing, about making art. So it starts with him picking up a paintbrush. Or rather, I was *so* sure, when I went for the operation, that Neil Pritchard, the surgeon, when he paints the marks on the patient, was using a two-inch paintbrush. And when I sent him the last draft, just to check it one last time he said, "I don't use a paintbrush," and I said, "But surely surgeons do," and he said "No, no." I was so disappointed personally. He dips the paintbrush in yellow paint and as the Aria of the Goldberg Variations starts, he makes his first stroke and it is a moment of artistic engagement . . . But very, very reluctantly I had to replace it with a sponge on a flap.

Smith: The joy of the extended analogy is that it allows you to write about writing as work. Usually when you read books about being a novelist, all you really get is the character at lunches and his publishing routines, and that's nothing to do with the process of writing. It's so hard to sit down and write about that procedure, but I feel that metaphorically it's done here.

McEwan: The dream, surely, Zadie, that we all have, is to write this beautiful paragraph that actually is describing something but at the same time in another voice is writing a commentary on its own creation, without having to be a story about a writer.

III. "I'm not against religion in the sense that I feel I can't tolerate it, but I think written into the rubric of religion is the certainty of its own truth. And since there are 6,000 religions currently on the face of the earth, they can't all be right . . ."

Smith: I want to ask you about the optimism in *Saturday*. There's this recognizably Updikean enjoyment in the book, which I love; you seem to relish the things of the world. And you're right; it *is* an amazing thing to be able to go and get a glass of fresh orange juice in England—these supposedly normal things that would have been revolutionary even sixty-odd years ago. But surely one of the problems we have with all this progress is that it has been at the expense of foreign places and foreign people who do not partake of the progress, and that's kind of exactly the reason we're in this shitstorm/"war-without-end" nightmare scenario right now. So I found it hard to celebrate with Henry Perowne, knowing what his privileges are based on.

McEwan: Yeah. Well, I guess this is writing against the current in as far as I would take your view to be one of the conventions of liberal intellectual anxiety, one of the spectral opponents of the pleasures of life in the West. Perowne has these, too. He has all these marvelous advantages and yet he finds himself in a state of anxiety—we have all the pleasures and yet we're looking behind our back. And the reason I wanted to make Perowne a wealthy man is because, actually, that's what the first world is.

Smith: But by any comparison, he's pretty damn wealthy.
McEwan: The fact that he's wealthier than some but not all journalists . . .

Smith: You knew you were going to be set up by that. Some people were always going to find the descriptions of Perowne's luxurious life distasteful.
McEwan: Yeah. That doesn't touch me at all. Because I know that these journalists are wealthy by any planetary standard. That's precisely why I had him gazing at the locks on his door, thinking about the bad people, the drug dealers who want to get in—there's an embattlement. They're on the other side. You block these people out of your world picture. It's a kind of framing. You cease to see a patient on the table because you only see the little square, the mole—

Smith: Exactly. But then you are saying that happiness is based on unreality or a bubble of unreality.
McEwan: It's a kind of framing, yes. But great things are achieved within that frame.

Smith: The other thing about championing progress is the danger that we go too far in the "celebration of all things Western" direction. I'm reading articles by Rushdie recently which rigorously defend Western thought, and because I've just reread *Black Dogs* (in which the character Bernard is a great defender of the principle of "rationality"), it did strike me that Rushdie has become Bernard Extraordinaire. He's defending the Enlightenment against all corners now, bravely and viciously, but very strongly. I understand his emotion, exactly. But it's strange when you consider where we were fifteen years ago when some of the more confident Enlightenment assumptions, the quasireligious worship of the rational, for example, were being radically questioned. And now we're at this point where it's three cheers for Descartes because we've got these mad men in their planes. It's like we've all become radicalized in response to that.

McEwan: When the Enlightenment was being sort of undermined by the theorists in the academies, that was done with a general sense of security about the ultimate cultural victory of Enlightenment values, and now I think that victory is a lot less assured.

Smith: And so would you say you've lost patience, if you've ever had any patience, with the idea of religion?

McEwan: Absolutely. I agree with Salman about that. I have no patience whatsoever.

Smith: I suppose I feel the same, but I feel strange about feeling it.

McEwan: I'm not against religion in the sense that I feel I can't tolerate it, but I think written into the rubric of religion is the certainty of its own truth. And since there are 6,000 religions currently on the face of the earth, they can't all be right. And only the secular spirit can guarantee those freedoms and it's the secular spirit that they contest.

Smith: You were asked once what you believe, truly believe though you can't prove it, and you said: the absolute belief that there's nothing after consciousness. But something about *Saturday* and its joy in the world and, again, that kind of Updikean pleasure, made me wonder whether you'd ever imagined yourself moving in that vaguely Christian direction . . .

McEwan: No.

Smith: Never? No change as you've got older, no inching fears or hopes . . .

McEwan: No. I don't see any paradox in that which celebrates all things within the context of the extremely brief gift of consciousness.

Smith: See, for a lot of writers even the phrase "brief gift of consciousness" is enough to send them into a fit, and I'm one of them. As a breed, we tend to harbor quite severe death fears.

McEwan: And *gift*, by the way, is a metaphor because—

Smith: Nobody gives.

McEwan: Indeed, there's nobody there.

Smith: But I think amongst English writers it's quite unusual to have such a solid, non-death fear.
McEwan: I have an absolute death fear! I don't want this thing to end. [Philip] Larkin expresses that feeling so beautifully.

Smith: But I think with Larkin, he's the kind of man who would have taken any religion that seemed even vaguely convincing, he wasn't fussy. He'd take anything—he didn't believe in being brave . . . but as it happened everything was too stupid to be acceptable to him. Anyway: enough about death.
McEwan: Yes.

IV. "I was trying to say . . . The erotic imagination does not necessarily need critical manifestos, that it can't be governed in that way."

Smith: I want to talk to you about sex and women. You said something once about *The Female Eunuch* being revelatory. I think that about that book a lot as well—as weird as it is to talk about that now, given all that's happened in the past six months. [Germaine Greer appeared as a contestant in Britain's *Big Brother* TV show.]
McEwan: Yeah. Is that the same Germaine?

Smith: It's hard to imagine. Anyway, I wasn't there in '75 to see the first book come out, but I would imagine the word "feminist" was not one often used much in the context of your short stories. But the women in them and the care and concern with women all the way through your fiction is really interesting to me. And there's a lot of honesty about the deep, masculine hatred for women.
McEwan: "About it." That's the key.

Smith: Right. Almost every dimension of it is looked at. Silent women, damaged women, sexually vulnerable women, little girls, everything.
McEwan: I got a good kicking over all that. I was trying to write about the very things that I felt the feminist discussion was involved in, and also to have some fun writing about them. The first story you get is of a man who falls for a shop window dummy and then I just let this man project every fantasy on to her, just see what happens.

Smith: There's an idea in those stories that sex is where things can go most right and most wrong. That seems to be a very McEwan idea. It'll save you and also completely destroy you.

McEwan: But also it seemed to me at the time, in the '70s, that there needed to be a huge realignment in the way men and women would talk to each other. And I'm absolutely certain if you were to get into some time machine and go back to the early '60s, the condescension and also the apartheid would completely amaze you.

Smith: It's like when I'm reading Kingsley Amis. Whatever the attitude is to women is not really the interesting thing, it's that the women are so *other*. It's as if they've come off a different planet. There's no communication at all. You want to say, "Go on, Kingsley, poke her with your finger, she's *real!*"
McEwan: There was no game about it, either. People lived it. I used to talk to Martin Amis about thinking of girls as real people and then he married Antonia and I think then he got it, he suddenly saw something he hadn't seen before and actually his books have changed. Meanwhile I was going in the other direction. I remember going to a conference on the erotic, I don't know why I'd been invited, it was a time when the left, they were tough cookies, there were many separatists. Anyway, I gave a very good talk and what I was trying to say was the erotic imagination does not necessarily need critical manifestos, that it can't be governed in that way. The erotic imagination can be very interested in unkindness, for example. In sadism. I was booed offstage. I said, until you take that on board, then your picture of this is not accurate. I said, let's talk about masochism for example, male *and* female masochism.

Smith: That's the basis of *The Comfort of Strangers*.
McEwan: Yeah. So that's what I then went on to write. I felt: Oh, well, there must be other terms for discussion about what takes place between a man and woman beyond sociology and critical manifestos. What about the sort of thrilling notion that you could test love, test trust, that you could experiment with un-freeing yourself?

Smith: So the stories are news in a way, news from the male consciousness. And the news is: male consciousness ain't always the happiest place to be. And it's news unattached to dogma, which in 1985 I would imagine was a pretty out-there thing to do.
McEwan: 1981.

Smith: Oops.

McEwan: But, yes, and actually within a year or two there were American feminists writing about the erotic in ways that were really much closer to what I was trying to write about. British feminism is very rooted in Marxism, so it was very much about wages and matters of real concern, but it sat very uneasily in any discussion about the erotic.

Smith: Certainly in the past ten years feminism has become much more willing to talk dirty. There's a kind of cheap, fetishized version that you get in the women's magazines, trumpeting women who are able to say, "Yes, I am a feminist, but I still quite like being tied to a doorknob for three days." It's easy to satirize that stuff, but I feel you really believe in the underlying argument that there's no point in feminism ignoring the female instinct for the perverse. And then you get the other side of the argument, typified by my husband, who believes masochism and sadism will always be found to have its root cause in some kind of emotional damage, that there's no other reason.

McEwan: No, he's absolutely wrong. Madonna famously said being tied down gave her the thrill and comfort of being strapped into a car seat when she was three. I thought, Ah! She's said it.

Smith: The quote at the end of *The Comfort of Strangers*: "She was going to tell him her theory, tentative at this stage, of course, which explained how the imagination, the sexual imagination, men's ancient dreams of hurting and women's of being hurt, embodied and declares a powerful single organizing principle, which distorted all relations, all truth."

I'm a writer who never writes about sex. It's so far from my own fictional world, and it unnerves me when you say "powerful, single, organizing principle." You mean that sex is the pole that everything else moves around—in which case, I'm really missing a trick. That seems to be what you were saying in 1981. And I wonder if you still feel that.

McEwan: No, I don't.

Smith: Because it's a very a big thing to say.

McEwan: That's a very big thing to say especially in a tiny novel. But it's something that someone who had just gone through what the character had gone through might well feel. But no, I have now reached the stage where as soon as anyone says life moves around a single, organizing principle I stop listening to them. I don't feel that life organizes itself around any single principle. It's a religious impulse to only grasp at one thing, one explanation.

Smith: I understand.

McEwan: That's interesting, though . . . I don't know where things stand now in the sexual debate. I've just started reading *Villages* [John Updike's new novel] . . . plenty of sex in there.

Smith: I know. It's unbelievable. I don't know how he stays interested. I find it amazing, not just purely technically, but the virility of the man, the continued interest.

McEwan: The virility of the man!

Smith: You know what I mean. He's still bothered. He loves women and he says, somewhere in that book, that he can't believe that women "tend to us" or "care for us at all" or something like that. As if to say: what a miracle it is. He doesn't seem to have ever gotten over the idea that women don't mind making love to men.

McEwan: I like the bit at the beginning when he's being shaved, the hero, and it's like: the girls all worship us but of course they don't have enough intellect to be able to worship us. *If only they knew how vast our consciousness is* . . . But seriously, it still remains difficult, more difficult now than it was, to understand what the true relation is between men and women. Back then everything was being stirred up, it was a blizzard, it was an argument you had to get involved in. Now it all seems to have slowed and settled. A sort of muffled silence.

Smith: In a lot of the chick lit, depicting women slightly older than me, the sexual maturity is that of a nine-year-old, maybe. The sex is just this giggly and ridiculous activity one is subjected to in order to make a man stay in your house and marry you. There's no honest expression of female sexual desire, the kind you find even in those old cheesy feminist manuals like *Our Bodies, Ourselves*. We've gone backwards. I mean, if you had a daughter who believed this stuff they're printing now, you'd be devastated.

McEwan: I keep hearing that song "Too Drunk to Fuck"—have you heard that?

Smith: Yeah. Things have not gone well in the past ten years.

McEwan: What a shame.

Smith: What about your two boys? Are you conscious of bringing up different kinds of men from the ones I had to date?

McEwan: Yeah, I think so. They're both very rapid in their development. When they got to the age of about sixteen or seventeen, they had their first girlfriends, and stayed with them for two or three years. I think it was enormously healthy. And they remained friends with them afterwards. And now Will is in his second long relationship and Greg has just finished his first, but they still meet and it's very touching. Three-hour phone conversations still go on and they seemed to have had lots of sex. Far more sex than I'd *ever* imagined at the same age. I find it deeply enviable.

Smith: One of the critical standards I remember being levied at all your generation of male writers was: *does he write women well? Can he write a convincing bird?* Do you think about that still? Does it concern you? Do you think you've improved?

McEwan: I think I'm sort of gender-blind on this. I think it was Fay Weldon who said that a man could never write a woman properly, which I thought was ludicrous. Taken to its logical extension, novelists could only write about themselves; you couldn't write about an old person, a young person, a person you didn't know. Henry James said that in the contract between writer and reader one thing we must accept as given is the subject matter. I accept that wholly. It's a great contract. There's nowhere you'll not let your imagination go.

V. "As you get older you feel the need to make yourself clear . . ."

Smith: Ah—I wanted to talk about the places you let your imagination go. Dark places. The most striking thing in *Saturday*, I think, is the final scene, in particular, the sadism of it. Now, either I'm an idiot or—well, I just didn't expect it, I was caught out completely. I was having a lovely time in a lovely world with lovely people and I went upstairs to read the last hundred pages—Nick [Nick Laird, Smith's husband] was downstairs watching TV with friends—and was sitting alone with this book feeling like I was being attacked. My scalp was prickly, I was sweating, I kept wanting to shout downstairs but then there's no point trying to explain what's happened in a book if somebody's not reading it . . . I felt physically assailed. And maybe there's a lot of fiction which does that and I just don't read it. I'm always reading this flowery literary fiction. But I'd never had that feeling before. And I never expect that response from my readers, I never expect anything physical from them. I know I can't make them cry and I can't make them go [*sharp intake of breath*] like I was doing with your book, yesterday. So I wonder if you sit down and aim for that response and how you can possibly pace a novel, bargaining on that result? Because what if it didn't happen? What if I just read that scene and went, "Uh, yeah," and moved on?

McEwan: I knew what I wanted to get, I had no idea exactly how I was going to get it. I leave blanks in my planning, and there are bits it's best not to think about till you get there. I didn't know whether he had a knife nor did I know what he wanted. I had to write it to find out what was going to happen. I mean I knew that he would end up being thrown down the stairs, and that the operation would happen but I was looking for my . . . well, to go back to where we started this conversation, to 9/11, and the sense of invasion, one can only do it on a private scale. If you say the airliner hit the side of the building, a thousand people died, nothing happens to your scalp. So I, in a sense, tried to find the private scale of that feeling.

Smith: But what advice would you give regarding how a writer might *earn* that moment? Because when I finished reading I thought you'd done exactly what you needed to do, to earn that moment. I didn't feel that you'd tried to scare me in a cheap way or you'd taken a backdoor. More could have happened in that scene, in fact. I was interested, in my mind, as to how far you could have gone with that narrative before I was angry with you for a manipulation. All the narrative decisions you make in a scene like that are ethical decisions, and also aesthetic, and you have to make them, they're serious. And someone who can't write makes them very badly.

McEwan: Especially if you're going to have a young woman with no clothes on, being looked at in that way. How long you dwell on it is key. And I felt I was taking a risk having Daisy naked. And the risk was—well, first I got it completely wrong, I didn't make it frightening enough and the reason I didn't make it frightening was I didn't want to humiliate her. But then it was unreal. So I had to go back and I made her defiant. But it just didn't stand up.

Smith: I would never be defiant in that situation.

McEwan: There's no way anyone could be defiant with this man holding a knife to your mother's neck. But again the question of the amount of time one dwells on the nakedness. And I thought if I was Updike now Perowne's gaze would be relentless and we would have to have Daisy's body described. And I thought: there Perowne cannot go. So I went to fear and fear did what

I thought a brother and father would have to do in an emergency. Look to the floor, think of a way of attacking. And in a sense so did I, I looked to the floor. Apart from the swell of her pregnancy. The whole thing is four pages. It's narrative time enough but not particularly long to dwell.

Smith: In the past you worked more on the complicit nature of the reader-writer relationship. That story about the father with the two little girls, "In Between the Sheets," makes you complicit by constantly allowing—without authorial comment—these descriptions in which the father makes the children sound older than they are. Several times they're described as looking older, speaking like women, moving like women. This makes the reader complicit in the pedophile's idea, or potential pedophile's idea, that these girls could be his. And that's an incredibly uncomfortable experience as a reader.
McEwan: Yeah. I was very keen on making readers uncomfortable. I think I've lost that ambition now, it doesn't interest me so much as a project.

Smith: It's a kind of cruelty.
McEwan: Yeah. Leading the reader into siding with the murderous pedophile or rapist. It's not so interesting.

Smith: Or offering the reader an extreme, antihumanist perspective on a human being. In the story "Homemade" you describe a young boy running a race as a "tiny amoebic blob across the field . . . staggering determinedly in its pointless effort to reach the flags—just life, just faceless, self-renewing life . . ."
McEwan: Yeah. I was trying to be funny. Because he comes home thirteenth.

Smith: But the reader is also being forced to see people from perspectives the novel as a form doesn't usually encourage.
McEwan: Absolutely.

Smith: Do you think your taste for that has lessened a little?
McEwan: It has lessened a little. Because I think death anxiety or numbers-of-days-left anxiety make me keen to make sense of the human, rather than to distort it. I think there's a wonderful recklessness you have in your twenties and thirties as a writer, you can do terrible things because although intellectually you know your time will end, you don't yet feel it in your blood,

in your gut. It's a recklessness I think one should really enjoy, relax into it, spread out. As you get older you feel the need to make yourself clear.

Smith: Right.

McEwan: There are a couple of things. One is you have children and as you age, there's some growing sense of wanting the human project to succeed. Not fail. Or you no longer wish to dwell quite so much on the possibility of it all going wonderfully, horribly wrong. You begin to wish it would go right.

Smith: So, in conclusion: what are you going to do about your mellowing coinciding with the world's hardcore radicalization and madness? That's a strange mix. You feel it in *Saturday*. The collision of somebody in that moment of their life where they're feeling satisfied and fulfilled and unfortunately that moment's happening on a planet that's losing the bloody plot entirely.

McEwan: Yeah, it is an extraordinary moment. It's like we've engaged ourselves in some medieval struggle. We had our Diderot and Voltaire and now you'd hope we'd at least now investigate the structure of DNA, and the origins of the universe, and the possibility of understanding more about ourselves with a new metaphysics—but that's not the focus right now. The struggle is a medieval one between faiths.

Smith: Yeah. It's all gone wrong. When I was in America around all these classic left-wing intellectuals, the feeling was one of literal despair. They just run through the streets screaming. That's basically their only reaction to the moment they're in, as if this moment were unprecedented. But that's the interesting thing—it's nowhere near unprecedented. I liked the fact that in *Saturday* you seemed to be saying, instead, what we were getting here is a madness that, in truth, has always accompanied progress.

McEwan: You know, twenty-five years ago or twenty years ago, all we talked about was the possibility that the Soviet Union and the United States were going to have a global conflict and do it in Europe. That was the unprecedented moment.

Smith: You wrote your own apocalypse story at the time as well.

McEwan: It felt like a real possibility. And we got very indignant, caught between two empires, we thought we might all die. Martin Amis famously said that if the war started he would drive home, shoot his wife, and then shoot his children.

Smith: He doesn't do things by halves.

McEwan: As a humane act. So the liberal Left went around saying, "Dear sir, in your interview, you said you'd shoot your wife and children. Do you really think that's an appropriate response?" But anyway it was on our minds. And madness was in the air.

Smith: In *Saturday*, Henry Perowne wonders whether the madness and trauma of 9/11 will take a hundred years to resolve itself. Do you believe that?

McEwan: At the end of *Saturday*, I think of a figure like Perowne but a hundred years earlier, 1904, and of what terror lay ahead then. We've almost forgot the First World War, Stalin, and then the Second, the Holocaust—if we had a fraction of that we'd be very fortunate. At least we know what we're capable of. But the moment is not unprecedented.

Smith: Maybe everything takes a hundred years or more to play itself out. Look at the bloody Treaty of Versailles. Now: next question is utterly unrelated.

McEwan: Good.

Smith: I read your back catalog over a month or so and I felt very satisfied merely having "read all of McEwan." And then I thought, fuck, imagine *having written all of McEwan.* So I was wondering what it feels like to look at your own bookshelves and see this nice little backlog of work. This little stack. I don't know what that would feel like. Amazing, I would think.

McEwan: It's not amazing because you get there by very slow increments. If you think of Updike—*that's* amazing. Updike's "Also by" page is now a few pages long in itself. An insane amount of books.

Smith: That is insane. He has a condition I think. It's a disease with him—he can't stop.

McEwan: Graphomania. Well, it would be easier to dismiss if it wasn't so good.

Smith: Does it give you pleasure, though?

McEwan: It's like a family album, the consciousness of your own past—well, you must find this already. I certainly find it. People say what were you doing in such and such year, and I know exactly what I was doing. I know I was publishing a particular book, or halfway through one. These books are the spoonfuls with which I've measured my existence.

A Conversation about Art and Nature

Antony Gormley/2005

From *Kenyon Review* 28.1 (Winter 2006): 104–12. Reprinted by permission of publisher.

I came to know Antony Gormley during a week we spent together far inside the Arctic Circle in March 2005. We were sharing a miniscule bunk room on board a converted Dutch lighthouse ship which was frozen into a fjord a few hours by snowmobile from Longyearben on Spitzbergen Island. We also took turns driving and riding pillion on these untrustworthy machines, and we managed some spectacular hikes onto a high plateau above the fjord. We were in a good position, therefore, to have a number of conversations about landscape and art. We continued those conversations one warm afternoon in June 2005 at his workshop in north London. All around us various people working for Antony were busy with his various projects. He was just about to install *Another Place*, a hundred cast-iron figures molded from his own body, set along the tidal shores of Merseyside. The solitary novelist is bound to feel admiration for a man whose art provides a small army of specialists—computer program designers, welders, foundrymen, and so on—such gainful employment. We spoke for about ninety minutes. We each made edits of the typescript and merged our versions. —Ian McEwan

Antony Gormley: What is the consolation that we seek into going into the elemental world and how do we use it?

Ian McEwan: I feel bigger, freer. I remind myself (not having any religion) of the arbitrary fact of existence, that it could all be the consequence of an extraordinary chapter of accidents on a beautiful rock surrounded by sterile space. So to cross a landscape is a kind of necessity, and the longer I'm out there—if I can get time to walk days on end—that feeling grows. It's hard to describe without falling into a well of clichés. It kicked in for me with the hormones, the first stirrings of adolescence. It was very strong, that sense of the earth, the rocks, the trees, the earthly realm really filled me at that

134

age with joy, and nothing, not literature, not even sex could fulfill me in that way.

Gormley: It's interesting that you associated that with the burgeoning of sexuality. You say that it makes you feel bigger. For me the wonderful feeling when we went up to the Arctic was actually how tiny one was, how tiny the boat was, and the way that the rhythm of the arctic ice forming, freezing, melting, breaking, the sense one had that those things have been going on for time out of mind, way before any complex evolution was possible. It is contradictory that, on the one hand, you feel tiny but you also feel completely free. If we think of the male sex drive as an attempt to go back to the place where we came from—is the urge to experience landscape similar in a way? There is a sense that one of the things one looks for in going to these uninscribed places of the world is a sense of origin. This is the place from which we came.

McEwan: Yes, ultimately life is cooked up from the stuff of landscape—rock, or the minerals from rock, and water and energy from the sun.

Gormley: My first encounter with the elemental world was going north to Yorkshire, to school, somewhere that was so totally different from Hampstead Garden suburb with its box hedges, a kind of suburban landscape of rural architecture redescribed for the middle classes in safe, bite-sized, packaged bits. To escape from that into real landscape, with stone walls and amazing skies and the grit, the sense of the peat and the underlying shale and the color of the water in the rivers—it was revelation to me. Finally there are real places.

McEwan: My earliest experiences were not so gritty as yours because this was rural Suffok. But the ingredients were there—a big tidal river, big skies, mud, trees, salt creeks. But Suffolk, in fact, is a giant garden—everywhere you look is human history.

Gormley: And on an amazing scale—Suffolk is a very particular thing, the size of the fields and the arable intimacy that you don't find on the moors.

McEwan: This kind of English landscape was an extraordinary achievement. Bountiful food production living alongside rich biodiversity. A deal was struck with nature. Smallish fields, hedge rows, boundary trees, occasional copses to harbor foxes. It seemed like a balance had been reached by accident, with the maximum amount of wildlife in an area that's growing food. We met our own needs and kept alive populations of insects, plants, birds, mammals, and the apex predator, the fox. A beautiful creation, such a landscape, and a tragedy to see it replaced by the desert monocultures of intensive farming. Fox-hunting country is often the loveliest because to sustain a fox you have to sustain so much else. All the things it needs to eat—the rabbits, the voles, the slugs—and the space. The urban romanticism that banned fox hunting opened up possibilities for worse kinds of savagery— the gross philistinism of agribusiness. Yes, man-made landscapes can be truly beautiful.

Gormley: It's interesting, isn't it, in Hugh Brody's *The Other Side of Eden* he asks Anaviapic, an Inuit friend, whom he had invited south for the first time, when motoring through the west country, "How do you like the countryside?" and he says, "Where is it? I don't see any countryside, this is all made, all built." The English sensibility, our relationship with the countryside is very much a response to the history of its human occupation.

McEwan: Enclosures, clearances, emparkment—some of our finest made-landscapes are filled with a history of suffering. We've got nothing like the human emptiness of the Arctic.

Gormley: I think we're describing significant differences. When I think about Suffolk, I think like you do about the hedgerows, trees, plantations, the amazingly huge sky over and above this quilted mass; that's a relationship with a place that is qualified by human history. But what's wonderful about the sea is that it is not like that. It's an element which is endless and uninscribed. What I like about the beach is that it's a place that attracts people and engages them in a dialogue. The last place I installed *Another Place* was in De Panne, Belgium, where bourgeois flats are built eight stories high right on the beach and there is this amazing dialogue through the lace curtains between total elemental chaos of water, wind, sand, and western comfort domestic culture: a real border.

McEwan: The beach is also the place where white and pink people attempt to be brown, which is an odd development in our recent history.

Gormley: It's all part of the regressive behavior—we want to play—all of us play by the beach. It is also a deep memory of the early times of the sense of sun and wind on the skin. I love the way that we regress at the beach and we do silly things that are really necessary—we understand ourselves better.

McEwan: One useful service rendered by this beach-lust is that the interior empties just when you want to be walking. It's great that not everybody wants to be on a mountain. When you're up there, it's an interesting experiment, to try and see mountains from a pre-romantic, pre-eighteenth-century point of view—as ugly, chaotic, threatening, a punishment for man's first disobedience. No one much thought of wandering around up there for pleasure until the English began the cult of alpinism in the late eighteenth, early nineteenth century. When the weather closes in and suddenly you're cold and wondering if you've gone too far and not left yourself enough time to get down, then landscape takes on this other aspect. Its indifference can be a shock. You could fall off here and die, and it doesn't mind. It doesn't care what you do.

Gormley: Those are the best moments. We've been going to the Lake District for twenty years and the best moments are when the classic sun-filled afternoon turns rotten on you and suddenly you're on the edge of Wetherlam or the Old Man and you know on the other side of the cairn there's a forty-foot drop.

McEwan: The great biologist E. O. Wilson uses the term *biophilia* to describe how our interest in and love of landscape, plants, and animals have been inscribed in us by our evolutionary past. He's suggesting that our ideal of the perfect landscape, of open grassland with spaced clumps of trees, is formed by our ancestral environment, the savannah. It's a lovely and unprovable idea. We've been talking of this call of the landscape as if it were a universal. But we know this is not historically so, and I have plenty of friends who could never see the point of traipsing around in the countryside. They'd rather be in a restaurant or an art gallery.

Gormley: So how do they escape? I think of landscape as an engagement with the elemental world, as an antidote to urban anxiety. You have just described it as being a source of its own unique anxiety, but somehow they are of a different kind. One of the things that one goes hiking for is to actually encounter real danger rather than that mentally produced anxiety to do with deadlines or the fear of being knocked over by a car, something that's more chosen.

McEwan: I guess people find danger in other ways. But did it make sense to you when I said at the beginning of the conversation that landscape makes you feel larger? I didn't mean more important. I've just remembered a certain moment when I lived with my parents in north Africa. I must have been about eight or nine and my mother had a job in a shop in Tripoli. We lived on the edge of the city and my father was at work, so she used to drop me off at the beach alone with a packed lunch and she would come and collect me four hours later.

Gormley: Who else was on the beach?

McEwan: No one. So there I was with my book, my trunks, my snorkel, and a towel (these were in pre-paranoid days when kids roamed freely), and the minibus had just dropped me off, and I went down these little wooden steps that take you to the beach. There was a sandy cliff, maybe thirty feet high, and I paused at the top of the steps—the whole beach was empty and pure white, the sea was clear and sparkling and invitingly blue, and I knew it would be warm and I had it all to myself. I was just filled with this wild joy and the joy was, "I'm here, I exist!" Being in a powerful landscape does what we hope art does—it enlarges your immediate mental arena.

Gormley: I guess I am trying to make art that is part of that widening. It's a very cheeky thing to think you can make a bit of real coastline into an imaginative or dream place, but the idea of *Another Place* is you're using a hundred memories of a particular body at particular times in its breathing cycle all looking out to the horizon as a catalyst to thinking the very thoughts that you're intimating. The human perceptual world is limited by a horizon, but there is always that human need to imagine what's beyond it. That's what this piece is about and why it's called *Another Place*. It's an open question where that place might be—mental or physical. The Mersey has a particular association with a memory of those people who left England to find a new home in America. I feel that now in a postcolonial, globalized world there is no other place really. There are bought utopias and sold dreams of otherness, but we have to deal with the here and now even if the here has become a globalized here—someone called it "now-here." The idea of *Another Place* is precisely to provide people walking the dog with an extension to their experience of the beach. They witness that they themselves are part of a field of witnessing.

McEwan: *Another Place* seems to suggest the power of collective dreaming. All these figures are facing out to sea. The work has great power because they're facing the same direction and thinking the same thing—well, I think they're thinking the same thing. It's not just a solitary thought, it's a collective ambition.

Gormley: It's a congregation, a communion of attention, but the location of the work has to be inside people as well.

McEwan: A field of dreams.

Gormley: For me it's very important that the relationship between the dog-walking, intelligent, mobile bodies going up and down the beach and these static objects that continue from the near to the far is that they connect them—by being between them—they participate in the field, become part of it.

McEwan: It wouldn't work for a moment if it were a field of triangles. These are human forms and we automatically anthropomorphize the chunks of iron. The impact comes from their shape, and that's what I like about your work. It suggests a new form of humanism. It looks at the relationship between an individual or a group with the landscape, and it also includes us in the landscape, gazing at these idealized or minimalized forms.

Gormley: I don't think they're idealized. I think it's important that they tell the story of their making: you can still see traces of the cling-film and places where the mold has been cut, so I would say they're very straightforward man-made industrial fossils that take a particular life form at a particular moment and register it in elemental terms. I think of iron as being a concentrated earth material; it's the most potent element, it's the thing that makes the red in our blood. It's the thing that keeps the whole jolly planet on its course in space. Something like eighty-five percent of this planet is iron. If you go down in the magma, you don't have to go very far, and you are in iron world. So these objects are, on one hand, honest, straightforward indices of a particular human body, but they are also a bit like meteorites made of planet stuff: a useful material for thinking about the relationship between the human body and more enduring bodies in space.

McEwan: Time is very important in this. I'm talking about time in a landscape—geological time, evolutionary time, human time. Time does a curious thing to human sorrow—it weathers it, the way water might weather rock. So you might stand by a ruined croft in Scotland where a family was driven away, and all that remains in the landscape is an echo of the human tragedy. Your sculpture has something of this weathered quality.

Gormley: I believe it has something to do with the weather being the thing that everything suffers but is also the elemental condition that carries on, and in it there is another form of consolation. I think we learned that from the tsunami and the Iraq war. Human-based tragedy in the context of natural disaster and the pain involved is perhaps more bearable; there is no one to blame. Which reminds me that I wanted to talk about anxiety. I'm aware that you've become more forgiving and articulate more positions, but when I first read your early work I recognized and responded to a difficult and "uncertain-about-everything" world. The feeling of the foreignness of territory inside other houses, the feeling of not knowing what's going on in somebody else's head. So perhaps there's also inspiration to be taken from discomfort and uncertainty?

McEwan: A young artist can be dark and reckless and indulge a savage pessimism. It's a thrill, like driving round corners too fast. You're wild and free because you're never going to die, your infinite days are stacked up ahead of you. Then, after an endless transition, you realize fully, sensually, right there in your body, that your days are numbered, that life is going to shrug you off. It's all going to go on without you. And you've come to love the human adventure. It's enraging, tragic, joyous, and unbelievably diverse. You want it to go on, to succeed against the odds. A sense of obligation develops towards the joy as well as the terror. What I was trying to do in *Saturday* was describe private happiness against a background of gathering fear.

Gormley: Joy is very, very difficult. You can paint things pink but they often as not end up looking tragic.

McEwan: There is a line of Peter Medawar, the biologist, which I had my character in *Saturday* invoke—to abandon all hope of progress is a meanness of spirit. One has to be wary of the delicious, seductive joys of pessimism. In art it can turn into an empty mannerism. And in the universities, in the humanities, all intellectuals are required to be card-carrying pessimists. You have to go to the sciences today to find any real sense of wonder, any real joy in the intellectual life. I think in some ways you are among the most optimistic artists I know. You're not telling us that we're doomed when you set your hundred figures in the landscape, or ask us to contemplate what it might mean to be made of a mess of moving particles. It's pleasure and wonder.

Gormley: I think the story is far from over and what precisely the part that we might play in the unfolding story of the evolution of matter. It is completely an open question. I go to science in the most crude and amateur way as a huge resource and everything to do with post-particle physics for me is extraordinarily rich, both in its language and the cosmological idea of an event horizon. We are being forced to try to imagine something beyond language. This is another horizon of imagining that we have to cross over; it's fascinating to me that we're given that opportunity. Physics, and particularly string theory when expressed in mathematical terms, takes us somewhere unimaginable in the terms of our physical universe and that fascinates me. The possible is just out of reach . . . every hour I need to wake up . . . it is like this invitation . . . so much still to do.

McEwan: I'm writing the introduction to a book in which a hundred and forty thinkers, most of them scientists, answer the question "What do you believe that you cannot prove?" What comes across in the contributions is the excitement among these scientists—whether string theory is going to accommodate quantum mechanics, or what the interface is going to be between the machine and the brain, or whether we will find life, or intelligent life, beyond the earth, or how computer software is going to change this and that.

Gormley: Isn't there much more crossover than there was before, so artificial intelligence now is informing neuroscience and neuroscience is informing evolutionary psychology and psychology is informing the development of biochemical therapies?

McEwan: Exactly so. They appear to be working towards the formation of a common language. They need each other. The biologists need the mathematicians, as do the neuroscientists, and the physicists and biologists have a strong emerging interface. To understand each other they have to speak in common English, which is what makes it accessible and interesting for the layman. The old Enlightenment dream of a unified body of knowledge is beginning, only just beginning, to emerge. Were you to ask cultural theorists and literary critics the same question you would get a much darker view, and no solutions. When it comes to the intellectual landscape, I'd rather cross it with scientists like these, and with artists like yourself.

A Conversation with Ian McEwan

David Lynn/2006

From *The Kenyon Review* 29.3 (Summer 2007): 38–51. Reprinted by permission of publisher.

Ian McEwan received the 2006 Kenyon Review Award for Literary Achievement. He is the author of nine novels, with a new one to appear in the summer of 2007, along with many other works of short fiction, plays, screenplays, and other work. He has also received the Booker Prize and many other honors. David Lynn interviewed Ian McEwan at Bloomberg News on November 9, 2006, in New York.

David Lynn: Thank you for taking the time to come in and have this chat.
Ian McEwan: Sure.

Lynn: Early on in your novel *Saturday*, the central character, a busy surgeon, who is anticipating a day of rest, is thinking about literature, specifically fiction, and how it's never appealed to him. This is the passage:

> His free time is always fragmented not only by errands, and family obligations, and sports, but by the restlessness that comes with these weekly islands of freedom. He doesn't want to spend his days off lying or even sitting down, nor does he really want to be a spectator of other lives, of imaginary lives, even though these past hours he's put in an unusual number of minutes gazing from the bedroom window, and it interests him less to have the world reinvented. He wants it explained. The times are strange enough, why make things up?

It's a wonderful passage—obviously this sentiment establishes among other things that Dr. Perowne is not Ian McEwan. But does this reveal any kind of ambivalence on your part with the role of fiction in our culture?
McEwan: Well, there are two things really for me to say about that passage. One is it's really setting out the manifest, as it were, for this book. In other words, this book is going to be tied right into a world that is public, shared, recognizable, real. All the external events—the Iraq invasion and so on—are

definable, clear, checkable in your newspaper. The other thing is yes—Henry Perowne is not me, although I gave him one or two elements of my own life.

Lynn: Such as your house.
McEwan: I gave him my house; I gave him little bits of my children, of my wife. I gave him in its entirety, a relationship with my mother, who also suffered from a neurodegenerative disease. But for the purposes of this novel, it seemed intriguing to me to have a man who is not an intellectual, but nor is he stupid. And he does share with me something that I felt in the months after the Washington/New York attacks in 2001, a sudden restless urge to know more things. I felt we'd been missing something all through the nineties. Our backs were turned on certain events that clearly were linked. And like many other people, I went out and bought numerous books on the history of the Middle East and the nature of Islam and actually the tenets of belief of Islam, which had never really bothered me before, books by a whole range of scholars, historians, and historians to colonialisms. I did an awful lot of reading as I think a lot of other people did too. And at the time I wasn't reading a lot of fiction. So I captured that little sense of impatience of imagined lives and urgency that I felt for some months and just gave them to him as a sort of mindset.

Lynn: Terrorism does of course come up in the book—but it's of a very homegrown order. A deranged group of young men, or at least one of them is suffering from, as you say, a neurodegenerative disease—the leader of them, and it's specifically not Muslim terror intruding, it's something very local, very immediate . . .
McEwan: But the issue still remains, what does a rational person or a society that regards itself as rational do in the face of irrational behavior? And there's something very contaminating about aggressive and irrational behavior. In the Second World War, for example, the allies had to become genocidal in themselves, they had to firebomb, they dropped nuclear weapons. Genocide became an aspect of foreign policy. In that sense they began, horribly, to resemble the people they were bound to defeat. It's always an interesting issue, how do you defeat a vile opponent without becoming a little bit vile yourself?

Lynn: Or is that inevitable?
McEwan: Exactly.

Lynn: I've always felt that the role of fiction, one of the roles of fiction in our lives, was to give shape to the chaos of human experience. That we tell stories in order to shape a world that resists shape. Does that tie in with what you're saying now, that you're using this novel as one way of dealing with the irrational? That you're trying to contain it within the form of a novel?

McEwan: I do think of novels in terms of investigations, journeys, open-ended pursuits in that sense. The reader is bound to be aware that when Henry Perowne says he's not interested in invented imaginary beings, he himself is an invented imaginary being, and therefore there is a paradox. I mean, he might not like novels, but he happens to be the hero of one. In other words, for all his struggles, he is another mind that has been invented. And he belongs in that project, I think, of literature—showing us what it's like to be someone else, but someone with whom we might or might not share some vital aspects. Containing the irrational, I don't know—all you can do is describe it and describe the dilemma, never really resolved in this book and I don't see how it can be resolved, of when you're confronted in the street as a doctor and you somewhat abuse your professional authority to escape a good kicking, but then afterwards feel somewhat besmirched. You feel you've told a lie, but you haven't.

Lynn: There again you've been tainted by the encounter with that behavior.

McEwan: Exactly, and if we're just to talk outside the novel, politically the United States and its allies have found themselves besmirched through their struggles against an enemy, that is, I think, completely vile in its totalitarian instincts. It's very hard to remain good and to enter battle.

Lynn: You were speaking of Henry Perowne with a little distance, as if for you he had achieved a sense of independent status. Did you feel that at some stage in the writing he'd become a being unto himself? With a mind—that's the word you just used . . .

McEwan: He became that for me in the very first paragraph when I wrote in longhand, "Henry Perowne comma a neurosurgeon," and then rather like Joseph K., he wakes from troubled dreams. But finds himself waking in the act of rising from his bed. Standing in the darkness utterly naked. My pleasure in creating that moment for myself was, I have a character in the dark, as it were, just emerging, waiting to be dressed. I didn't know who he was at that point, apart from his profession.

Lynn: But he lived for you, the heart was beating for you.

McEwan: Yes, he was already there and it was a rather pure feeling of just having this character stand naked by the bed, feeling rather elated and then crossing to the window. And yes, he is distinct from me, but more than in any other novel of mine I've drawn on a recognizable world to fill out the details. Of course, one is always giving every character some aspect or other of oneself. But, I gave him, as we said, my address and I gave him some of my . . . well, the tortured ambivalent feelings about the impending invasion. His utter impatience for, say, magical realism in fiction is not really mine. But it's something that I have sometimes fleetingly felt, not as a dismissal so much as a sense that I really want the real world plausibly reenacted.

Lynn: And that's obvious in your fiction.

McEwan: And I'm fine with much magical realism. I have read *The Tin Drum*, and I adore the work of Borges, and have actually started rereading Garcia Márquez with some pleasure.

Lynn: I like the later Márquez myself—he became famous for *One Hundred Years of Solitude*, but I actually think the later work is better.

McEwan: I'm with you on that, and I do feel sometimes a little impatience when characters sprout wings and fly out the window. I think the laws of physics are intricate and wonderful enough and the world that greets us is wondrous enough and difficult to reenact.

Lynn: One of the traits that *Saturday* does share with most of your fiction is very much that what is presented is a real, solid world of blessed normalcy. The characters are lucky to be where they are. And then, over and over again in your work, something extraordinary intrudes. There's something from the outside that's unexpected, sometimes irrational, sometimes just physical, something totally unexpected that alters that real world irrecoverably in some ways. Every writer I've known has his or her own way of making their way through the process of writing. I've never heard two people describe it the same way, but generally they either have a pretty good idea where they're going from the time they start or they discover the story in the process of telling it. How do you make your way?

McEwan: Well, if I had to opt for one of those two, I'm in the latter. I write to find where I'm going. But sometimes a scheme doesn't emerge very rapidly in the early part of writing, sometimes in the first five or ten thousand

words. Sometimes I just blunder into a novel and start out thinking I'm doing one thing that I had asked myself to do in a note ten years before and
end up doing another thing that I had asked myself in a note three years
before. Sometimes I have to trick myself into doing things. But I do see writing, the actual physical matter of writing, as an act of imagination. And the
best days, the best mornings are the ones in which forcing down a sentence
might generate a surprise. A combination of ideas, or simply a noun meeting an adjective that suddenly gives me pleasure. Whole characters have
sometimes emerged for me simply out of a sentence. Not out of the need to
describe a character, but the need to make this kind of a pattern on the page.
And then I've gone on to build on that and found myself again pleased that
something has come up, a little serendipity that's taken me in the direction.
I'll give a concrete example: When I was writing *Atonement*, I was setting
out to begin the Dunkirk section, and I decided that the central character,
Robbie, was going to simply make a three-day walk towards the coast, alone.
As I wrote the first paragraph, I suddenly found myself inventing two names
and two other characters, and as I did so I thought, of course, this is going
to be a lot more interesting, for him to have company. Suddenly, the whole
matter thickened for me, and I didn't know who these people were. The
writing unfolded it for me, too, and those are nice discoveries—to end up at
lunchtime with two people you didn't know about at breakfast. That's what I
mean by the pleasures of surprise and of not having too strong or too rigor-
ous/prescriptive a scheme. But on the other hand I do, or with *Atonement* I
did have, a pretty strong sense of how it was all going to unfold. Once I got
going, once I was three chapters in, I suddenly realized that I was writing in
the voice of a seventy-seven-year-old woman novelist. That I would put her
initials finally at the end of the main body of the novel and that there would
be a coat and so on, all those things were quite clear.

Lynn: Speaking of the pleasures of the language, that reminds me of the
great American stylist John Updike. In an earlier conversation you mentioned to me that you particularly liked and admired his work. How have
you found Updike important for you?
McEwan: I can't claim him as an influence, much as I'd like to, because I've
never really written like him. But, there is the little twitch or spring or little
"knight's move of consciousness," a phrase which I know I read in a book of
his, but he claims not to know where it is, we can't find it and he thinks he
almost certainly stole it from Nabokov.

Lynn: Sounds like Nabokov.

McEwan: A scientist friend of mine says that actually a famous neurologist of the twenties used this phrase. So, anyway that's a hunt to be conducted. Still, it nicely captures the spring in the step of a good Updike sentence. Sometimes it's a matter of a word inversion, slightly off the normal nature of Standard English. He is a natural metaphor maker, simile maker. He has a marvelous eye. He is the one who follows Conrad's prescription to make you see. I mean I think he is the most extraordinarily visual of writers, and maybe that's what I admire in him above all and aspire to in my own writing—to make you see, to get to the heart of any emotional exchange or any transaction or any set piece. It's crucial, in my view, to have the reader see, and that is not to say that you've got to lard the page with masses of description, but key, vivid, specific details, like little starbursts in the darkness, I think have emotional consequences. If you can see this then you can feel it.

You don't want to get bogged down in metaphor. But Updike is full of these superb descriptions. When Rabbit, for example, rows his granddaughter out to sea and has a heart attack, the description before this terrible event happens of the vividness of light and water and sound. Clearly you're being set up or sense that there's some great physiological change occurring within Rabbit and in this indirect free style you know that it's Updike, but it's also Rabbit, and that something terrible is about to happen. Why is the world becoming so vivid? Or in *Roger's Version* when the character takes a thirty-page walk through a decrepit part of town and there's a description of a puddle with a bit of oil slick in it refracting light as in a rainbow. A couple of paragraphs I think there are just exquisite.

Lynn: Do you think that this facility with images has something to do with Updike's fascination with visual art, his work as an art critic?

McEwan: I'm sure—I think it must be inseparable from it and I mean, no question that it's a different side of the same coin. He has a very strong visual sense. I like writers generally, and Nabokov is another who is supreme in this respect, who recognize that forty percent of the brain's processing is given over to the visual, and the visual region projects deep into other parts of the brain, of language and emotion. We are visual creatures and the novel, more than cinema, for me is ultimately a visual medium. Perhaps too, Updike's poetry, which again is highly descriptive, is of importance here too. But I like, myself, to be able to see a scene. And in the opening scene of *Enduring Love*, for example, the most important element of that set piece was to make the details in the relationship, of all the different bits, the people running across a field towards a balloon that was in trouble, to make that clear, as clear as . . .

Lynn: I have to say that when I talk to people about your work, that's the image that over and over and over comes up. People remember that opening scene of *Enduring Love* more than any other moment in your fiction.

McEwan: Yes, it's funny how that seemed to have made such an impact. I wrote it when I was two-thirds of the way through the book; I'd been looking for an opening. What I wanted was to sort of hit the ground running, to have a sense of urgency and visual clarity with something knocking the heart, or making the heart knock and get a sort of drumbeat of prose. But, I couldn't find it, not that I even looked, I just knew it would come up; I hadn't yet found the event, the thing that would embody all this. Until a friend of mine, we were hiking in Ireland in a high wind and he suddenly remembered he'd read in a paper of a balloon and a father and son who had tried to tether it and dropped to their deaths. I never could find the newspaper piece 'til long afterwards. But as soon as he told me, I thought—now that's it. And I need more than two people, I need six or seven around that balloon. What better enactment of morality? This notion that if we all hang on we can hold it down, but if one breaks rank then there's no point in being good anymore. How perfect that was for me. So, that was a gift really. I just couldn't wait to get back to my desk. Well, in two days I think it went down.

Lynn: What other contemporary authors do you read for pleasure or with admiration?

McEwan: In fiction or nonfiction?

Lynn: Well, either.

McEwan: Well, in nonfiction, I'm reading and rereading now the great American biologist E. O. Wilson. I think he is a superb writer, as well as a great scientist. I'm just reading his book called *Creation*, in which he pleads with Christian fundamentalists. At the beginning of each chapter he says, "Pastor, may I now bring your attention to . . ." and what he's arguing is that, although he knows he can never get an agreement between one who thinks the world was created and one like himself who is a secular humanist, who believes firmly that evolutionary theory is beyond doubt. At the same time, since science and religion are the two most powerful forces in the world today, they have a joint mutual interest in saving its environment, the environment of the earth. So it's an elegant plea, probably a hopeless one, because

I can't imagine any pastor wanting to read E. O. Wilson, they'll just want to reread those familiar verses, from those same old Apostles and bearded prophets. But it's a bold attempt to put a hand out across the divide. I've admired his work for a long time. I like the roll of his prose. As a stylist alone, even if he wasn't a scientist, I think he would have made a colossal impact in the literary culture. I'm interested too in the way certain scientists, and I include Voltaire for example in this, write so well. When they're forced, when people are forced to actually describe their best summary of the thing as it actually is, I think that's quite a strict discipline for the prose. I'm a great admirer, for example, of the letters Voltaire wrote when he visited England. He wrote some letters back. They're called "Letters from England" or "Lettres Philosophe." He describes witnessing Newton's funeral and then just gives a couple of long letters to the theory of optics. Some of the best explanatory writing for the layman on science that I've ever seen. There are great moments in Darwin, too. So I think there's this hidden literature which really needs to be brought, molded, talked into a canon that lives alongside our literary canon. And I hope one day a publisher will make a science library that is about the literature, the poetry of science writing, because it's certainly there and is a marvelous tradition.

Lynn: The distinction between fiction and nonfiction is one that really fascinates me, and I think some of the most interesting writing done in recent years has deliberately played with that boundary. W. G. Sebald, someone I admired a great deal, he plays with this over and over again. Recently in the U.S. we've had things that amount to scandals, although they don't strike me as that, where some writers have presented what are essentially novels or pure fictions as memoir or biography in some sense, and people have felt strangely betrayed by that, really furious and angry, as if there's a moral dimension to that confusion. What do you think of that? I think it is very recent that people have a faith that there is a truth that can be told so readily and are so abused when it turns out not to be that way.

McEwan: Well, I feel a mixture of things. On the one hand, I think that there are things that are the case and there are certain other things that are not, and I'm not much in sympathy with the kind of relativism of, say, postmodernist criticism. I think we do know more now than we knew ten years ago about the natural world, for example. Fiction has always, right from its inception, certainly in the eighteenth century, liked to blur the distinctions. "In the town of M, stroke, in the year of . . ." So why is he not telling us the name of the town? Well, because he doesn't want to offend the real people who are living there. That old trick is one that we've all learned. I've constantly made use of real events, real people, or have my characters meet real people. In *Saturday*, Henry Perowne gets to shake the hand of Tony Blair, and it's the real Tony Blair, not the imagined Tony Blair. When someone says, "this happened to me" and it didn't, well I think the most fascinating thing about that is the outrage that follows, not so much the deceit. I know in certain recent cases there's been another matter, which has been plagiarism. In other words, you've stolen someone else's experiences or even imaginary experiences and claimed them for yourself.

Lynn: That seems a different order of crime.

McEwan: Yes, so this does seem more like pickpocketing to me, and for that you need to be fingered and named and shamed. But I don't know, it does show us that we care about these lines, and I think they ought to be drawn actually. I do. I don't think we could just drift away in a cloud of unknowing relativism about this. Something happened to you or it didn't. Of course we all know that travel writing is fantastically smoothed and fictionalized and many travel writers know that they collate events, miss out great stretches of boredom, make certain things happen in one place that probably happened in another, but it suits their purpose better or whatever . . .

Lynn: It would be like actually transcribing the way people speak into dialogue. You would never write dialogue that mimics the way people speak; it would be boring and wretched. You're creating the illusion of reality.

McEwan: Exactly. I mean there have been cases, and it happened last year here in a big way; there was a Swiss writer who claimed to be a Holocaust survivor and wrote a very successful book. And I wonder why that writer didn't simply say it's a fiction, because I think it would have been a very successful fiction, because it was all imagined and rather brilliantly so. Somehow, that this really happened is of great consequence to readers. Briony Tallis, at the end of *Atonement*, having shown her hand on this, says you know there's always going to be a certain kind of reader who's going to say, "but what really happened?"

Lynn: But that's an astonishing moment, when she appears for the first time at the very end of the novel. My head snapped back with that. It's very, very interesting when, as you say, she pulls the curtain aside.

McEwan: There's one bit of that book I never published. I thought, "No, it's too tricksey," but sometimes I regret it . . . that you would turn the page and you would get, "About the Author." And it would say: Briony Tallis was born in 1922 in Surrey. Her father was a high up civil servant. Her first novel published in 1951, and I gave her some titles, very period titles. Her first novel was called *Soho Solstice*, and then various others, then her career dipped for a while, but then in the sixties she was taken up by the feminist Virago press and her novel *The Ducking Stool* was made into a film with Julie Christie. I say she died in July 2001—which is when I finished the novel. Then I chickened out. I thought, No—time for the tricks to end. It's got to actually end with acknowledgments to the Imperial War Museum and set the reader down on terra firma.

Lynn: Do you, as you're writing, ever think about your audience, whom you're writing for? Do you have an ideal reader in mind or are you at the point of your career where you just don't much care, that you're writing what you need to write?

McEwan: I have a kind of being, not really a reader, a kind of entity whose dominant disposition is utter skepticism. And this being wears a constant snarl, and is always muttering, "Come off it, you're never going to get away with that," or "This is feeble." It's all the hostile reviews or reviewers that I've ever had in my life. And it's quite a useful being. But as for readers, readers are too diverse and the thing that we all learn about contemporary literature is that there are no standards; there are no common standards of taste. You can get two perfectly intelligent, widely read people in the room who've read the same book, and one thinks it's a disgrace from one end to the other, and the other thinks it's a masterpiece. How is it that we don't have a common view of what even constitutes a good sentence? There's nothing, our feet can't touch the ground on this, and it's no good to try and sort it out by voting—these sorts of lists that you get in newspapers.

Lynn: Oh, but they are popular those lists.

McEwan: Maybe the lists are our desperate plea for some certainty, given that we just don't know what a good book is or we can't agree on what a good book is. It decimates me every time the Booker Prize comes around, what's on it, what's off it, you know, outrage, delight, someone says it's a master work, someone says it's a piece of crap. How is it we have not taught ourselves in university courses the elements of a good book? It's fine about the past, we can say in a letter, a few hundred funerals go by, and we can begin to build a consensus. But what follows from that is, it is impossible to constitute a reader in your head, except a strange, skeptical, critical, un-impressed one that I have who makes me take things out, generally. It's not about putting things in; it really makes me take things out.

Lynn: You touch on an interesting quandary. Updike, for example, for all his high acclaim, has never made a lot of money with his novels. His sales have always been fairly modest. You're incredibly well thought of—no, that's not the right word—you have sold many, many books on both sides of the Atlantic. Do you have any ambivalence about that or are you just thoroughly pleased?

McEwan: No, I have no ambivalence about it. I think I represent the standard author in that, you know—I would like more readers. It's a sort of colonizing instinct. For a long time I have thought that the novel, not in its modernist form, but in its nineteenth-century form, is a popular art form, it's a demotic one. It should reach large numbers of people and there's nothing shameful about it . . .

Lynn: And that's the irony, that someone like Dickens could aspire to the highest literary qualities as well as try and reach as broad an audience as possible. But in the twentieth century that was thought of as somehow soiling.

McEwan: It was modernism that promoted the notion of the artist as a sort of severe high priest who belonged to a small elite and was not going to ever have his pages dirtied and grubbied by the hoi polloi. I think it was a nonsensical view. Writers like Virginia Woolf saying, "Character is now dead," helped push the novel down some very fruitless impasses. And although I think in the United States, literature, fiction, largely bypassed all the problems posed for it by modernism, in continental Europe there was a long fading off through the fifties, sixties, and seventies of authors still writing novels that never really engaged the world in the way that, say, Saul Bellow could. When I was researching *The Innocent*, set in Berlin during the cold war, I spent good time in Berlin, walking and cycling all around the perimeter, walking the whole length of the wall with a good German friend. And I remember asking among my German friends, "Well, where are the good contemporary novels on the German wall, on the Berlin wall?" And they said, there's Peter Schneider's *The Wall Jumper*, but no, there's nothing, because it's not a subject for novelists, it's a subject for journalists. And you got a sense that they were still in this aesthetic, that the proper business of the novelist was to write about an alienated figure in a hotel room in an unnamed city staring at the wall, waiting for the appearance of another unnamed character in order to accomplish some unnamed pursuit.

Lynn: So you're not a fan of Beckett?

McEwan: Not of the later Beckett, I'm afraid I'm not, and I think what would Roth, Updike, Bellow, just to take the obvious three, have done had they been Berliners? . . . They wouldn't have ignored that wall.

Lynn: No, in fact they were just who I was thinking of as you were making that description. I was thinking that the American realist novel, even someone like Toni Morrison, really is there as well.

McEwan: I think the wall did not find its literature, I hope it does in retrospect. I mean part of the problem too, was, the wall was a fantastic shaming monument to the dreams of the left or of Soviet Communism. And it was odd that so many people, so many writers on the left felt that if they were going to condemn the wall in the madness of polarizing thought, people would think they were right wing, working for the CIA. To call the Berlin wall a monstrosity was what American presidents were doing, so it couldn't be right. As Orwell says, it's a terrible thing that if your enemy says something, it becomes an untruth. If your enemy points to a fact and you therefore are forced to think it's an untruth, that is a terrible, terrible mind-set to get into.

Lynn: So if you're not an heir to the modern novel or the modernist novel of the twentieth century, whom do you look back to as a kind of literary mentor in the sense of someone that you would like to be seen as following in the steps of?

McEwan: I'd have to qualify what you say, because *Atonement* could not have been written without all the experiments in fiction and reflections on point of view. And tricks with those and that sense drawn from modernism and postmodernism of having other writing, other texts, the spirits of other writers moving through your pages as if they, too, were as much a part of the real world as forests and cities and oceans. I feel myself to be absolutely not someone, as it were, trying to write Mozart symphonies in the time of Stockhausen. But, I do think that the nineteenth century invented for us some extraordinary things and we'd be crazy to turn our backs on them. And one is the notion of character. We run narratives about other people in our real lives, we make characters of them, necessarily, because it helps us to guess what they might do next. Intention is very much bound up with the notion of character, the sort of person who might do this or that. It's all part of the way in which we instinctively judge other people's behavior and see ourselves reflected back in their own view of us. So I think the nineteenth century formalized this for us, and the creation of character and the mapping out of other minds and the invitation to the reader to step into those other minds seems to me very much the central project of exploring our condition. So it is connected with what was achieved by Jane Austen or Balzac or Flaubert or Dickens. But now it's become much more complicated, we can't simply take a point of view and omniscience for granted and there's a kind of innocence that's lost there. But still I think, people do hunger for the complete immersion in a fictional world that seems real. We still have that.

Lynn: I think that's a lovely place to end the conversation. Thanks so much for speaking with me today.
McEwan: Great pleasure, David.

Naming What Is There: Ian McEwan in Conversation with David Remnick

David Remnick/2007

From the *New Yorker* Festival, 6 October 2007. Reprinted by permission of the *New Yorker*.

David Remnick: We are extremely lucky to have the last minute addition of Ian McEwan who was good enough to wedge the *New Yorker* Festival into his schedule. Ian, I suspect that we have here maybe more than one or two potential writers who would like to get a sense of how you become . . . *you*. You were not born in the midst of literary London, and your education is not to the one or two fully-approved universities of the elite. You come from a military family and a town called . . . ?
McEwan: Aldershot.

Remnick: You went off to boarding school at a very young age with dreams of doing what?
McEwan: My parents were living in North Africa at the time. My father was a soldier, as you say. I was sent off to a state-run boarding school, mostly for working class lads from broken homes in central London, and the school also took a handful of kids from the military. It looked like a grand, English private school, with a Palladian building, beautiful grounds, and a wide, tidal river winding through the distance. It was a meritocratic experiment of the old Left, the old London County Council, and the experience freed me somewhat from the niggling irritations of English class. These were nearly all working class lads, most of whom then went to university. Very untypical in those days. Remember that this was the sixties when only something like seven percent of the population went to college. In 1967 I went to the University of Sussex, a brand new university, again also slightly dislodging me from the usual educational progress of English writers. Sussex had decided to "redraw the map of learning," as it famously described it.

Remnick: This is at a "red brick university," I suppose?
McEwan: No, the red bricks were slightly older. This is what's called a "plate glass university."

Remnick: What does that mean?
McEwan: It was nicknamed by the press, "Balliol by the Sea." It took many of its best teachers from Oxford and it intended to redefine the boundaries of the traditional subjects. So, on arriving, all kids in the humanities were required to read three central texts. One was Tawney's *Religion and the Rise of Capitalism*, the second was Jacob Burckhardt's book on the Renaissance, and the third was the Turner thesis on the expansion of the American West. It considered historiography—not simply the history, but the study of the means and processes of writing history—fundamental to all discussion of either literature or history or anything else in the humanities. It was very stimulating.

Remnick: What did you have in mind to be or become? What were you like when you were sixteen years old?
McEwan: Sixteen? I had Buddy Holly glasses . . . I think I resembled a Margarita pizza with a fair display of acne. And I had fallen in love with English literature. I had a Leavisite English teacher who inculcated me with the notion that studying literature was a form of priesthood and that the noblest thing in life would be to teach English literature at a university.

Remnick: How much had the mid-sixties taken hold of you?
McEwan: I loved blues and rock-n-roll and jazz. I also listened to a lot of classical music. Music swept through me.

Remnick: What was the study of literature like for you? The "becoming" as a reader?
McEwan: In my early teens I read contemporary literature—Iris Murdoch, Graham Greene, John Masters, John Fowles. Then, from sixteen on, well, there was the canon . . . No one disputed it much at the time. There were all the usual suspects: the Elizabethan poets, Shakespeare, obviously, the metaphysical poets, through Dryden and Milton. I was rather obsessed by Swift when I was still at boarding school. Then Wordsworth, Keats—all the usual stuff. I also got my first taste of Yeats, Eliot, and Auden. I think I was reasonably well read by the time I got to Sussex. There I was taken by Richardson,

Sterne, Fielding. So, all white, all male, but I didn't notice. At university no one discussed contemporary literature, but we read a lot.

Remnick: Is this exactly what kids *didn't* get years and years later?
McEwan: Until recently, the air, the life was choked out of literary studies by theory. You'd visit a campus and find that the kids had not read much at all in terms of the primary sources. And that was sad, it was joyless. The orthodoxy was you could not read the poets and novelists until you'd learned how to "read," until you had read up on the theory. Of course, that immediately invoked an infinite regression, because in what language were you going to read the theory? That's all beginning to fade, thank god. I was in Princeton yesterday, and kids seemed to be much more engaged by the literature itself rather than pronouncements about it. This was a twenty-five year madness that swept through the academic culture. Mercifully, it was unsustainable.

Remnick: When did you start writing or start thinking of writing? What was the impulse to write as an undergraduate?
McEwan: Well, because of this redrawn map of learning, by my second year I was immersed in Kafka and Thomas Mann and Robert Musil, even though my subject was meant to be English literature and French. I began to feel such a new excitement about the writing. I thought of it rather as a conversation between great minds. I thought that, in a humble way, I could join in. Anyone could. I began to think that I didn't really want to have a job in a university now that I could see what a university was like—not as thrilling as I thought. Still a source of great pleasure to me, but it wasn't quite like my ideal—a monastery on a craggy mountain in an eighteenth-century gothic engraving.

Remnick: Oh, the fact was that it was *too* exciting, not that it wasn't exciting enough?
McEwan: No, it seemed rather humdrum, you know—there were the professors, here was the notice board outside their offices, there was the car park. I began to think that I would like to write short stories, and then I had a curious stroke of luck. I came to the end of my degree with no idea of what I wanted to do. I hitchhiked around Italy with my girlfriend, came back, and found that the government had given me money to go off and do a Masters degree. But I hadn't chosen a course. I saw in a prospectus that at the University of East Anglia you could do a general literature MA, but that for just one part—I think it was 1/16 or 1/12 of this MA—you could submit some

fiction. So I phoned the place up. Malcolm Bradbury actually answered the phone—in those days there weren't so many people on the planet. It was like that Ry Cooder song: "Call Him up and tell Him what you want . . ."

I spent a very productive year at UEA. Malcolm had told me when I met him that they had opened up this tiny concession from the university administration only with a great deal of effort. In Britain then creative writing at universities was not generally accepted. I was allowed to submit some fiction in place of one essay. That was all it was. I was the only one taking that option. There was no course. I didn't ever attend a creative writing course. I think I met Malcolm Bradbury maybe on two or three occasions for five or ten minutes in the whole of the year.

Remnick: So it wasn't the sort of American style workshop?
McEwan: No. We were writing essays on *Anna Karenina* and *Middlemarch* and we were looking at theory. Theory in those days was looking at Bergson and reading Henry James on the art of fiction. We also read a great deal of contemporary American fiction. It was my first encounter with Mailer, Bellow, Roth, and Updike.

Remnick: Now, the scene—you've talked about this before, but I want to clarify—the contemporary literary scene in Britain and the books that were coming out were utterly unexciting to you.
McEwan: Very dull.

Remnick: How would you sketch out what it was at that time?
McEwan: Well, the pastiche would be that it was about a slowly dissolving marriage somewhere near Hampstead . . .

Remnick: [Laughs]. Somebody very sad in a bed sit . . .
McEwan: Yes, afterwards, it was usually the guy that got the bed sit.

Remnick: Right.
McEwan: Written with no formal ambition, in a sort of social documentary style of an unreflective realism.

Remnick: What had happened? How had English literature, which had been what we know it to be, gotten in this kind of condition by the fifties, sixties, and early seventies?

McEwan: I don't know. It's a kind of weariness, really. There were some notable exceptions. Let's not forget that Golding was writing at that point and he was a law unto himself.

Remnick: Kingsley Amis was someone you were interested in at that time?
McEwan: No, I wasn't at the time, actually. I didn't get those jokes. Later I really came to like him, but at the time it made me impatient. It all seemed so . . . fussy, and smothered in the writer's private likes and dislikes—it oppressed me.

Remnick: And you weren't keyed into it socially . . .
McEwan: No. Socially, as I said, my background had made me rather indifferent to the maneuvers and textures and comedy of class. I preferred the dissociated fictions of Kafka. I thought it was extraordinary to have a character wake up in a room and the reader is unaware what year it is, what city this is, what language, what culture. At the time this seemed to me a liberation. Now I take a completely opposite view. I think that the lifeblood of the novel is, in fact, much to do with the specific, the local, the actual, the naming of things.

But running against this preference for the existential, I was fascinated to be reading the Americans I've mentioned. Writers who were free of the shadows of modernism, though they had learned all its lessons. They were formally ambitious; they seemed to have made their peace with the nineteenth-century novel and seemed assured that they could continue some of its central traditions. If you'd gone to Germany and France in the sixties, seventies, and eighties you did *not* get writers producing for you Paris and Berlin in the way that Bellow could do Chicago or Roth could do New Jersey or Updike could do small town life of the North-East. These were bustling, rich novels, often with a kind of hilarious sexual freedom.

Remnick: Did you go in for conscious imitation in these first stories?
McEwan: That's what I think is valuable about the short story. That's the advice I would give to any young writer. Do *not* sit down and write a nine-hundred-page novel, because you're likely to write a bad one and waste five years of your life. Waste three weeks writing your homage to Philip Roth, and if it's a terrible homage, then . . .

Remnick: It's just three weeks. Who were you writing in conscious imitation? Those Americans?

McEwan: I did. I wrote a *very* conscious homage to Roth in a story called "Homemade," which is in *First Love, Last Rites.*

Remnick: In which there is an incest moment with the ten-year-old sister.
McEwan: Well, I had to sort of move things on a bit . . .

Remnick: [Laughs]. And how did Malcolm Bradbury react when he got a story like that? It probably wasn't the usual thing.
McEwan: He would say, "Well, I read the story about the boy having sex with his sister. When can I have the next one?" It was just like that.

Remnick: That's very encouraging.
McEwan: Yes, and he'd say, "Keep going. Yup, yup. So, what's the next one about?" And I'd say, "Well, it's about a boy who murders a . . ." And he'd say, "Well, fine. I want it by November the 3rd."

Remnick: [Laughs]. So he was a very engaged teacher in that way.
McEwan: Yes.

Remnick: And took full credit for your rise.
McEwan: Well, one of the difficulties now is that I'm claimed as the product of a writing course. I don't think any writer—maybe in the States it's different—but I don't think writers generally like to feel that they're the product of a course.

Remnick: At the *New Yorker,* where we receive hundreds of stories in a given week, a lot of those envelopes are coming from the University of Iowa and Columbia and places like that. It's where stories come from. Stories happen from younger people and then for the most part stop. In your career that's mostly the case too, isn't it? You wrote stories in the beginning of a career and then you tired of it. Why?
McEwan: I find beginning any fiction difficult. I have to really write my way, stumble my way into anything I'm doing. To do it ten times for a book, as opposed to once, there's the difference. Maybe you're right, it's the form for youth, but it's the form for old age, too. Great stamina is needed to write a novel—it feels like physical effort. Perhaps stories will be the *last* thing I do.

Remnick: But you notice in some of the Americans that you just talked about, the novels in their sixties and seventies started to get shorter and shorter. Mahfouz, the great Arabic writer, who had written these massive novels about Cairo, toward the end of his life, when he was in his eighties and nineties, he was writing little dreams—they weren't even stories, just paragraphs. That holding it all in the head became the thing that was so hard.

McEwan: Look at Bellow—*Ravelstein* and those other small novels. Also, just that weight of organization of a massive amount of material becomes burdensome.

Remnick: What were some of the sentimental events that formed you as a young writer? What family events, family relations, or other things went into getting you started as a writer?

McEwan: Well, by the seventies the sixties had arrived in the small Norfolk town of Norwich where I was. I got swept up by this wave of friendliness and freedom. I'd always been a rather conventional boy—and now I found myself striding through the English countryside with my head full of mescaline and thinking, "If there isn't a god, well then there jolly well ought to be." Then I met up with two American pals and we went to Amsterdam and bought a microbus and drove it to Munich and then to Istanbul and then to Tehran and then to Kabul after a long stay in Kandahar and Herat.

Remnick: What did you see there? What struck you in Afghanistan?

McEwan: Afghanistan was in a blessed hiatus, before all the disasters that have befallen it since. An intensely poor country with some of the most beautiful buildings, mosques, I've ever seen in my life. Harsh scenery and a Homeric form of hospitality. People, however poor, invite you into their houses and lay out their best food. We ended up in Peshawar, having spent some time along the Khyber Pass—really frightening area actually. The Pashtun tribes were there. Stateless pride—they were controlled by nobody and never would be—and there they still are. We couldn't get to India because of a war brewing between India and Pakistan at that time, then we turned back. I was about nine months on the road and there came a point bouncing around these desert tracks coming westwards at ten miles when I thought, "What I really long for is a white-washed, small, bare room in a house in a quiet city under a very gray sky . . . and I want to get back to writing."

Remnick: Did you go about acquiring it?

McEwan: Yes, I did. I never had an idle thought like that and acted on it so clearly. I went back to Norwich, found just that room, and started writing much more seriously than I had. I found a benefactor in one of the great American editors, Ted Solotaroff, who ran *The American Review*, which then became *The New American Review*. Published every three or four months as a book.

Remnick: This is where Roth was publishing excerpts.

McEwan: The most exciting moment in my writing career was when I got my new issue of *The New American Review*—it was shocking pink, the cover, and in white letters it said, "Philip Roth, Susan Sontag, Ian McEwan" in a row.

Remnick: In the same typeface . . .

McEwan: In the same typeface, yes. It was 1973. I was twenty four. I had not published a book at that point. Nothing since—no prize, nothing—has given me such a thrill.

Remnick: In the *Paris Review* you describe your own style, your own approach in the first ten years of writing as "formally simple and linear short fiction, claustrophobic, desocialized, sexually strange, dark." The books we are talking about—*The Cement Garden, First Love, Last Rites*, and *Comfort of Strangers*—what was the conscious project to create that kind of tone, such that the journalistic handle many years later became "Ian Macabre"? In *The Cement Garden* it's a kind of *Lord of the Flies* situation in which the kids live in this brutal and sexualized, parentless world, and the macabre really does enter. What were you after?

McEwan: I used to be accused of writing to shock, and I denied it vehemently, but looking back, I think I did want bold colors—perhaps this was a young man's insistence on being noticed. And I'd led a very quiet life. I was a shy child and pretty shy teenager—at an all-boys school, not coming to sex until seventeen or eighteen, never having made my own choices in life. So, when I started writing it was as if an explosion went off in my head. I had an exaggerated desire to be vivid, loud, dark, whatever you want to call it. But, of course, these things must have had roots and, without actually allowing myself to be psychoanalyzed on stage, I can't really give a full answer to "Where do ideas come from," that chestnut of a question. It's very hard to answer.

Remnick: It must be an interesting process for you at fifty-nine to look back and see, not only the man you were in your twenties and thirties, but the writer you were. Does it feel terribly distant? Does it feel *you*?

McEwan: No, it doesn't feel far away. I do understand it. I certainly understand the narrow ambition. I think it connects with that tentativeness I described in my mother. I thought I could only write short stories, not novels, that I could only write about very tight, claustrophobic situations. I learned only slowly to spread out. I didn't really *dare* write a novel until the late seventies. I spent *years* messing around with short stories, and even when I wrote my first two novels they owed their structure more to the short story than to the great sprawling things that I loved in other writers.

Remnick: More like blown out stories.

McEwan: Yes, they ran from A to B. There were no subplots. They moved through time in a completely linear way.

Remnick: Describe this hinge moment, beginning with *The Child in Time*, which I think you would agree is a really important moment in your career and path as a writer. The great novel about, for those who haven't read it, a mature man who goes into a store with his child and comes out without the child—the child is lost—and the effect this has on his life, his wife's life, and the paths they take.

McEwan: Well, I took a break from writing fiction. By the time I'd finished *The Comfort of Strangers* I felt I'd really written myself into a corner and that I had to do something else. I started writing for television. I wrote a TV film with Richard Eyre.

Remnick: To just get away? Or for mercenary reasons?

McEwan: No, to get away. I couldn't see any future in the kind of fiction that I was writing. I had to stop and do something entirely different. I wrote a play set in the early stages of the Second World War about a young woman who gets caught up in the Bletchley code breaking operation. I then got involved with a friend, Michael Berkeley, a composer, and together we wrote an oratorio performed by the London Symphony Orchestra and Choir. That was an exciting process. It was concerned with nuclear weapons, which was a great worry in the early eighties. The notion that the superpowers could conduct a limited war using Europe as their battleground was one that was terrifying us in Europe. And then I wrote a movie with Richard Eyre called

The Ploughman's Lunch, a political movie set against the background of the Falklands War.

After those three projects, I felt renewed, and more engaged. I was no longer interested in this existential fiction which refused to locate itself in place and time and, I suppose not for nothing, I wrote a novel about time itself and all its manifestations, how we experience it subjectively, how it's described in quantum mechanics as against Newtonian physics, how certainties and uncertainties in all this are reflected in our different moments of being. The loss of a child is perhaps the worst thing that can happen to anybody. I don't know if it's played in the press here—the disappearance of Madeline McCann, a little girl snatched from her parents in Portugal. It brought it back to me, the fact that here is an event that probably will have no closure for these parents, and they will live in a kind of hell of imagining.

Remnick: And accusation, too.

McEwan: Yes, the accusations are without base. So that really was a turning point for me, to come back after a long break. I also wrote journalism and that too helped me out of these tight circles.

Remnick: Has the process of writing a novel changed for you radically? Beginning and sort of screwing around with little bits until you find your way? Has it been mostly the same since you came into this more mature period of your writing life?

McEwan: No, I am terrible at beginnings. I never know what I want really. I think there's something lurking there, but I can't quite see it. I can spend a year just writing out opening paragraphs of things. I have a book of plots— loads of unused plots if anyone is looking . . .

Remnick: How much each?

McEwan: $4.99. And then suddenly I will turn up something that makes me think that there's something in there for me, and I don't even dare tell myself what it is.

Remnick: Take *The Child in Time*—how did you stumble in there?

McEwan: That's rather too long to tell . . . A good example would be *Atonement*. Well into a year of pursuing various little things and then, one morning, I wrote a paragraph about a young woman coming in to an Adam style sitting room in a country house with a bunch of wild flowers that she's just picked and she goes across this room—there's morning sunlight, there's a harpsichord that no one ever plays—and she finds a very expensive vase, a Meissen vase. And, rather than put water in the vase first, she puts the flowers in the vase and then thinks about where she's going to get the water from. Something about the room, the woman, the wildflowers in a precious vase—I knew that I'd finally started a novel, but I didn't know what on earth it was.

Remnick: In the previous days, the previous months, you hadn't had in mind the setting in time, the milieu? The day before you could be writing about a forest in Brazil and then two days before could be the Vietnam War or something?

McEwan: Yes, I'd thought of how someone might commit a mistake—a mistake that might be confused with a crime—and suffer for it for a lifetime. For a while I thought it might be a story of someone who in their youth shoplifts something from a store and, from then on, the consequences ripple outwards and shape that whole life.

Remnick: Like the forged coupon or something in Tolstoy?

McEwan: Yes, exactly that. But I wasn't thinking of *that* when I was writing of this. Then I left that paragraph—it was about six hundred words—for about three months. I couldn't quite bring myself to continue it, because I thought I'd make a mistake. Then I sat down to it and I wrote what is now the second chapter of *Atonement*. At that point, I have to confess, I thought that I had stumbled into a science fiction story . . . a future in which wealthy elites were tired of technology and preferred to live the lives of the landed gentry in the late eighteenth-century. And that it was only the middle management and blue collar people who took full advantage of technology and had implants in their brains that gave them direct access to the Internet. So when Cecilia takes these flowers out into the garden, the young man that she both wants to talk to and doesn't want to talk to has got a shaved head with a small antenna on it.

Remnick: You want $4.99 for *that*?

McEwan: Well, you could have had that one for $3.00. I realized that at best this was a second-rate short story, and by the time I had finished that chapter it was 1935, and all I had to do now, I realized, was to give this young woman a younger sister. So I wrote what is now the *first* chapter of the story.

And by the time I'd got *that* down, Briony had cousins from the north, the little play "The Trials of Arabella." I thought, "Ah! *She's* my shoplifting story. She's going to commit the mistake." It all suddenly just rolled out in front of me. I saw it—I saw Dunkirk, I saw St. Thomas' hospital in 1940, and I saw an old woman at the end of her life who will tell the reader that she has spent a lifetime atoning for her error by writing various drafts and the novel that the reader will read will be the final draft. I only had seven thousand words, but I could see all this ahead of me and, like a lot of writers at this point, I thought, "I must make sure I don't get run over by a bus before I get this down."

Remnick: And then it comes quickly?
McEwan: Yes, fairly quickly.

Remnick: And that means what?
McEwan: Two years.

Remnick: Do you wish you could do it otherwise?
McEwan: Yes. I really wish I could be lying in the bath thinking, "Ah! The whole thing."

Remnick: And when you go over this process with your friends who are in the same racket, do they describe a similar process?
McEwan: No. Martin, for example, says, "I've got this great idea for a novel," and he tells me what his great idea is.

Remnick: At a certain point, history comes into your writing. With *The Innocent* and, in a very different way and in a later time, history comes pouring in to the seemingly satisfied domestic life of a neurosurgeon in London the day of the anti-Iraq War demonstrations leading up to the war.
McEwan: Well yes, *The Innocent* is a novel about the transfer of power from one empire to another. It's about a young British telephone engineer who gets called to Berlin to help in a project which was an actually existing Anglo-American tunnel into the Soviet sector—this was long before the wall was built. A two or three hundred yard long secret tunnel that went into their sector to tap into the telephone lines that connected East Berlin with Moscow. The tunnel was betrayed by an English spy called George Blake. It was one of a series of betrayals that made the Americans immensely distrustful of working with the British again. It was a perfect background for

a discussion of political power. The British still enfeebled by the Second World War, the depths of the Cold War, American power beginning to establish itself globally. The historical element was strange because the novel ends in . . . well, I was writing it in June 1989, the very last pages . . .

Remnick: Not long before the fall of the wall.

McEwan: Yes. The last couple of lines of the novel describe its hero much older now resolving to meet his former lover, the woman he knew in 1955. He wanted to meet her again in Berlin and stand and look at this wall before they pulled it down, which he knew was going to happen soon. And that was really fanciful. I had no idea that a few months later this wall *was* going to come down and that I *would* be celebrating with the crowds in Potsdamer Platz and at the Brandenburg Gate.

Remnick: Now, this bringing in history and reading up and research would have seemed to be, I would think, anathema to you as a younger writer.

McEwan: Exactly so. I was absorbed by an idea of the novel without being fully aware of it. Apart from Kafka, I was rather impressed by the existential qualities of Peter Handke. I'm not sure he's very much read these days, but I liked *The Goalie's Anxiety at the Penalty Kick* and *The Ride across Lake Constance*. Sometimes the aesthetics are invisible, and you're not fully aware of how they are selecting out, narrowing down the content. Ted Solotaroff wrote a wonderful essay called "Silence, Exile, and Cunning," about his attempts to become a writer. He thought that the proper subject for him as a poet was to write about the fall of Christian civilization, because his head was full of Eliot. Meanwhile, he was working in a bar in Manhattan frequented by mobsters. In the evenings he was in a rooming house in some stinking tenement where suicides and marital rows were going on all around. But there was only one subject for him—the collapse of Christian civilization, about which he had little to say. Years later he saw how he had this *amazing* material, the things he overheard in the bar as he was making margaritas for Cosa Nostra.

Remnick: There are writers who fight like hell to reject the notion that they use this bit of their life in their novels. You don't at all. You give an interview or write an article and say, "Well, I took . . ." Your mother, for example, when she was very ill with dementia toward the end of her life, and you used her, as it were, in *Saturday* when the doctor goes to visit his mother. In other words, you fess up. Do you think the other point of view is fussy and dishonest?

McEwan: No, no, not at all. In fact, *Saturday* is the only novel in which I've done this. I was moving from Oxford back to London after many years. I'd already decided I wanted to write a novel set in the present and about the present. I didn't realize how horribly interesting the present was about to become when I made this decision in the summer of 2001. I gave my hero my new house. I gave him one of my children. I explored my new neighborhood with him; the hospital where he worked was where I did all my research. I thought I'd let life around me flood in. As for my mother, I hoped the novel would be a memoir, a testimony to this process of slow disintegration. I had talked to her about it a great deal. What else? Yes, the squash games, everything . . . I just let it all pour in. And yet there were many things I gave Henry Perowne that were *not* mine—his loathing for literature . . . his views on politics are not entirely mine—sometimes mine exaggerated, sometimes the reverse of mine.

Remnick: So, view of politics being a kind of modest liberalism, an unsureness . . . ?
McEwan: Yes . . .

Remnick: There's a passage in *Saturday* . . .
McEwan: Henry Perowne is trapped in a traffic jam and looks across to a shop selling TVs—fifty different models, different screens all showing the same thing. [Reads from "In its window display are angled . . ." to "In neurosurgery he chose a safe and simple profession."][1]

Remnick: And how do you feel about that passage reading it several years on in the wake of disaster?
McEwan: Well, we made the wrong decision. I don't think there is anyone on the planet who . . .

Remnick: There's one . . . There's one.
McEwan: Well, if you were this powerful man, and you got up in the middle of the night and went into the Oval Office and there on the desk was a

1. McEwan, Ian. *Saturday*. London: Jonathan Cape, 2005. 140–141.

history reversal machine with a button that said "Rewind" and you could take the world back to, say, June 2002, and no one would know a thing, it's my sincere conviction that this man would press the button.

Remnick: I think you're right. Ian, I wonder as you look ahead as a writer what it is you feel you have to do, what you have to or want to get done—or do you want to write less? Does it mean less to you now? Does the obsession stay as heated as it was when you were thirty?

McEwan: Well, think of the career of Philip Roth. At the beginning of his sixties he stood at the start of a most extraordinary sequence of novels. He is a stern reminder that there's always work to be done, and that this work *can* be done. I feel I haven't yet written the novel that I really want to write. It's just beyond the edge of recognition.

Remnick: And when you think about that novel, it's a novel that you're thinking about a subject or a level?

McEwan: No, I'm thinking about a reader, an ideal, ghostly reader, and that reader can't turn away. And I'm not talking about suspense, I'm talking about how wonderful it would be to erupt into such clarity and precision in the naming of feeling or shifts of consciousness that the act of recognition in the reader would be too powerful to resist.

Remnick: Such as happens with what book for you, or what career and what moment in a life?

McEwan: If you ask me to name one moment in prose where I think this happens, I would say the last ten pages "The Dead" by James Joyce. When Gabriel and Gretta come back from the party and snow is falling, they go up to their hotel room. He thinks they're going to make love; she upset by a song she's heard sung at the end of the evening. She tells her husband that there was a man who loved her once, and he feels a quick flash of jealousy. But of course this is long in the past and that man was a seventeen-year-old boy dying of TB, Michael Furey. After weeping she falls asleep; he goes to the window and reflects that the aunts will soon be dead, soon he must make his own journey westward. The snow is falling on the "mutinous Shannon waves" and on the grave of Michael Furey. I don't think Joyce wrote anything more beautiful than the ending of "The Dead." But I don't think *anyone* wrote anything more . . .

Remnick: You pay it homage at the end of *Saturday*.

McEwan: I do. More than once have I raided it, as it were. But no one could better it. Here is one of the big questions, the biggest question there is—the nature of death or the fact of our mortality—played out within the beautifully observed threads of a marital spat, a bit of disappointment about sex, a sudden confession about a love. Gretta says, "He died for love of me . . ." Well, to write something, say, a quarter as good as that would be my ambition.

Remnick: Updike is very good on this subject. He's brutal about himself. Somebody asked him once, and he made no bones about it, "So, you're at age X and you look back—what's the lasting bit of you?" It's early days for you to even think about that, but when you look back at the books you've written, when do you smile with at least some satisfaction? Where are you pleased?

McEwan: It's bits and pieces, I suppose. I liked the way the Dunkirk section of *Atonement* worked out, partly because it was a tribute to my father, who was there. There are certain passages of *The Innocent* that I like. There are some reflections on death in *Amsterdam* that I might return to and expand in some way, I don't know. But there's always a sense—I think writers *have* to have this sense—that they have not found the perfect thing. It's something to do with how you could bring together the metaphysical, but do it lightly, or intimately and warmly in a recognizable personal moment.

Remnick: I have one last question, and then we're going to open it to the audience. I wonder whether you're pessimistic or optimistic about moving forward in terms of literary culture. In the age of not one screen but three consuming screens, beeping blackberries, and all the increasing distractions, how confident are you that younger people will put themselves in front of an enigmatic text two or three nights a week with the phone quieted and other distractions ignored?

McEwan: I'd like to think that the technology, the means of delivery, is secondary. If you can download *Middlemarch* into a little slab and take it on holiday, that won't make the difference. Someone is still affecting your mental state by means of symbols—a neurological miracle, that these marks can generate such scenes in your head. It's a form of telepathy, a writer transferring thoughts into someone else's head. And we'll always crave these re-enactments. We're a gossipy species; we're curious about each other, and literature is in a sense a higher form of gossip. Think of just one aspect of the novel—dialogue interspersed with analysis of a character's inner thoughts. Where else in life can you get this, except in gossip? "Guess what he said next?" And "What I was thinking was . . ." For a troublesome, squawky, social animal, such as we are, we'll need this mutual scrutiny. The novel has survived so far, despite the gloomy predictions. I think it will hang on in there. I mean, it's refused to die yet, even faintly, so I live in hope.

Audience: Mr. Remnick asked you a question about looking back on your works that give you moments like the end of "The Dead." There is a section in *Saturday* that I love that I thought you might have mentioned—where you've given your neurosurgeon, toward the end of the book, his joy in his work. That section of what work does for him—he compares it to sex; he compares it to the love of his children, the smell of his children, and the utter joy that his work does for him. You said you gave the neurosurgeon parts of yourself and parts not, and I couldn't help thinking when I read that section, "That must be how he feels about writing."

McEwan: Well, it's interesting this, because sometimes you come across an experience for which the language lacks a word. You might find that this word exists in another language. I was informed by a classics professor yesterday at Princeton—we were talking about this very thing—that the word does exist. It's called *energia*. That is that complete loss of self in an absorbing task. Now, the trouble is that the word *energy* is already firmly staked out for us in English. Psychologists have suggested the word *flow*. I don't think that quite does it. There is a form of intense human happiness, often not recognized in the moment, that comes from losing yourself in something difficult. You cease to be aware of time; you cease to be aware of self; you experience no particular emotion because you're inseparable from the task. And sometimes it can happen with something as complex as writing, but it can also come with the making of a good meal. A game of tennis, a team game can do it too—you forget that you exist, everything goes except the matter in hand. It's bliss. I wish it happened to me in writing more often. I think it happens maybe a few times a year. But, of course, I'm pleased that passage meant something to you.

Remnick: So most days feel like laying pipe, and the rare moment is as you've described?

McEwan: Yes. It's a form of grace. The words flow and you are completely at one with the thing it is you're describing. You don't even pause to pursue a word—it's simply there. For me it's never lasted more than a half an hour. It's really not only to do with writing, as I say. It's to do with a form of absorption and difficultly in which we then feel as if we've finally justified our existence with the gift of consciousness . . . *this*. Happiness isn't the word. It's beyond emotion, really. Often only known in retrospect, too. It's a great subject.

Audience: In *Saturday* you thanked the neurosurgeon you studied for the text. I was wondering how much time you spent with him and how you sublimated yourself into his craft?

McEwan: I spent two years with the neurosurgeon, Neil Kitchen, who at that time was head of neurosurgery at the National Hospital, which is the main neurosurgery hospital in the UK, and where neurology had its beginnings. First of all, I used to meet him and talk with him, and addressed the reading list he gave me on the anatomy of the brain and various pathologies. And then I started attending his theatre mornings. I used to scrub up and gown up and just stand around—he'd often let me stand at his side while he worked. He was very generous with all this. He let me into the very heart of his operations and many procedures I saw more than once. I saw quite a few MCA (middle cerebral artery) aneurisms. I began to think I could even *do* one . . . In fact, on one occasion he *was* clipping an MCA aneurism and I was standing to one side in my gown—by the way, the guys, all the surgeons, have a V-neck here, and you have to get your chest hair to curl over it, if you're going to be a properly cool surgeon—so I was there with my one chest hair curling free and into the operating theatre came two fifth-year students—they were allowed in to watch neurosurgery. They came over very quietly and said to me in a respectful whisper, "Excuse us, doctor, could you explain what's going on here?" So I took them to the light box and I said, "Well, yes, we're making an infratentorial route here . . . the aneurism, as you can see here, is on the CT scan. We'll be taking the classic route . . ."

Remnick: The lawsuit would be fantastic!

McEwan: And they thanked me and watched for awhile and left. I always wondered how they did in their exams.

Audience: I'm always impressed with how you explore the intricacies of relationships. My question is about *The Child in Time*, particularly, because I thought you were able to get into the woman's point of view very insightfully. I wondered what insight you could provide about that.

McEwan: Well, I've *known* some women . . . We used to have this debate in England—I hope you didn't have this mad discussion here—in the eighties a wing of the feminist movement insisted that men mustn't or can't write women. It was never mandated the other way around, I noticed. Fortunately, that's died. I mean, what we have in common is too overwhelming, and anyway who'd want to write or read a novel that only had men in it? Well, you'd read Hemingway, I guess. Aren't novelists supposed to be professional empathizers? It's all down to observation, isn't it? And there's a vast sea of misery and comedy and pleasure and pain to be observed in the ways in which men and women misunderstand each other. Young Briony in *Atonement* discovers after she's written many fairy stories that you can write fiction in which no one has to be bad, and yet bad things can still happen. *On Chesil Beach* is in part about how two well-intentioned, loving, but innocent young people could cause each other such pain. And there's a comedy in that, too. One of the pleasures, I suppose, of being a novelist is to play god and watch it. Make it happen and watch it.

Audience: I wondered how you came to the subject of *On Chesil Beach*. It's relatively small for you, I thought, but perfect and jewel-like. I found it kind of Chekhovian, as well.

McEwan: It's odd that you should mention Chekhov, because I had been rereading the stories. The honeymoon night that fails seemed to me an obvious subject for a short novel. I asked around since writing it who has done this. Well, I've now got a Joyce Carol Oates novel in my suitcase called *The Falls*, which is about a honeymoon during which a man throws himself over the waterfall. There is a Maupassant story which I've never read called "Une vie." So my reading list is going to extend itself. The setting seemed a gift—an enclosed and intimate situation, which is also deeply connected socially.

How did I start it? In just the way I described to David. I didn't know what I was doing. I fumbled around. And then, suddenly, I found myself writing the first sentence, more or less as it appears in the published version. "They were young, educated, and both virgins on this, their wedding night, and they lived in a time when conversation about sexual difficulties was plainly impossible. But it is never easy." As I saw it, these lines offered a whole story, waiting to be unpacked. After writing a page or two, I wrote notes, not about the novel in terms of what would happen—but about the implied narrator, about the tone. I used words like, wry, tolerant, forgiving, and all-seeing. For the first two or three months, that's all I did—write and re-write the first chapter trying to get that tone. When that was done, it was relatively straightforward.

Remnick: A last question . . .

Audience: This is a continuation of the previous question. I heard you read *On Chesil Beach* on CD and realized as I lay there at five o'clock in the morning listening to you that this was a way I could understand my own life and a conversation I was unable to have in 1963. It shattered my life, and it's never been the same since. I've never thought of it as something that other people knew about. So I wondered whether others have spoken to you of a similar experience and whether you yourself have ever experienced anything like that?

McEwan: When you say experience, do you mean your own of a disastrous honeymoon or are you referring to something within the novel specifically?

Audience: The idea that you live in a time that doesn't give you the language to speak about something crucial with someone you love.

McEwan: It's odd that, isn't it? You can be afflicted by some mental torment, and if you haven't got the means or entitlement or, as you say, the language to shape it, to describe it to yourself, all you can do is suffer—and often not be fully aware that you *are* suffering. Children in particular can suffer in this way. This is why language is such a precious tool. And this is really what that short novel was about.

Remnick: Ian, thank you so much for coming. And thank you all.

Dual Purpose

Ashutosh Khandekar/2008

From *BBC Music Magazine* 16.9 (May 2008): 38–41. Reprinted by permission of publisher.

Michael Berkeley and Ian McEwan have been friends for almost thirty years. Although both highly successful creative artists, they have only collaborated once before, twenty-six years ago, on an anti-war oratorio *Or Shall We Die?*, which will be performed in Cardiff this May as part of the composer's sixtieth birthday celebrations. The two are preparing to unveil their new opera, *For You*, to be given its world premiere by Music Theatre Wales at the Hay Festival. This will be Berkeley's third opera, following in the wake of *Baa-baa Black Sheep*, based on a novella by Rudyard Kipling, and *Jane Eyre*. McEwan, meanwhile, is making his first foray into opera, though *For You* picks up several themes—secrets, lies, sex, and obsessive love—that will be familiar from his hugely popular novels which include *Enduring Love*, *Atonement*, and recently, *On Chesil Beach*.

The bittersweet plot of *For You* follows the damaged lives of an ageing composer/conductor, Charles, and his wife Antonia as their marriage unravels through a series of betrayals. The couple are embroiled in a fateful *ménage à six* involving a nubile horn player, a doctor, a Polish maid, and a gay secretary. The opera's title is ironic in that all the characters act more out of selfishness than generosity. The plot has its comic moments that border on bedroom farce; but there are also poignant shifts to a much darker, tragic mood. The work ends with Charles pouring out his soul as he conducts his latest symphony, the climax of his creative career.

Ash Khandekar: Charles, the opera's principal character, is a composer, which is bound to seem self-referential in the case of Michael. Was it difficult to write music for a character who himself writes music?

Michael Berkeley: I don't think you feel it's self-referential when you hear the music. I've kept my own musical voice rather separate from Charles's though inevitably the two get entangled occasionally. For example, there's a scene where Charles looks back nostalgically at the music of his youth, and I've quoted from my own youthful oboe concerto at that moment. The point is that I had to create a musical voice for Charles that says something about his character and that fits into the organic whole of the opera.

Ian McEwan: I found it irresistible to write a story about a composer, because I find the act of composing such an interesting metaphor for creativity in its purest sense. Having said that, the main character is nothing like Michael and I didn't really ask Michael what it was like to be a composer. I wanted to explore the world of a creative obsessive and the way people are mesmerised by the power of that sort of genius.

Khandekar: The language of the libretto is very terse and contemporary, but it has clear references to the Mozart/Da Ponte operas in its interaction between servants and masters, in the twists and turns of the plot, and in its rather cynical yet tender exploration of love.

Berkeley: Yes, there's a lot of Mozart in this, though I hesitate to mention anything so sublime in this context. We wanted the piece to be about human behaviour, its foibles and deceptions and what can happen as a result of those things. There's almost a *Don Giovanni*-like conclusion to the opera.

McEwan: One thing I took from the classics is the ensemble pieces. It was good to write sextets. I love *The Barber of Seville* and we were very keen to have ensembles that grew in complexity, where all the characters end up expressing themselves at once. I'm always amazed at how opera can do this— it's unique in that respect, but it's something I haven't heard very much in contemporary opera.

Berkeley: I'll tell you why, it's because it's bloody difficult to do!

Khandekar: So back to the basics. Which did come first: words or music? This is an original story, so presumably it all had to come out of Ian's head first before Michael could add his musical voice . . .

McEwan: Actually, it was more collaborative than that. Our starting point was that we wanted to explore the idea of sexual obsession. We went on several quite long walks where we worked on the opera's plot, and we gave each other things to read that might have the kernel of a character in them. I listened to Michael and he listened to me. Simple as that!

Berkeley: I never felt that I was being given a *fait accompli* which I then had to go away and set to music. One of the great things about working with a writer on an original libretto is that it unfolds as you go along. Ian would feed me the text as he wrote it and I would play back to him what I'd done with it. He then used that as a reference point for what was coming next. So that meant that the music itself was integral to the narrative.

Khandekar: No artistic tears and tantrums to report, then?

Berkeley: Neither of us are natural conflict mongers—after all, our first collaboration was about the evils of warfare, you may recall! We work with an intellectual understanding that is mutual. There were little things that we smoothed out by talking about them.

Khandekar: There's quite a graphic sex scene that could be tricky to stage. Sex in opera can be cringe-makingly embarrassing.

McEwan: Actually, although the opera is infused with sexual intrigue, the sex scene itself is really a piece of situation comedy. Its climax is interrupted as all the characters file on stage one by one—another Rossinian moment which I loved writing. In terms of the performance of Charles's manhood, is this the first operatic "no-show," Michael?

Berkeley: I need to give that some thought! But seriously, it strikes me that so many contemporary operas don't explore the tension between comedy and tragedy enough. You can only have real blackness if it comes after a flash of light, and music can deliver this sort of abrupt contrast supremely well in conjunction with words. Ian writes very precisely, and I needed to negotiate the shift of musical mood from comic to tragic equally accurately, which was a real discipline. Again, Mozart provided some inspiration here.

Khandekar: Ian's novels contain some breathtaking descriptive writing, such as the portrayal of military life during World War II in *Atonement*. An opera libretto, however, is based on inner monologue and dialogue. Was it difficult to pare down your writing to these basics?

McEwan: I rather enjoyed it actually. Michael talked about the inspiration of Mozart, and for me, writing this libretto had me looking up to Shakespeare. It made me realise how powerful the iambic pentameter is. Sometimes I'd find I'd written five of them in a row without realising it! The libretto isn't poetry, but I became very aware of my inner ear and its sensitivity to what you might call "sprung rhythm." Basically, it's measured prose. I didn't try to think about what Michael would do with it musically, but I did imagine breathing the phrases.

Berkeley: I actually found Ian's words very powerful to set. The language has a stark intensity and even the shortest phrases pack a lot of meaning.

The libretto is not like one of Ian's novels. The thing about opera is that it's all delivered with a degree of hyperbole. The emotions are heightened. A lot of dramatic things happen in a short space of time.

Khandekar: You pushed hard for the opera to be performed with English surtitles—especially Ian. Is this an admission that the text in opera tends to be lost at the expense of the music? Or just that singers are bad at projecting words?

McEwan: This is psychological drama as well as music theatre. And I think these days audiences are so used to engaging with opera through surtitles, that they've just become a normal part of the interaction between music and words.

Berkeley: I think you've also got to bear in mind that Music Theatre Wales is a pioneering company that goes around the country introducing new work to places that are often rather unprovided for when it comes to opera. Anything that gives audiences a chance to engage with a new work, with a new libretto and a psychologically complex plot has to be seriously considered.

Khandekar: What are your hopes for this work? New operas don't exactly have a good track record of surviving as repertoire pieces.

Berkeley: I've been lucky—*Jane Eyre* has been taken up into the repertoire, with productions in Australia and the US after the British premiere; and *For You* is going to be developed into a larger version which is being performed in Germany and Switzerland. I think actually we're living in a bit of a golden period for new opera in Britain at the moment. The Barbican has just celebrated Judith Weir, Harry's [Harrison Birtwistle] got a new opera being premiered at the Royal Opera House, *The Minotaur*. George Benjamin, James MacMillan, and Jonathan Dove have all had major world premieres recently. So it's not a case of doom and gloom—far from it.

Khandekar: Will there be other collaborations between the two of you in the near future or will we have to wait another twenty-five years?

McEwan: There are all sorts of possibilities of course. I couldn't sustain myself as a librettist, though it has been artistically rewarding and the collaboration is great. I've written screenplays, and in the ranking of things, I'd say a scriptwriter is as a Corporal to a librettist's General.

Berkeley: . . . and The Author?

McEwan: Oh, The Author is god!

Shadow Lines

Steven Pinker/2008

From *PEN America* 9 (2008): 131–38. Reprinted by permission of the publisher.

Ian McEwan: Let's talk about what is actually happening when people engage in a conversation.

Steven Pinker: Well, if you look at the transcript of a conversation, it's remarkable how little communication of data there is. So much is innuendo and euphemism, and we count on our listener to fill in the blanks. If you look, for example, at the Watergate transcripts—which were probably the first conversations that many people saw reproduced directly on the page—they're very hard to follow. The context, which allows you to get away with saying very little, knowing your interlocutor will read between the lines, is absent. Simple politeness may be the clearest example. Someone might say at a dinner table, "If you could pass the salt, that would be awesome." Why are you pondering counterfactual worlds there at the dinner table?

McEwan: It's a blatant lie. It would not be awesome.

Pinker: No, it wouldn't be. And when there is a fraught topic under discussion—say, sexuality—people rarely say what they mean. There's an old cliché, "Would you like to come up and see my etchings," which was meant as a sexual come-on. James Thurber drew a cartoon of a man in the lobby of an apartment building saying to his date, "You wait here, and I'll bring the etchings down." We get the joke, because we know that question is not supposed to be asked literally. Veiled threats are another example. Anyone who watches mafia movies knows what it means when the wise guy says, "Nice store you've got there. It'd be a real shame if something happened to it." The target understands that comment as a veiled threat. This becomes a practical problem in, for example, the prosecution of sexual harassment and extortion and bribery. How do you interpret Clarence Thomas when he said to Anita Hill, "Who has put pubic hair on my Coke?" Was that an innocent observation or a sexual come-on? It's also a problem in the design of computer programs. If you program a computer with an atlas and an understanding of English grammar, for instance, and then ask, "Can you tell me the best way to get to Minneapolis," the computer will answer, "Yes." Of course, when you couch the question in those terms you have a different question in mind. Actually, you don't have a question in mind—it's really an imperative. So what's going on? Why don't we just say what we mean? The answer is that conversation does two things at once. It does convey information—you really do want the bloody salt—but what you say also presupposes the relationship you have with someone. Issuing a command or floating a proposition can change that relationship in a way that neither of you wants. When I say, "If you could pass the salt, that would be awesome," I'm able to ask for the salt without bossing you around as if you're an underling. And yet I still convey the imperative.

McEwan: These things vary enormously between cultures and nations. I noticed the first time I came to the States that people were blunter. A handbook was reprinted recently that advised American troops in Britain in 1943 or '44 how to order a pint of beer, among other things. It was not considered rude by most Americans to say "Gimme a beer" with no modifiers. But it would seem insulting in a pub in England—especially in 1943. You'd have to add something like "Would you awfully mind" or "Excuse me."

Pinker: "If it isn't too much trouble . . ." A lot depends on how particular pairs of people are categorized in a culture. Do you treat a salesperson as an underling? And these customs change over time.

McEwan: One of the things that all of us must do as readers is open books and read artificial accounts of conversation in literature—in other words, dialogue. And it's very unlike reading the Watergate transcripts, isn't it? It's the duty of the novelist, first of all, to let you know who's speaking, and the novelist can give that information an adverbial construction ("she said happily") or can even provide paragraphs describing the speaker's mental state. Does that seem to you, as a cognitive psychologist, a terrible corruption? Do you find yourself frustrated by the ways those interactions are set forth?

Pinker: I never thought of it. I suspect if you compared several pages of dialogue from a novel with several pages of transcribed conversation, they would look very, very different. In addition to that explicit fleshing out of a character's intentions and mental states, I bet that the content of the conversation itself would be crafted in a way that sounds natural and elliptical, but nonetheless is quite different from real conversation—so that the conversation can be meaningful to someone who doesn't know the entire biography of each character. I often fall for the scam of being invited to give a lecture with the accompanying obligation of having to submit a written paper. I say, "I'd be happy to give a talk, but I don't have time to write up a paper," and they say, "Oh, no problem. We'll run a tape of you speaking, we'll pay someone to transcribe it, and then all you have to do is clean up the punctuation, and you've got an automatic paper." It never works that way! No matter how articulate and eloquent I might feel myself to be in the moment, when I see my words on the page I'm appalled at what a gibbering, inarticulate bumbler I seem to be.

McEwan: Nabokov once said, rather humbly, "I think like a genius, I write like a distinguished author, and I speak like a child."

Pinker: And even when you touch it up, you don't want to turn it into a bit of turgid writing, you want it to sound conversational, but you have to apply the artifice of what you imagine spontaneous articulate speech should sound like. I expect there is a similar relationship between convincing fictional dialogue and actual human conversation.

McEwan: There's also the immediate impulse to make yourself a lot cleverer than you really are. You get caught in the same trap of in the end having to write a lecture using the transcript as a prompt. You've written very entertainingly about the nature of seduction and the ways we cannot speak our minds. I've never spoken of this terribly embarrassing thing, but when I was seventeen, I'd been at a boys' boarding school for seven years, and I knew very little about girls. I went to university and there was a big rock 'n' roll concert to welcome us all, and I thought, "Well, it is my duty to have success with a girl." I saw a very pretty girl standing alone—or so it seemed to me—and I thought, "I know what, I'm just going to cut through all the bullshit," and I said to her, "Look, would you like to come back to my room and fuck?" To my amazement she said, "Fuck off." So I learned the lesson that Jane Austen should have taught me long before. Of course, we know, in literature as in life, the business of seduction has to be hedged around at every stage by plausible denial. All I meant was, "Come and see my etch-ings." She is allowed to say no, and we both save face. She can reject me by simply saying, "No, I don't want to see your etchings," not "I don't like the shape of your body."

Pinker: It's a profound puzzle, I think, why we don't just blurt out what we think, as you did. Why should the woman take offense? She's perfectly free to say no. Why would there be the angry refusal? There's a bit of dialogue from the movie *Tootsie* that made this hypocrisy clear. Dustin Hoffman is disguised as a woman and engaged in late-night girl talk with Jessica Lange. Jessica Lange says, "You know what I wish? That a guy could be honest enough to walk up to me and say, 'I could lay a big line on you and we could do a lot of role-playing, but the simple truth is I find you very interesting, and I'd really like to make love to you.' Wouldn't that be a relief?" And, of course, later in the film, Dustin Hoffman, now out of his disguise, unrecog-nized by Jessica Lange, approaches her at a party and says, "I find you very interesting and I'd really like to make love to you." She throws a glass of wine in his face. So why the hypocrisy? The answer, I think, hinges on a concept that economists and logicians call "mutual knowledge." That is, the differ-ence between two people knowing something and each one knowing that the other knows that they know that the other knows ad infinitum. Which makes both a logical and a psychological difference. So if Harry says to Sally, "You ought to come up and see my etchings," and Sally says, "No," then he knows that she's turned down a sexual overture, and she knows that she's turned down a sexual overture, but does she know that he knows that she knows? And does he know that she knows that he knows? In the absence of this higher-order knowledge, you can maintain the fiction of a platonic friendship. Whereas overt language leaves nothing to the imagination. I think the difference between individual knowledge and mutual knowledge is the basis of "The Emperor's New Clothes." When the little boy says, "The emperor is naked," he isn't telling anyone anything that they can't see with their own eyeballs, but he *is* conveying information—because everyone now knows that everyone else knows that they know. This changes the relation-ship. They can now challenge the authority of the emperor in a way that in-dividual knowledge didn't allow them to. So blurting things out, as the little boy does, and as you did to your misfortune, creates mutual knowledge, and thus forces the relationship to change in a way that is not forced when you use innuendo.

McEwan: Representing this in fiction is of course a matter of endless fascination. In James Joyce's story "The Dead," Gabriel comes away from a party given by his two aunts, an annual affair that happens around Christmas, with his wife, Gretta. Gretta pauses on a landing to listen to some singing and piano music from the drawing room, which Gabriel himself can't hear. She then comes down, and they go out into the street with the singer, who's quite famous. It's a cold night, and slushy, and Gabriel begins to feel an overwhelming desire for Gretta. He wants to cut through all the years they've spent looking after children and worrying about household cares, all the sorrows they've endured, and get back to the moment they first met. They find a cab after some difficulty, a horse-drawn cab, and he's dying for the moment that they'll get back to the hotel room. There then proceeds an awful set of misunderstandings. He thinks that she's aware of his desire. She kisses him lightly, but there's something on her mind, and he's irritated that something stands between them. Then she blurts out her famous confession that the song she heard earlier, "The Lass of Aughrim," made her think of a seventeen-year-old boy, Michael Furey, who was once in love with her. Gabriel feels a flash of jealous anger towards a rival and says rather bitterly, "Perhaps that was why you wanted to go to Galway with that Ivors girl?" This couple is in their late forties or early fifties. And she says, "He is dead. . . . I think he died for me." She then tells the painful story of how this boy, dying of TB, came out in the rain, stood under her window, and sang that song. She had to go back to Dublin to convent school, and when she was there she got the news that he had died. It's one of the most beautiful representations of two people's minds running along entirely different lines. He thinks he's beginning a seduction and she's wrapped up in a sorrow that then becomes his. He reflects on the dead, and Joyce makes the famous evocation of the snow falling outside on the central plains and into the mutinous Shannon waves and the graveyard of Michael Furey and the treeless hills. I think that late-night conversation between Gabriel and Gretta is probably the best thing Joyce ever wrote. I often regret that he got drawn by literary and aesthetic ideologies into such a colossal cul-de-sac as *Finnegans Wake* and never again gave us so touching or human a moment as he did in that short story.

Pinker: It is immeasurably rich, the number of psychological phenomena captured in that sequence. Fiction can shift across points of view and get in the heads of different people as they deal with inherently ambiguous bits of communication—and this allows us to interpret what other people must mean when we can't take words at face value. You asked at the outset how we do this, how we figure out what someone means when he says something that is ambiguous, as most things are. And the answer is that we exercise our intuitive psychology. We get inside the head of the speaker and think, "Given that what he said, taken literally, can't make any sense, what did he mean? What are his thought processes, his intentions, what's his relationship with me such that he would utter that strange sentence?" Anything from "If you could pass the salt, that would be great" to far more fraught topics. Fiction allows us to exercise that part of our mind in a much deeper way, because the author can control how much we know about the state of mind of the person who utters an ambiguous sentence. We can alternately see it from the point of view of the speaker, the listener, and an omniscient narrator, and this gives that part of our mind an invigorating workout.

McEwan: And the crucial thing here is that Joyce withholds information. His narration moves in and out of Gabriel's mind, and he could simply tell us what Gretta is thinking when she stands at the top of the stairs. Instead he makes us complicit in Gabriel's misunderstanding.

Pinker: This reminds me of your own novel *On Chesil Beach*, which hinges on a failure of sexual communication. The agony of the book is that the two characters, newlyweds in 1961, are unable to communicate even the simplest sexual desire in language, and various misunderstandings and consequences unfold from that. In intimate relationships—our close friends, allies, soul mates, lovers, sexual partners—there's a part of us that strongly resists articulating the terms of the relationship in explicit language. There, more than anywhere else, when we express heartfelt loyalty and fusion, we do it physically—by eating together, hugging, exchanging bodily fluids, moving in synchrony. To the extent that language is used, it's formulaic. "I pledge allegiance": that's how you indicate you have solidarity with your tribe or your nation. "I believe with a perfect faith": you have fidelity to the religion. "I love you," which is an invitation for the other person to say "I love you." You're not conveying a proposition, you're engaged in a ritual. You don't say, "Let's fall in love. I'll support you when you get sick, you support me when I get sick, and I'll do the following chores, I'll bring in this amount of money, we'll have sex so many times a week." Anyone who did that we would assume doesn't understand the terms of an intimate relationship—which has to be felt in the marrow and has to appeal to a primitive intuition of being one flesh. That's the primitive level of communion that we need to feel to have an intimate relationship—presumably because the overt language system is connected to the rational, deliberative, conscious parts of the brain, and that's what controls conversation.

Whereas if you convey that this is under the control of some deep, primitive emotion, then you're giving the other person some reason to believe that it is a heartfelt commitment and you won't be out the door just as soon as it's in your interest to do so. *On Chesil Beach* works in part because people were painfully, pathologically inhibited from talking about sex in the early '60s, in a way that is less true now. As I recall, the first sentence hedges the particular inhibitions of the early '60s by saying that it's never easy. The question is, now that we've gone through the sexual revolution, and there have been a couple of generations since, is the premise that people are skittish about talking about sex obsolete? Many people informed me that all this talk about "etchings," innuendo, "you wanna come up to my apartment," the young people don't do that anymore. It's business-like, matter of fact, they hook up, there's no emotion whatsoever. I was a little skeptical. So I asked my class of undergraduates. I said, "People tell me that people your age no longer have to use innuendo about sex. They just blurt it out." Laughter across the classroom. One person says, "Isn't that what old people always say about young people?" And I was informed on no uncertain terms that one doesn't just approach an attractive stranger and ask, "Do you want to have sex?" It's still, "Do you want to come up to my room? I have a very nice view."

McEwan: Clearly there's a massive gap in popular culture between the representations of sexual behavior and what actually happens. I've had many, many letters from readers of *On Chesil Beach*, some of them from people in their sixties and seventies—but also from seventeen-year-olds and eighteen-year-olds. The actual language people use might change, but the underlying reality is that for most people, to have sex for the first time is to cross a line—a shadow line, to use Conrad's term—and it's fraught and it's comic and it can be very sad. By the way, the young lovers in my book ate a hearty meal together and that didn't help them one bit.

Pinker: People of my generation and yours have a morbid fascination with the world of instant messaging. It's a whole medium that we were born too late to weave into our lives. The students told me the thing about instant messaging is that there's a lot of ambiguity—because the bandwidth is so slow that context becomes enormously important. And for that reason, one of them said, you can get away with being a little more overt in an instant message, because when you make a proposition—say, "You wanna have sex?"—if it looks like it's going to be rebuffed you can, as she put it, "LOL it away." So there's a different deniability.

McEwan: This is a LOL-a-by . . . I wanted to ask you about Bartleby the Scrivener, because he seems to break every rule of human communication. He will not play the game, and he drives the narrator of Melville's story nuts. At one moment the narrator realizes that this is his fate, that God has sent him Bartleby, and his role in life is simply to provide Bartleby a place behind the screen in his office where he can stay. Then you turn the page and he just wants to get rid of this dreadful incubus. He switches from one mood to the other. It's a parallel story to "The Dead," in a way, because Bartleby's death also evokes such a powerful sense of humanity. The narrator's discovery of the one small fact he could glean about Bartleby's life—that he had a job in another office opening up dead letters whose addressees had died—sets off that famous cry, "Ah, Bartleby! Ah, humanity!" at the end of the story. But I wonder, from a cognitive point of view, what is it with Bartleby? I always thought he was autistic.

Pinker: It's possible. The most obvious cognitive deficit in autism is a failure of intuitive psychology, which is exactly what we use to read between the lines, to get in someone's head and figure out what they mean. Often, autistic people lose the subtleties of conversation, at least in comprehension. My friend, who has an autistic son, called home one day, and the boy answered. My friend asked, "Is your mother home?" and the boy said, "Yes." And that was the conversation. His mother was home. He didn't realize that this was actually a request to speak to the mother.

McEwan: Bartleby has this lack of awareness. He gives up copying but still keeps coming to the office—is, in fact, living in the office and won't even go down to the post office and post a few letters. He starts off copying, but his role shrinks and shrinks and shrinks. And he has no awareness of the frenzy that this causes around him.

Pinker: There could be a failure of what linguists call the cooperative principle—if you have two adversaries all of the ordinary rules of charitably interpreting conversation break down. Or it could be a case of Asperger's or autism where there is, rather than an unwillingness to be charitable, an inability to be charitable. Being charitable partly entails filling in the blanks.

"A Thing One Does": A Conversation with Ian McEwan

Ryan Roberts/2008

Interview conducted in London on 12 June 2008, specifically for this volume. Printed with permission of author, with special thanks to Ian McEwan.

Ryan Roberts: Throughout your work, you have dealt with various aspects of relationships, often setting these relationships against external forces or individuals, but, as with *On Chesil Beach*, also exploring the intimacies associated with being a newly formed couple. What is it about such relationships that interests you?

Ian McEwan: My first reaction is to say, well, you'd have to be a psychopath or suffering from autism not to have an interest in relationships. We are social creatures, and relationships are where we live, unless our lives are spent tragically alone. And it's really where literature in the modern age—over the last 400–500 years—has lived. And the novel in particular has become the form to investigate them. So my own interests are fairly conventional.

I used to be drawn to the idea that any *sexual* relationship was a microcosm of power, but I feel less strongly about that. It's less the power aspects of the relationship that appeal to me these days and more the intricacies of misunderstanding, and for breakthrough into self-knowledge, for the ways in which relationships can disintegrate—and what makes them endure. *On Chesil Beach*, I suppose, was a small-scale investigation of some of those elements, particularly the misunderstandings that arise when people not only are unable to describe their feelings to each other, but can't even describe them to themselves.

Roberts: There's a bit of that in *The Innocent*, too, where Leonard and Maria murder Otto—there's an inability to come back from that, to find a way of communicating again.

McEwan: There are ways back, in all things, but often it simply doesn't happen. Emotions get in the way—emotions like pride, self-persuasion. That's another aspect of this that interests me, and it's a concept associated with Bob Trivers, the evolutionary psychologist. I think it was Trivers who first said, when talking about deceit, that the simplest way to deceive someone is first to deceive yourself. If you want to cheat, it's far more effective to per-suade yourself, because then you have nothing to hide. You're speaking your truth, as it were. I don't know how true it is in evolutionary terms, but this seems to say a lot about the way people are in confrontations or difficulties, personal difficulties. And we see it, too, in larger political terms. People dis-tort or are selective with their memories and with evidence. It's that element now, in relationships, that seems to me so rich for investigation.

Roberts: Since we have this ability to self-persuade, what is your sense of the idea of a "truth" that is out there? If you only talk to parties who have been aggrieved, I assume that's just their perception of some greater truth?

McEwan: I don't hold with the sort of postmodern relativist view that the only truth is the one an individual asserts. I do believe there are realities that await our investigation. In that sense I'm an objectivist. I also accept from biology that through perception, cognition we have to construct the world . . . I mean, the extraordinary advances made, say, in the neuroscience of vision show that only a tiny portion of the retina actually shows us the world in detail. The rest is constructed around it. But there's something out there, and it's consistent and we've evolved in it and can operate in it and can successively refine our descriptions of it. In our perception of the truth, self-persuasion does play a role. We all stand somewhere on a spectrum. There are people who can be quite clinical about their own feelings in relation to what they think is really there. And there are other people who really cannot see the world apart from their feelings and projections about it. Somewhere along there we all must stand.

The pleasure and interest of writing a novel, of course, is that you can dictate all those terms. You can set the dials, as it were, of the narrative in such a way that the only truth you can know is through one character's eyes, or conversely, you can vary it as you go along or opt for some god-like om-niscience.

Something rankles in me when people talk about "My truth." You must be more familiar with this in the universities than I am, especially in the world of literary theory. There's a strong anti-rationalist streak that I find intellectually repellent. I can't engage with it at all. That's one more reason why I find that I would rather read a cognitive psychologist, or an evolution-ary psychologist, or a neuroscientist on human behavior, than I would, say, Jacques Derrida, Lacan, or Baudrillard.

Roberts: How do you view attempts by, for instance, the academy to lay on theory or to approach your work from that angle?

McEwan: Well, critical writing varies enormously. There are people still writing in terms that I can identify with—writing at the higher end of literary journalism. I'm happy reading Frank Kermode on Shakespeare. I don't even know what it's called—moral criticism perhaps—it's in the language that we speak. It's gratifying to a writer, to come under the gaze of a mind that has read a lot and thought a lot.

Clearly, the postmodern bandwagon has come to a halt, because it has lost a wider readership, and can't engage with the culture. For the first time in years I found myself reading a book about literary theory—it's by Edward Slingerland—on what science offers the humanities. It's a superb book, actually. But that's a bit of a digression.

Roberts: This ties in with the question of human nature that you wrote about in your piece about your expedition to the Arctic with Cape Farewell (and it sounds as if your new work will also focus on aspects of human nature). The essay revolves around the boot room, a place where equipment is put on, then shed, then taken by other members of the expedition as their needs dictate. There's a crucial passage in the article about human nature, art, and our ability to effect change: "But we will not rescue the earth from our own depredations until we understand ourselves a little more, even if we accept that we can never really change our natures." And you talk about the need for rules—boot room rules. How do we resolve within ourselves this sort of engagement with global issues (and there are many, not just climate issues, but AIDS, tyranny, poverty, etc.)? How do we engage with such issues when we're so inept at managing ourselves? Do you see any hope for engaging with any of these larger issues?

McEwan: I *do* see hope. We clearly are inept left alone to flounder, but we make societies, we live in cities, by and large they function, because we've devised rules, we've made social contracts that all trump our private needs for immediate gratification—to have what's not ours is pursued at a cost. Most of the really perceptive writers on climate change accept that the problem has to be addressed within the context of global poverty. Burning fossil fuels has driven our civilization and has lifted millions, tens of millions *out* of poverty. Moral considerations apart, poverty is very bad for the climate.

The issue challenges our nature. Individually, we're competitive. Nations are competitive. They have to collaborate on this, and they can only do this if they exercise their rationality and agree on a set of rules within which they can compete. We get these standoffs between the United States, saying it won't sign up for anything unless China and India do, and they say they won't sign up because they have to lift millions out of poverty and, besides, they are not the real problem, the United States is. We need good rules within which these circular problems are going to be resolved.

There hasn't been much ground for optimism lately. CO_2 is rising two or three parts per million every year. We're now approaching the 400 level. The talk of trying to stabilize at 560 parts per million this century is looking increasingly shaky. And yet we know enough science, technology, and negotiating know-how. People know what needs to be done. In the end, self-interest rather than idealism is going to focus our minds. And even greed can be regulated in our favor—an effective carbon trading system could help drive down CO_2. And as I said in that piece, we're used to doing good works for those who might return the favor. We're fine-tuned to that process. Now we have to think outside the framework of an individual lifetime and start doing favors for unborn people.

The time scales are longer than what human nature is evolved to deal with. We're really looking at the next hundred or two hundred years. The severity of this is going to really hit people later in this century when you and I will be gone. So it is a challenge, and I *have* been writing about it. I'm writing a novel that has at its center a character who has rather too many weaknesses and faults. He's determined to do something about climate change. But what keeps getting in the way are all his defects. That's the simple premise.

Roberts: There's another quote from the same article in which you say, "Leave nothing to idealism or outrage, or even good art—we know in our hearts that the very best art is entirely and splendidly useless." In the face of needing rules to regulate us and to help push us along, could you elaborate on this idea? Do you think writing a novel that has at its center the subject of climate change will spark discussion? What can art do in such cases?

McEwan: I don't think it can do much. And I don't think it can do much about climate change. I suppose it can reflect the problem and pose the problem in terms that might be useful to people. I think we *do* face a test of our nature, and the more we know about that nature, the better we'll be able to face that test. That is why it's so important to look empirically at what we are, how our cognitive abilities shape our interactions with the world and with each other. But, no, when I'm writing this novel I don't think I'm going to save the world, that's for sure.

Roberts: When it gets reviewed, the headlines will undoubtedly bring up the issue of climate change. Green is "in" now—there's a lot of fashion in the idea of "going green." Do you see that as just dressing up? As something that really doesn't have a lot of impact—the marketing of "going green"?

McEwan: What will really matter is when a country like the United States starts to build massive solar energy installations and, in doing so, decommissions something that's pouring CO_2 into the atmosphere. Using less of this or that helps in that it delays the problem, but it does not solve it. Driving a smaller car, turning down the thermostat might make us feel better. But ultimately we have to shift to clean energy sources.

There are many ways of seeing this problem. One eminent writer on climate change, Wallace Broecker, has made the analogy with sewage. In the nineteenth century, many large cities in the West started to deal with the problem of sewage disposal. There were people writing at the time saying that sewage is just a part of what we are and it's part of what we must pay for the privilege of living in a city. The cost of doing it is estimated at something like a hundred billion dollars, and it was done in the West over a period of a generation or two. *Huge* underground networks built at *fantastic* expense. Now, we might have to think of CO_2 as our new sewage.

But I don't mind the fashionability of it; it is important either way. There is a quiet industrial revolution taking place. Those hip West Coast guys who refined the internet want to relive their youth by developing clean energy technologies. There is a huge amount of innovation in solar energy going on. Then there is the boring economic stuff. The Germans allow people to sell the electricity they generate on their rooftop back to the utility companies at a highly subsidized rate. It's created a quarter of a million jobs in the solar and wind sector. Again, it's boot room rules stuff . . . within which consumerism could still go on. People could be just as greedy and competitive and say, "I've got a better solar roof top than you." That's fine. Human nature can flourish within that enclosure.

Roberts: There's so much to deal with when you think about such larger issues that it's hard to grapple with just how the different levels play with each other—how the popular, fashionable movements play in with the politics and how much the politicians are influenced by those fashionable movements.

McEwan: Yes, well within a democracy it is very useful that there are fashions and that politicians who want to be reelected must attend to them. But it also suggests a receptivity to anyone with enough vision to take a lead. From this point of view alone, what a great tragedy of wasted opportunity it was, the election of George Bush. And we just have to hope that whoever is next (and I hope it is Obama) will take a lead on this.

Roberts: Again, it's that acceptance of change, acceptance of the reality around them. In the U.S. we've seen gas go up 50 percent, then double, and now when you look around at prices you find yourself saying, "Oh, this is the cheap gas. It's under $4.00!"
McEwan: Yes, and we think your gas is free. It's amazing what everyone gets used to. I mean, we're living with, I would guess, the equivalent of about $8.00 a gallon. It doesn't stop people filling up their cars . . .

Roberts: Related to the issue of politics, I wonder about the issue of a nation atoning for its past, its actions. Is there atonement on a national level, do you think? How does that differ from our personal atonements?
McEwan: I think it's quite difficult to do anything about a deed done in the past. But there are some things you can do. This year I was in Australia on the day that its prime minister apologized to the aboriginal population. Even in the cynical Australian press, it was very significant, although mostly symbolic. I see the same has happened recently in Canada. Some nations have confronted their past more effectively than others. Atonement is simply being aware of the past rather than repressing it or distorting it. So on the one hand the commission set up in South Africa after the apartheid regime fell did enact for the national conscience the cruelties of the regime. I think the Germans have been better than most in dealing with their past. In contrast the Turks are still in denial about the Armenian massacre and are prosecuting writers for mentioning it. The Japanese have their own forms of denial. Atonement on a national scale is about dredging up the muck rather than burying it. This can't be played out before any supernatural entity that can forgive you. It's really about how the national narrative incorporates what happened.

Roberts: What do you feel is the role of an author related to political discourse or such social issues? What sort of voice or what impact do you think authors can have on such issues?
McEwan: Well, writers have to be careful about being drawn in to a celebrity-opinion culture that has a view about everything. Yet, on the other hand, sometimes it's important to speak up when certain public issues cross

your own concerns. The media now are so relentless and hungry and ubiquitous and permanent. They roll through every hour of the day and night. And in their hunger they constantly, *constantly* churn out opinion. Opinion is cheap, I guess—you don't have to send anyone anywhere—and it's sometimes difficult to take it seriously.

So it's really a matter of balance. The other thing is that writing fiction is a private, obsessive business, and as soon as you come out . . . there's never anything final if you say something in public. You are likely to get misquoted, then attacked on the basis of something you never said. It's like shaking one of those little snow storms in a jar—a million blogs float up. The levels of debate are pretty low, with much fury and spite. And yet, there are quite sensible things, but finding them is difficult. Still, for all the noise and pointlessness, it is still worth speaking up if you feel strongly.

Roberts: You say that writing is very personal and obsessive, that it takes a lot of quiet and a great deal of introspection. How has that changed over your career?

McEwan: The world is louder. The internet has made it loud, and rolling news has made it loud. Also adding to the volume, and this is a local matter in Britain, the national temperament has changed. It has become a lot more febrile, more emotional, idiosyncratic, labile. The nation has constant mood swings. The prime minister can be God one week and Satan the next. Every small remark can create days of pointless rumination by professional rune-readers. I'm not saying you can't have solitude these days, but the difference now is that you have to work for it, whereas in the seventies and eighties it was there anyway. It was the air you breathed and, if you wanted to be in public, *that* was the effort you made. Now it's the other way around.

Roberts: Let's turn to music. It features in several of your works, and you recently mentioned to Ivan Hewett in the *Telegraph* that "music can tie itself to memory in a special way."[1] Other than serving as a subject for your work, to what extent does music or other artistic forms influence your writing?

McEwan: It's very simple: I take a lot of pleasure in it. I admire musicians and composers. Perhaps more than any other art form, music consistently delivers satisfaction and formal perfection that are only ever found in the best poetry. Novels, and even great novels, are never perfect all the way

1. Hewett, Ivan. "Ian McEwan: Opera? Great Music, Terrible Plots." *The Guardian*, 26 May 2008. http://www.telegraph.co.uk/arts/main.jhtml?xml=/arts/2008/05/26/bomcewan126.xml.

through—*Anna Karenina* or *Madame Bovary*, and certainly *Ulysses* have their longueurs. The Goldberg Variations do not. Also music's lack of meaning has infinite appeal. Of course we all bring meaning *to* it, but what it actually is saying is beyond us, beyond words. Last night Annalena and I were with Julian [Barnes] and his wife Pat [Kavanagh] listening to Paul Lewis at Wigmore Hall playing Schubert and Mozart. And I thought, not for the first time, that I could never get such pleasure, and in every realm—emotional, intellectual, sensual—from going to hear someone read from their latest novel, or from reading it myself.

On Chesil Beach was my first attempt at using music as a marker of character and also as a vehicle of misunderstanding. Edward's love of rock and roll and Florence's love of the classical repertory are part of their mutual incomprehension. I've used it in the opera and in *Amsterdam* as a means of talking about overweening ambition, of wanting to really create this perfect thing.

Roberts: And does this have an analogy to writing? Especially when you think of the composer as author? Charles Frieth, the composer in your libretto *For You*, mentions at one point, "No religion, no purpose except this: / make something perfect before you die. / Life is short, art is for all time— /." You discuss with David Remnick in your interview for the *New Yorker* Festival this idea of trying to achieve something in writing, something that would have a similar effect. Is perfection easier to achieve in music? Do words get in the way of achieving that idea of perfection?

McEwan: Well, words inevitably get in the way because they mean different things to different people. But that doesn't stop me believing that I could reach for something beyond anything I've ever done. All writers need this illusion. But even as you were posing the question, I was thinking, "Yes, whatever that thing is it would have to be short"—that it's not possible over length. Maybe I'm not a good enough writer, but the sprawling capacious inheritance of the novel seems to forbid perfection, whereas the novella might just, at its very best. Certainly the best poetry does. There are many poems of which I'd say, "I wouldn't want a single word changed."

Roberts: I just re-read *On Chesil Beach* and, as far as its form or shape, it is amazing how wonderfully balanced it is. As far as I can see as a reader, it's a perfect length for the content, for the relationship it describes, for the issues it touches on. Were you thinking of music when you wrote it or this idea of achieving something nearing perfection? I think the last time we talked you mentioned you sort of had a particular form in mind or a particular length for the novel.

McEwan: I think that I did say to you before that one of the first things I thought of when writing it was its length and structure. I wrote in a notebook "five times eight"—five chapters of about 8,000 words. In fact, it came out at 39,000 words. Five chapters of equal length.

In *Amsterdam* I tried to imagine what it would be like to compose a piece of music. I saw it in visual terms, of something half-seen, a shape, a set of stone steps, a plateau.

Of all music, it's Bach that continues to hold me. There are pieces that I first heard when I was sixteen and loved, and they haven't dimmed. I wouldn't cross the room to play a CD of *Rubber Soul*, which also captivated me around the same time in my teens. But I listen to the keyboard partitas or certain cantatas and enjoy them with the same intensity I did in 1965.

Roberts: How did you prepare for the writing of *For You*? Did you think of potential music at all, other than perhaps the rhythm inherent in the language? Did you look into other librettos, for instance?

McEwan: No, I steered clear. I didn't do any prepping, apart from a couple of walks in the woods with the composer, Michael Berkeley to outline to him the story as I saw it. We had agreed that sexual obsession would be a good subject. My interest in music made me want to put a composer at the center of the story. This composer will conduct the pit orchestra, in the first and last scenes. Music is constantly there, as a matter of discussion. I wrote it in tandem with *On Chesil Beach*. Again, arithmetic for this was "ten by ten"—ten scenes of ten minutes each. It came out slightly longer in the end. But that was the discipline. I would send off a scene to Michael and then get on with the novel. When I thought that he was catching up with me, I would look for a point to stop with the novel and start again on the opera.

Roberts: Getting back to form, you were talking of the possibility of reaching perfection with poetry. In early interviews you mentioned you had written poetry, telling Ian Hamilton that some of your earliest writings were sonnets. So why is it "Novelist Ian McEwan" and not "Novelist *and Poet* Ian McEwan"? Do you write in that form from time to time?

McEwan: No, I don't. I take the rather severe view that if you are not training your hand and ear in your early twenties as a poet, then you are not going to really be a serious poet. I don't hold to the notion that anyone can do it. I mean, anyone can do it *badly*, in literature. It requires a lifetime's commitment. It isn't something one can do lightly. And if a novelist occasionally writes a poem, that's not the same thing.

I have written a couple—I wrote a villanelle that was published in *The Observer* a few years ago. And then a willfully unrhyming pop song. But this was something on the side, a bit if fun.

Roberts: I suppose the same question could be applied to the short story. I know you've had the question from time to time of whether you'll return to that form. Do you view the short story as you do poetry, as something that needs to be constantly kept up with?

McEwan: I do like the idea of writing more short stories, but the novella— the 20,000- to 40,000-word novel—appeals to me more. In the literary culture, there is a strong virility fixation. If you publish a short novel, people think you just can't get it up for the full stretch. I suspect that the majority of fat contemporary novels are only quarter read, at least if my bedside table is anything to go by. Many 150,000-word novels would have turned out better at a third the length. It's formidably hard for a writer to sustain quality at great length. Few achieve it. Henry James wrote in "The Art of Fiction" that the first duty of the novelist is to be interesting. It's good advice, but it's not easy to follow, and I'm not sure that even James always followed it either.

Roberts: Quite. Let's turn to something different. I'm curious about your trip to America early on in your career. You wrote about it in a piece titled, "1976" for Picador, and what intrigued me wasn't just the perspectives or ideas you had about America going in—the fear of being mugged or being followed by "Men with guns, some hard American craziness"—but also your meeting with Philip Roth in New York. How did that come about?

McEwan: It's overlaid in memory by the fact that Roth then came to live in London in the early eighties, and I used to see him then. Yes, he took an avuncular interest in my writing, and was very encouraging and kind. I gave him a draft of my first novel *The Cement Garden*. I remember him coming to my flat in South London and spreading the chapters on the floor, saying, "It's all great up to here . . . the children . . . both parents died . . . *Now* what you've got to do is let all hell break out." He may have been right, and who knows, it might have been a better novel, but it would have been a Rothian novel. I resisted his advice, but I was incredibly flattered by his attention. Along with everything else, he is a very good critic.

When I started writing in 1970 Roth's work had an imaginative freedom, hilarity and expressiveness and wildness that was completely outside the contemporary English novel. It was a liberation. That sainted triptych— Roth, Bellow, Updike—have always been fully aware of modernism, and yet escaped its shadow. They also found a way of taking all that was best from the nineteenth-century novel and incorporating it into a modern self-consciousness. All those tools were there—character, digressive sprawl, and a powerful sense of geography or place. Bellow's Chicago, Roth's New Jersey, Updike's New England were almost like characters. They seem to have been able to engage fully with what it means to be alive now in the United States, in cities or provincial towns, happy to hold with the idea of the social novel as a viable form, with moral sense, and that it has a demotic quality, a classless or plural aspect.

While, in Europe, the novel shrank in the postwar years, even if the pages got more numerous—it shrank into a pursuit of something rare and perfect and difficult and *bleak*. It had less engagement with the world. This wasn't true of the English novel. It had other problems. It rather shriveled into a tiny bourgeois universe, it seemed, of rather minor concerns. So, while I've often said that Kafka was an important writer to me, those three were even more so, even while my own writing was hardly like theirs.

Roberts: You've mentioned being somewhat influenced in writing *Saturday* with Updike's Rabbit Tetralogy and the idea of bringing the contemporary into it. It brought to mind Updike's constant use of media—you hear it through the radio and advertising and television—it's a constant flow of that same media that we experience every day. This is reflected in *Saturday*, this bringing in of news reports and bringing in of the outside into Henry's world.

McEwan: You have to be careful. You don't want to overwhelm a novel with news reports. But we go about our days with half an ear to the news—it's a parallel story unfolding around you. How many did the bomb kill? Will Gordon Brown get his extra votes? How many refugees crossed the border? If you're directly involved it's another matter, but for most of us it's background music, the soundtrack of our daily existence.

Roberts: Speaking still of Updike, he tends to rewrite a lot, as when he collected together his Rabbit Tetralogy and rewrote passages so that reading them as individual novels differs slightly from reading them as a collection— he smoothed out redundancy to make them flow together as a whole. I'm interested in how you approach your editing process.

McEwan: I don't touch things once they're published, except maybe to correct the occasional fact. I generally feel what I did in the past is all part of the story and can't be changed. If I open one of my early short stories, my fingers twitch to get in there and change the punctuation. I experimented for a while with using commas in place of full stops. Now it looks pretentious. I was too influenced by Beckett. And the paragraphing . . . the paragraphs seem too long to me, too undigested. But I do nothing. I feel it would be a betrayal of my former self to go in there and start messing about.

Roberts: Are you involved with other aspects of book production?
McEwan: Yes. I get involved in the cover art.

Roberts: For just the UK editions, or others?
McEwan: Mostly the UK editions. My publisher here asked me if I had anything in mind for *On Chesil Beach*, and I said, "Well, I'd like a figure, walking away from us along the strand." So they sent a team to Dorset and came back with just that picture. It's perfect. I wanted to give the reader a sense of what that geological formation looks like—a narrow spit of land stretching seventeen or eighteen miles, surrounded by water, lagoon on one side, sea on the other.

Roberts: These types of decisions we're talking about (making edits in drafts, cover design, etc.) are often reflected in an author's papers or archives. What do you make of the occasional calls, by Andrew Motion and others, for the British government to support the retention of manuscripts within the country? Have people approached you about acquiring your papers?
McEwan: Yes, I get approached sometimes by intermediaries who say they can secure me a deal with this or that library. And I either don't reply or say I've got no immediate plans to dispose of my papers. But I'm going to have to do something soon. All things being equal, I would rather have my papers here. But if I was offered a large sum of money, I'd have to be feeling very rich to turn it down. There must come a point when I stop writing. What would I do for money in my eighties? But I think Andrew's dead right to raise this matter.

But, yes, I've walked around the vaults of the Huntington and looked at Kingsley Amis's papers, all the scraps and bits and pieces of a life, desk drawers upturned and catalogued, invitations to lunch, forgotten public readings, train tickets . . . it's spooky, how a life can be filed.

Roberts: As a librarian I find the issue of great interest and wonder whether the draw, the wanting to keep one's papers in England, might have anything to do with your perception of yourself as an English writer? Do you see yourself in these terms?

McEwan: Yes, I think so. My novels have been largely set here. I think I've been shaped by an English education, by English literature, and of course living here nearly all my life. I don't think of myself as belonging to any movement or school—what English writer does?—but I'm certainly not an American writer or French writer.

Roberts: The idea of placing your papers plays a role in the future study and examination of your work. I know Julian Barnes has written recently about death, so as an author, what are your views about death or your legacy, as it were? When you start hearing these sums from people interested in "preserving" you, preserving the train tickets of your life . . .

McEwan: Well, I don't think it's much of an afterlife, to be in the vaults of some library, but it's probably the only afterlife I'm going to get and I'll be luckier than most. I see no good reason to think anything will survive the extinction of my brain and my body. As you enter your sixties, a stronger awareness of your finite term finds its way into your work, inevitably. It's almost like a discipline, really. Even at a trivial level I think how expensive it is to have another wet, cloudy summer when you might only have ten or twenty left. So there's a real sense of time being short.

I once asked John Updike about this. He said that he was thinking of getting rid of a lot of books because he thought he might move somewhere smaller, and I said, "Well, that must give you such anguish." And he said, "Well, I would have thought so too, right up into my mid fifties, but something happens. You start to care less. It's notable," he said, "that the thought of your own death does not fill you with the sort of sorrow or fear that it did when you were in your thirties." And I think I'm just getting a whisper of that. So, perhaps, without religion, you become biologically reconciled anyway. You just care a little less.

Roberts: Does having children affect that, do you think?

McEwan: It helps, for sure. Although, it's sad not to know the story of your children's lives. But infinitely preferable to them not knowing the story of your life. In other words, you must pre-decease your children or face tragedy of the kind that's probably the worst thing that could happen to anyone.

Roberts: Yes, of course . . . Well, this brings us to our last question, which is about the process we've just been through. What do you think of the interview as a genre? Does it bring to mind Henry Bech in "Bech Swings?" when his interviewer tries "one more degrading time to dig into the rubbish of his 'career' and come up with the lost wristwatch of truth"?

McEwan: Sure. Well, I spend a lot of my time avoiding interviews, and still I end up doing an awful lot. I probably refuse five times as many or ten times as many as I do. It feels more like a duty, part of one's professional terms of engagement. It's mostly about pleasing others. I mean, obviously, I don't get much from it, you know. It seems to be a thing one does, that all writers have to do.

The form itself? Relatively modern, curiously set in its form, it owes something, I think, to the form of a play—a two-hander. Perfected by *The Paris Review*, it probably grew out of Hollywood, my guess is. I certainly don't think that the modern interview is, as I've heard some people saying, dumber or more stupid than interviews were, say, thirty years ago. I listened recently to Evelyn Waugh being interviewed by three people at once. It's on the sound archives of the British Library. The questions were just asinine. Unbelievably stupid. And Waugh kept his temper almost all the way through. At one point he almost yodels in despair. You know, questions like [imitating a clipped BBC voice], "Mr. Waugh. Do you write longhand or by typewriter?" And he says [normal voice], "No, I generally write on a block of foolscap." [Interviewer's voice] "Is that lined or unlined?" So it goes on. Not *one* question about his work. Nothing! [Interviewer's voice again] "Mr. Waugh, do you think one day you'd like to obliterate somebody?" [laughs]. It's a great resource, that British Library sound archive. It reminds us that we should not be too hard on ourselves.

Roberts: You've interviewed others, such as Updike.

McEwan: Yes, I enjoyed that. But mostly interviews are a form of public obligation.

Roberts: Well, thank you very much, Ian. I appreciate your obliging me [laughs].

McEwan: Well, for you, Ryan, it's a whole other matter [laughs].

Roberts: I really do appreciate it. I know it does take from your time and writing.

McEwan: It's a holiday from writing, that's for sure.

Index